ALMOST HEMINGWAY

Almost Hemingway

➤•◄

THE ADVENTURES OF NEGLEY FARSON, FOREIGN CORRESPONDENT

Rex Bowman and Carlos Santos

UNIVERSITY OF VIRGINIA PRESS

Charlottesville and London

University of Virginia Press
© 2021 by Rex Bowman and Carlos Santos
All rights reserved
Printed in the United States of America on acid-free paper

First published 2021

1 3 5 7 9 8 6 4 2

Library of Congress Cataloging-in-Publication Data
Names: Bowman, Rex, author. | Santos, Carlos, author.
Title: Almost Hemingway : the adventures of Negley Farson, foreign correspondent /
Rex Bowman and Carlos Santos.
Description: Charlottesville : University of Virginia Press, 2021. |
Includes bibliographical references and index.
Identifiers: LCCN 2021023500 (print) | LCCN 2021023501 (ebook) |
ISBN 9780813946672 (hardcover) | ISBN 9780813946689 (ebook)
Subjects: LCSH: Farson, Negley, 1890–1960. | Women journalists—
United States—Biography.
Classification: LCC PN4874.F38657 B69 2021 (print) | LCC PN4874.F38657 (ebook) |
DDC 070.92 [B]—dc22
LC record available at https://lccn.loc.gov/2021023500
LC ebook record available at https://lccn.loc.gov/2021023501

To adventurers everywhere

CONTENTS

Illustration gallery follows page 132

ALMOST HEMINGWAY

➤ • ⬅

Remembering Negley Farson

PEOPLE FAMILIAR WITH THE sunny zenith of Negley Farson's life could not have foreseen that he would be so widely forgotten today. He would have seemed, no doubt, to them, as memorable as Babe Ruth's swagger or Dick Tracy's jaw. "Almost everything happened to him that befalls a living man," journalist Arthur Krock of the *New York Times* once remarked.[1]

He was a man whose life invited wonderment. His son, Daniel, who inherited his father's fondness for liquor, described him as a "smiling giant of a man" who "did the things that most men dream about."[2] Nobel Prize winner Sinclair Lewis called him "a grand man who found every hour exciting."[3] Taking stock of Farson's ceaseless rambling, one reviewer simply dubbed him a "mutinous existential renegade."[4]

The chain-smoking Farson was once known in saloons and taverns across the globe simply as Negley—in some remote valleys in the high Caucasus, he was known as "Negley Farson Chicago Daily News," thanks to a native guide who mistook Farson's employer for his full name.[5] Even Farson's boyhood defied convention: he was raised by his grandfather, a former Civil War general never too busy tossing creditors off his porch to spend time bringing up his ward. From the very beginning Farson lived a life of adventure, and he later chronicled it in clear, exhilarating prose, much of it crafted by campfires, on riverbanks, atop mountains.

Once a champion collegiate athlete, Farson was in St. Petersburg, Russia, when the 1917 revolution broke out, working as an arms merchant and spending his evenings drinking with the young, infamous journalist John

Reed. During World War I, Farson joined Britain's Royal Flying Corps—feigning Canadian citizenship to enlist—and flew as a pilot over the Egyptian sands. His daredevil antics led to a plane crash in which he sustained injuries that would plague him for the rest of his life, though they did not blight his zeal for dangerous exploits. He lived on a ramshackle houseboat on a remote Canadian lake for several years, surviving on the salmon he caught and the ducks he shot. He sailed a small boat across the entire continent of Europe, navigating swirling rapids to cross borders bristling with bayonets as European statesmen prepared for the next war. He traveled on horseback across the Caucasus before Stalin could finish closing off Communist Russia to Westerners; he witnessed Gandhi's arrest in Borivli, India; he met Hitler, who patted Farson's blond-haired son on the head and called him a good Aryan boy. He was aboard the RMS *Olympic,* sister ship to the *Titanic,* when it crashed into another ship in New York Harbor.

In the late 1930s, he traveled across South America by car; when the roads became too rough or disappeared altogether, by canoe and zipline. Looking for a greater challenge, he crisscrossed Africa, hobnobbing with Pygmies, witnessing tribal scenes previously seen by only the most adventurous white men. He lay abed recuperating from malaria in Accra, on Africa's Gold Coast, on the day that the great earthquake of 1939 destroyed much of the city. In an age when foreign travel was not as convenient or common as it is today, Farson astonished his readers by popping up in faraway places, occasionally in the custody of police officers. When World War II came, he was in London, watching as German bombs obliterated the neighborhoods around him. He then sailed across the submarine-laden waters of the North Sea to Murmansk in the hope of witnessing the Russian armies' herculean battle against their Nazi enemies.

All the while, Farson struggled to cope with an injured leg for which he suffered through more than two dozen surgeries, some of them botched, the frustration of a nearly sexless marriage that he eased by seeking solace in a string of mistresses, and an addiction to liquor that he developed to deal with his physical pain and marital agony. Though his hardships were many, and great, his appetite for life proved greater. He lived each day as if it were a door that needed kicking in. To his mind, men who spent their time merely trying to get rich were pitiably dumb bastards.

By the time he had settled into his secluded home in Devon, England, Farson had earned a reputation as one of the United States' greatest foreign correspondents, a world-famous trout bum, and a best-selling author of rumbustious adventure books. He had become one of the world's most recognizable rovers, quite a distinction given Americans' esteem for the talented pool of foreign correspondents, those plucky know-it-alls, who prowled the world's capitals during the 1920s and 1930s, the golden age of the foreign news bureau. In that troubled era, foreign news was the equivalent of today's reality TV; the correspondents were the stars of the show. As British journalist Malcolm Muggeridge once reminisced, "They were the Knights-errant of our time; rescuers of nations in distress, champions of the downtrodden and oppressed, who smote the offending dragons hip and thigh with breathless words rattled off on their typewriters."[6] Or, as the *New Yorker* magazine lamented in 1956, foreign correspondents were "an interesting creature, who flourished most luxuriantly in the 1930s and [are] now almost extinct. The men of Farson's breed—if such a congeries of eccentrics and prima donnas can be called a breed—were not so much serious as cynical."[7] British correspondent Alexander Cockburn was equally nostalgic for a lost era when he bemoaned that "correspondence has somehow lost its glamour and its career appeal. Gone are the great days of a [William] Shirer or a Farson, when European correspondents were cocks of the walk, face-to-face with Fascism, or watching bombs fall from the roof of the Savoy."[8]

Farson's physical strength, coupled with his striking good looks, set him apart from his colleagues, who likened him to a world-weary hero of a Lord Byron poem or the protagonist in an O. Henry story.[9] "He epitomized tough masculinity, and didn't give a damn for anyone," BBC journalist Cyril Watling noted.[10] Krock also admired Farson's physical magnetism: "He was a college athlete who never lost the consciousness of his tall, strong body and its well-being, of the love for the sports of wave, stream and field."[11]

The similarities between Farson and Ernest Hemingway were too obvious for their contemporaries to ignore. They were both big-chested lovers of life, barroom drinkers, sailors, fishermen, big-game hunters, womanizers, writers of magnetic, muscular prose, Farson reveling in the real world,

Hemingway inventing his own. Born in the same decade, they had life trajectories that were a series of parallels—never intersections, for the two men never met—that compelled others to constantly compare them. "Negley Farson was a reporter who lived an impossibly adventurous life," wrote Stephen Bodio in *A Sportsman's Library*. "As macho as Hemingway's image, he roamed the world with typewriter, fly rod, fedora, booze, and cigarettes."[12] "Negley Farson, the American foreign correspondent, writer and man of action, was in the years between the wars as famous a he-man as Ernest Hemingway," wrote the British newspaper the *Guardian*.[13] British writer Colin Wilson actually admired him more than Hemingway: "Farson was the only man I have ever met who seemed cast in a bigger mould than other men. Unlike Hemingway, who tried hard to play the archetypal hero, and who, as a consequence, often struck false notes, Farson's impressiveness was completely natural and unselfconscious."[14] Just as they were born only a few years apart, they died a year apart, and even in death were subjected to comparison. In a column in *Field & Stream*, outdoor writer and tough guy Robert Ruark wrote that both Hemingway and Farson "had died more or less by their own hands in the last year. Farson didn't actually kill himself—he wore himself out just living hard and free." He added that, to him, "both writers stood for something that we seem to be running shorter and shorter on—a simple appreciation of the things that FIELD & STREAM has stood for over so many years. I am talking of manhood, and the uncontrived joy that man has always derived from hunting and fishing and camping and firelight and a reeking pipe. I expect nobody ever wrote better of hunting and fishing than Hemingway or Farson."[15]

In addition to his fabled feats as a roving correspondent, Farson wrote more than a dozen books, several of which are still considered classics in their genre. Several more probably should be. Though his novels were lousy, his nonfiction was superb. His memoir, *The Way of a Transgressor*, shot to the top of the nonfiction best-seller list when it came out in 1936, and it still wins praise and inspires young readers to lead more daring lives, though few of them probably remember the author's name. Readers passionately embrace the book not as a mere biography, but as a how-to book on adventuring. Another title, *Journey across the Caucasus*, first published in 1951, remains an engaging tale of a daunting trek, prompting

Penguin to republish it in its line of Travel Classics; along with Farson's *Behind God's Back*—the tale of a mad journey across Africa by boat, bad roads, and bush plane—it frequently earns a spot on internet lists of top travel adventure books of all time. But perhaps the volume that goes the furthest in cementing Farson's literary fame is *Going Fishing*, a spirited, spiritual accounting of Farson's victories and defeats in small trout streams and swift rivers across the globe. Even today, many call it one of the greatest fishing books ever written. Some insist it is *the* single greatest fishing book ever written. Hemingway owned two copies.[16] Historian Charles Lillard contended that "as a man Farson outdrank 'Papa,' as a journalist he out-adventured him, and when it came to trout fishing Farson outwrote Hemingway."[17] Among all of Farson's books, it best reveals the man for who he was—a restless spirit who scorned the nine-to-five life and those who grubbed for money, a wounded alcoholic with inner demons who sought salvation—and respite from the bottle—in quiet places. Yet for the most part, Farson has been forgotten, and his books collect cobwebs on the rickety shelves of used bookstores.

America birthed twin literary lions in Farson and Hemingway, yet honors only one. Hemingway stands today as an exemplar of the Lost Generation, those troubled souls cut adrift and stripped of any idealism by the Great War, those Americans who fled America because they no longer felt at home there, those writers who moved to Paris—*la ville lumière!*—drank wine, and argued art and literature in the Montparnasse cafés and wrote astounding modern novels like *The Sun Also Rises* and *The Great Gatsby*. But Farson, a contemporary of Hemingway, and F. Scott Fitzgerald, and John Dos Passos, and e. e. cummings, and Gertrude Stein, and all the other luminaries of the Lost Generation, has been forgotten. He shared the Lost Generation's fame, but only briefly.

1

→ • ←

Europe, 1925

IN THE SPRING OF 1925, Negley Farson set out from Rotterdam to sail across Europe.

His plan, though ambitious, was simple: in a twenty-six-foot yawl he had christened *Flame,* he and his wife, Eve, would run up the lower Rhine through the Netherlands, navigate their way along one of its tributaries, the Main River, pass through the nearly forgotten Ludwig Canal— parts of which had been dug in the time of Charlemagne—and from there drop into the Danube, which would speed them down to the Black Sea. Altogether the trip Farson envisioned would take them some eight months and carry their little boat three thousand miles.

For a thirty-five-year-old Mack truck salesman pocketing a comfortable paycheck and settled into a plodding middle-class life, the sailing venture smacked of boyhood fantasy.

"To sail across Europe had been a day-dream with me," Farson explained at the very start of the book he was to write about the adventure.[1] But on this day in June, Farson was not just embarking on a long journey across a continent to fulfill a fantasy, he was determined to reinvent himself. Selling trucks in the heat of Chicago summers had sapped his spirit. The gritty streets of Prohibition-era Chicago, the noisy trains, the pungent smell of the rush-hour masses—all of it had conspired to make him and Eve doubt their decision to live in the metropolis. Chicago had become a prison, and they yearned to escape. The sailing adventure across Europe was the laborious scheme Farson hatched to win back their freedom and to craft a different life for himself.

The idea sprang into being the previous year, 1924, in the stifling heat of a typical Chicago weekend. Unusually, none of their friends had invited the couple out to spend time in the suburbs, so he and Eve sat at home and stared glumly at a pile of thick Sunday newspapers. Eve, three years younger than her husband, noted that, no matter how much money he made, Farson would still have only two or three weeks a year to do what he loved—travel—if he kept his job in Chicago.

They pulled an atlas from a shelf, and in the semi-darkness—the humidity and heat forced them to keep their lights off—they took a make-believe voyage in a make-believe boat, starting in Rotterdam, Holland. Later at dinner in Chicago's Loop, they ate cold lobster salad and continued their imaginary trip, cruising along with the sun on their faces.

"We're only going to live once," Farson said, edging his imaginary boat away from the safe shores of fantasy and into uncharted waters.[2]

They began to pore over the columns of their bank account. They had enough money, the ledger suggested, to buy that boat. In it they could travel the world without regard for hotel bills or railroad tickets.

So Farson began what he called his "almost insane efforts" to win an audience with Victor Lawson, proprietor and publisher of the *Chicago Daily News,* an evening newspaper and one of the many publications scrapping for readers in the ethnic cauldron that was Chicago's population.[3] To meet Lawson—with the naked aim of getting him to help bankroll the sailing expedition in exchange for a series of feature articles on the trip—Farson turned to his friends for help. First, there was Janet Ayer Fairbank, a Chicago suffragette, champion of Progressive causes, and daughter-in-law of industrialist N. K. Fairbank. Employing her status as a high-society matron, she dashed off a letter to Lawson, a kindred spirit when it came to Progressive causes, and promoted Farson as someone the publisher should meet. The second ace in Farson's hand was Walter Strong, an executive at the *Daily News.*[4] Strong, a cousin of Lawson's wife, had perspicaciously pushed the *Daily News* to become the first newspaper to own a broadcasting station in the United States.[5] Farson, who as a salesman had developed a knack for getting to know the right people, relied on Strong to offer advice on how to refine his sales pitch to Lawson. If Strong decided to personally put in a good word with the old man, that was fine too. A third accomplice was John F. Bass, the *Daily News'* war correspondent on the Russian front during World War I, where he was wounded by German shrapnel. His relationship with Farson dated back to their days in St. Petersburg, Russia. Bass, in addition to being a professional journalist whose recommendation might carry some weight with Lawson, also offered Farson encouragement. For Farson's grander scheme was to sail across Europe, send dispatches back to the newspaper along the way, then hope that the journey would end with an offer to join the staff of Lawson's newspaper. Farson was angling to become a foreign correspondent. "The *Daily News* Foreign Service is far and away the best in America," Bass told him. "Get a foreign job under Victor Lawson and you will have the finest job an American newspaper man can get."[6]

Bass's assessment was no schoolyard boast. The newspaper's reporters abroad were among the best in the world. During a quarter century they had helped usher in a golden age of American foreign correspondence. Lawson had built his foreign desk from scratch, sending his first correspondent to Europe at the turn of the twentieth century. Since then their numbers had swollen into the dozens, and they had covered themselves—and the *Daily News*—in glory. Though their names are almost completely forgotten now, in their day they were hero-worshipped and romanticized as maverick world-travelers, gifted linguists, fine writers, and hard drinkers not easily cowed by foreign policemen or regime apparatchiks. Among the best were Bass, Edward Price Bell, Paul Scott Mowrer and his brother Edgar Ansel Mowrer, Junius B. Wood, Raymond Swing, Bassett Digby, and John Gunther, who, like Farson, would later go on to wider fame. "Our men are journalistic intellectuals, with definite personalities, with considerable personal reputations, and charged with duties in the highest realm of newspaper work," Bell once opined.[7]

At the onset of World War I, a decade before Farson set foot in Lawson's office, the publisher's reporters had proven the worth of foreign news bureaus, sending dispatches from all corners of the conflagration. Following the first shots, countless Americans who found themselves stranded in Europe flocked to the newspaper's offices in London, Paris, and Berlin, forcing the correspondents to operate rescue centers as they labored to pull together the strands of the fast-breaking story.[8]

In Belgium, three correspondents rushed into action: one followed the first wave of German invaders while the other two mingled with the stunned inhabitants of the overrun cities and towns. Digby traveled to Siberia to cover the mass mobilization of Russia's citizenry. Another correspondent was in Warsaw to tell the story of the failed German push to seize the city.[9] In short order, Lawson had thirty correspondents in the field, some with the German army, others with the French. Publishers of other American newspapers watched in amazement as Lawson's well-oiled foreign desk swung into action. "He was the pioneer in planting his correspondents wherever he suspected that a news item might grow," said James Keeley, general manager of the rival *Chicago Tribune*. "When the war began Mr. Lawson's foresight was justified. His harvest was at hand."[10] The British and French governments snatched the *Daily News* stories from the cables and shared them with their own newspapers. At one point the London *News Chronicle* gushed, "The *Chicago Daily News* is by far the best evening newspaper in the world."[11]

The man who had created this engine of global newsgathering was, of course, Lawson. Born in Chicago to Norwegian immigrants, Lawson had inherited from his father the *Skandinaven* newspaper, which catered to the great city's Norwegian population. Lawson had no intention of remaining a newspaper owner and planned to sell the newspaper to the first comer willing to buy it. Before he could get out of the business, though, he became the landlord of an upstart newspaper called the *Chicago Daily News* in 1875.[12] The long hours and hard work necessary to make a newspaper successful prompted the paper's owner to give up the business, and Lawson became its owner by virtue of taking over responsibility for its debts. He was not yet twenty-six. By 1925, Lawson had been in the newspaper business for nearly a half century and had helped to reshape the industry. In addition to creating a first-class foreign desk, he had hired columnists who waged lengthy civic-improvement campaigns, maintained a Progressive, independent editorial line, and promoted serialized fiction, human-interest stories, and journalistic stunts. He had once invested in an attempt to reach the North Pole by dirigible. All of this drove up circulation into the hundreds of thousands, established the *Daily News* as one of the world's most formidable newspapers, and made Lawson rich.

When Farson at last opened the door to Lawson's office in the labyrinth that the old building on North Wells Street had become, he was met by a small man with a finely groomed beard and penetrating brown eyes. The elder man, known to show up at the office nearly every day in an elegant gray coat and flat-topped hat, had such a delicate manner that Farson sized him up as "almost a timid man"—a judgment shared by Lawson's father-in-law decades earlier.[13] Charles H. Dennis, who worked for Lawson many years as an editor, insisted that Lawson was not timid but was merely a lifelong believer in the virtues of humility and caution.

Lawson skimmed clippings of some articles Farson had written for the *New York Sun and Herald* and told the aspiring correspondent, "I like what you have written." He then began to talk reverentially about his foreign desk.[14] Farson sensed that Lawson almost resented the younger man's belief "that I should think myself fit to be taken into such company."[15] But by now Farson had honed his skills as a salesman. His pitch was simple: the *Daily News* foreign correspondents were outdoing themselves at covering the European capitals and developing sources in the diplomatic offices of the world powers, but Farson would find the "more realistic" face of Europe by sailing across the continent, where he would chat with peasants, workers, and tradesmen along the way and file his stories from the places that many of the *Daily News* readers had left behind when they immigrated to the New World.[16] With or without Lawson's support, he said, he and his wife were going to sail across Europe—so shouldn't the *Daily News* profit from his dispatches? In Lawson's era, newspaper editors considered such bold behavior, bordering on reckless, as the mark of a man with potential. For instance, William H. Stoneman, on the local desk of the *Daily News* for three years, simply sailed to Stockholm without advance notice and informed the newspaper that it now had a correspondent in Sweden. Editors were delighted. John Gunther, hired by the *Daily News* out of college, abruptly quit his beat in Chicago, sailed to London, and got rehired by the newspaper.[17] Farson sat in Lawson's office and hoped for that kind of response to his proposal.

"The great editor sucked his thumb like a child while my destiny hung in the air," Farson later recalled. "Then he nodded. 'It's a splendid idea!' he said. 'Do it!'"[18] And that was that.

The Mack company had bestowed on Farson an unexpectedly large bonus at the end of the year, and he used it along with a little money he and Eve had saved to pay their fares to England, where he scoured the marinas and harbors until he found a twenty-six-foot Norfolk Broads centerboard yawl. Before they left, his colleagues at Mack threw him a party at the Illinois Athletic Club and gave him, among other gifts, a Mannlicher rifle, a Graflex camera, and a revolver.[19]

Now, with Chicago a hazy memory, Farson set out from the harbor of Rotterdam alone on his little boat, leaving behind the group of drinking buddies he had quickly accrued at the Royal Den Maas Yacht Club. The date was June 19, 1925. Eve had gone ahead over land to do some sightseeing in the Dutch village of Gouda, where she hoped to get a view of a particular stained-glass window. Her father, Tom, had died five days before, and she was spending time with her mother in Holland before embarking on the journey with her husband. Farson was to pick her up on the riverbank at nearby Lekkerkerk at sundown. So, by himself he worked to steer his way out of the Meuse at Rotterdam, an ordeal he maintained was as harrowing as a drive in rush-hour traffic along Fifth Avenue in New York or Piccadilly in London. The river was a mad jumble of tugboats with trawlers in tow, wide Dutch vessels with large red sails, cargo ships heading toward the Rhine, others heading toward the ocean, for Haarlem and Delft, and coal ships arriving from the Ruhr Valley. In the middle of it all, piloted by a rusty captain accustomed to the wide waters of the Chesapeake Bay, bobbed Farson's boat, *Flame*.

Farson relished the fact that he was an American citizen sailing an English ship in Dutch waters, but he cursed his reliance on his German chart. From the outset of his trip across Europe, he realized that navigation would be problematic. The chart was in kilometers, not miles, none of the buoys were marked, and numerous waterways ran into the river from left and right to create confusion as to which stream was actually the Rhine and which a mere tributary. There were also bits of land that appeared as islands on his map, but not so much in reality. More than once Farson trusted his luck to pick the right course around a jumble of land in the middle of the stream. As the hours passed, he made it out of the thick river traffic and found time to take in the scenery. He saw ducks paddling out of rushes to take flight, a flat, green countryside dotted by clumps of willows, the red tile roofs of villages, the peaceful curves of the river. "Suddenly my whole soul filled with deep contentment," he later wrote. "I lay back in the cockpit, my elbow against the wheel-spokes, delighted that it was raining and that I could feel the roughness of that old tweed collar against the weather. Our lives and nearly everything we owned in this world were in that snug cabin at my feet. Life, I felt, could hold no greater feeling of comfort and independence—and it never has."[20] Arriving at Lekkerkerk at last, Farson put in to pick up Eve and dispatched a young Dutch boy on the bank to find her. The boy soon returned at the head of a group of girls toting parcels—his wife had taken care of the shopping to stock up for their trip.

Fitting everything into the boat presented another problem. *Flame's* cabin was six feet by eight, and both Farson and his wife had to duck to enter and remain in a stooped position until they sat down. Access to the cabin was on the stern side of the boat. The forepeak in front of the cabin, which Farson likened to the toe of a boot, was given over to storage. It contained two suitcases and two duffel bags of clothes, books, medicine, cans of food, and a spare anchor, as well as an American flag and, ominously, a leak. Two bunks, each a foot and a half wide, lined either side of the cabin. By tossing aside the green canvas cushions that covered the bunks, the Farsons gained an extra three inches of space in which to sleep. A compact toilet with a pump stood at the head of the portside bunk. The galley, which contained nothing but a single Primus stove, lay at the head of the starboard bunk. A centerboard ran down the middle of the cabin, and by raising the drop leafs the couple had a nice varnished teak table on which to take their meals. The Farsons stored their food in a frost box made of porous clay and soaked in water. A tank with ten gallons of fresh water was stuffed in a cramped space beneath the afterdeck, and an African water-bag used the process of evaporation to provide them with three gallons of fresh water daily.

As the days passed on the water, Farson and his wife—whom he whimsically dubbed "The Crew" in his dispatches back to the *Daily News*—endured burnt fingers and blackened food as they taught themselves to cook whole meals of multiple dishes on one small Primus stove. Their dinner bacon would be cold by the time the eggs were ready, potatoes came out mushy, and by the time the coffee was fit to drink they were dead tired and ready for bed. But as the days wore on, they acclimated to life adrift, and Eve picked up the knack of cooking in austere conditions. Farson noticed that "three course dinners would materialize in the middle of a howling gale."[21] Eve, he concluded, had begun to perform miracles. Breakfast offered no similar challenge: they merely dropped their eggs into the coffeepot and let the water boil them.

Despite the occasional rough weather, the small craft sailed easily along the 125 miles of the Lek through Holland. Bend after bend of the river gave way to vistas of well-tended farmland; church steeples appeared in the distance one after another; and the little pontoon bridges that crossed the river swung open to let the small boat pass. Farson would look back on these idyllic days fondly and recall the slow passage of time while he smoked cigarettes and they listened to the tinkling church bells on shore. The easy going was ideal for a sailor just stretching out his sea legs, and for a crew still unfamiliar with life in cramped quarters.

At Emmerich on the Rhine, the adventurers first encountered the heavy merchant marine traffic of Germany. For the next 265 miles, to Mainz, Farson had to pilot his fragile vessel among great clots of steamships, barges, and tugs pulling strings of ships "at least half a mile long."[22] In one stretch of the river Farson saw hundreds of barges afloat. The river's current also overwhelmed the strength of *Flame*'s engine and forced Farson to ask for a tow from a passing tug. With his boat safely lashed to its side, Farson enjoyed the sight of the picturesque German towns as they slowly drifted by and the naked sunbathers who lay along the banks. After anchoring at Cologne, he and Eve visited a garrison town where Eve had attended a finishing school before the war broke out. Eve wanted to see a family that included several German officers. However, when the Farsons arrived they discovered that only one of the officers remained alive, and he had suffered terrible injuries. He now worked as an interpreter for the Allies in Cologne. "I get along well with the British," he told the Farsons. "I like them. I am afraid to talk to the French. I am always afraid they will make me do something silly. I hate them so."[23]

It would not be the last time Farson witnessed the hatred that was brewing up another war on the continent.

But they also enjoyed the tranquility of the peasant countryside. Farson began one dispatch this way:

As I write this, we are lying off the empty *schloss* of the mad king of Bavaria. And one might think that I was mad, too, for in a boat that leaks through the roof I am praying for rain.

We passed through here yesterday, gaily waved good-bye to the good people of Aschaffenburg, who hung over the red limestone bridge to examine us, and entered the pleasant country beyond. Low, green farmland, rolling hills,—very much like Dutch Pennsylvania,—dotted with crooked little red-roofed half-timbered houses. We saw shepherds tending their flocks; little goose girls, with long yellow plaits, driving their hissing regiments to the stream. Conventional things which one had read about in Grimm's *Fairy Tales* as a child,—but never expected to see! Storks nests on the chimney tops! And one black and white patriarch flapped by us, dangling his red legs as though broken, and dropped into a marshy field by the riverside. We saw fishermen, with their "V" nets on long poles, poling along the edge of the rushes, the man at the stern thrashing about with his push pole, scaring the little fish into the net. Yellow perch![24]

Above the steep slope of the Lorelei, in the Binger rapids, the Farsons' trip nearly ended at the bottom of the river. The tugboat pilot charged with navigating the fierce rapids forgot that *Flame* was in tow. The white water dunked Farson's boat with such force that the bow bitts were yanked out. Fortunately, Farson had tied the tow rope around his mast, which held—just barely—as the tug yanked his boat through the white churn and into the placid waters running between rolling farmland and on to Mainz. Here, their boat entered the Main River, and the Farsons began a 240-mile climb toward Bamberg, in the mountains of Bavaria. They were able to lash *Flame* to the side of the Kette-boat, a monstrous machine whose engines ground away to climb along a 190-mile chain, swallowing the iron thread at the bow and disgorging it at the stern. From 6:00 a.m. to 8:00 p.m., the Kette-boat pulled on the chain, dragging eight barges and the *Flame* against the current and up into the mountains. They made thirty-three miles a day. The pace was slow enough to allow Farson to jump to the riverbank, find a yard in which he could buy eggs and butter for breakfast, then clamber back on his boat upriver.

At the end of the chain lay Bamberg, and after unhooking their boat from the chain-pulling monster, the Farsons took the opportunity to stroll around the city and relax. Here they were able to gauge the mood of the German people. In the Theatre Café, Farson told a young German student that he had been astonished to see so much physical activity—swimming, marching, rowing—along the banks of the Rhine. The nation, he offered, seemed to be in training. The student smiled and replied, "Would you like to see our aeroplane factory?"[25] The student led Farson to what had been a barracks before the war. Inside, a group of boys and girls studied the skeleton of a fuselage mounted on wooden horses. They were building a glider. (The peace terms following the war forbade Germany from building a motorized air force.) In return they were receiving training in aeronautics and flying. The instructor, who Farson was told had shot down ten planes during the war, openly bragged about the breakthroughs Germany was making in engine design. Forbidden by the Allies to build new armaments, they had learned to do more with older ones.

From Bamberg, the Farsons entered what Farson deemed "one of the most beautiful canals in the world—the old Ludwig's. It had been begun by Charlemagne and was now almost dying away. We were probably the first and last craft of our type to go through it. Four miles longer than Suez, twice as long as the Panama, it was then the only fresh-water link across Europe connecting the North and Black Seas."[26] The beauty also struck Eve. She wrote in her travel diary, "Canal lovely and peaceful beyond all words—a calm ribbon of green water between rushy bends with fine forests and hills falling away to each side as we go higher."[27]

Farson's elation turned to exhaustion. The canal ran for 107 miles through 101 locks but was so shallow and choked with weeds that the *Flame*'s engine might as well have been thrown overboard. For much of three weeks Farson towed the boat himself. Every morning after breakfast he tied a rope around his waist, stepped out onto the towpath, and strained to pull the two-and-a-half-ton yawl up and over the Frankischer Jura mountain range. As he pulled he could occasionally look down on the roofs of the villages below. In the warm afternoons he threw himself on the ground, drank his beer as slowly as he could, and chatted with the lockkeepers. This was the land of princes and bishops, Farson thought: "A deep land of convents and monasteries and castles on towering crags. A legendary land to which we had brought the *Flame*. . . . I was in no hurry to leave this gentle land. I shot deer up here with the burgomeister of Maiern. The great buck stood in a cleft in the forest, and above him I saw the turrets of a castle perched on its grey needle of rock. It was like an ancient tapestry."[28]

The Farsons, still in the early days of their marriage, traveled well together, and the trip through the scenic countryside became a delightful show of pink sunrises and golden sunsets that they enjoyed together on the deck of their boat. The shared adventure had brought them closer together. Not all evenings were rest and repose, however. He had to file his dispatches for the newspaper, a nerve-wracking process that involved a muscle-sore Farson copying out his notes into story form as the sun fell and rose. "Leave Negley to a terrible day of copying," Eve wrote on July 21. "The poor creature sits in that chair from 9 to 9, never moving or going out to a meal and working like a dog on those 6 articles to be sent off from here. I can hardly bear to see him. He *is* a brick."[29] To add insult to Farson's misery, while they hiked to a nearby post office to mail off the articles, someone stole every tool on the boat.

The Farsons were enjoying the sight of the lush forests, verdant hills, and tidy German villages as tourists, but for many of the people who lived in the area, they discovered, life had become unsettled and grim. At night, "Wandervögel," a population of homeless folk who wandered across the German countryside in protest of industrialization and the loss of traditional Teutonic values, came and rested near their boat. "Very awkward as we have to tie up beside a sort of high road, where *crowds* of people gather on the bank and watch us, thrilled, as we cook and eat our eggs and bacon and coffee," Eve wrote on July 22.[30] Displaced by the war, haggard, hungry, and tired, the Wandervögel trudged through the fields and forests. They told the Farsons their troubles, then moved on.

Farson began one dispatch this way:

"Many men and women sleep in these woods at nights."
We were tied up to the bank of the Ludwig's Canal in the pine forest beyond Nurnberg and, as always, a group of pedestrians had settled down to watch us cook and eat our dinner. The towpath of the Ludwig's is an open road across Bavaria. The wanderer's highway! Even then, a group of wandervogel came swinging past, the lilt of their guitars dying away under the stars.

"But they are not bad men and womens," came the voice; "they are the—how you say—the homeless. They can't find any work."

A guttural murmur of resentment came from the vague forms above us. Why speak of such things? There must be plenty of work in the country? One hastened to tell us that next year things would be better; Krupp's would open a big works in Nurnberg that would employ 30,000. Besides, these people weren't all Nurnbergers; the police had surrounded the woods and arrested forty-one only that morning. Five they had imprisoned—they were criminals.

An argument started; the group aligned itself against the youth who spoke English. What did he know of work—or an empty stomach? One bitter voice announced that its owner had waded knee deep through the snows of Bavaria all the previous winter.

Sudden silence!

Two figures had moved into the glow of our riding-light. Gaunt men with tight lips. Unshaved. They stood there, grimly silent, and examined us. A sinister scrutiny. No one spoke. Then they turned, slid down off the towpath and disappeared in the woods.

We slept fitfully that night, troubled with imaginings of pity and fear, of those furtive figures moving about in the woods. At daybreak I awoke, heard voices and, looking out, saw a man washing his face in the canal. He was old with grey hair. He washed himself very carefully. A woman stood above him doing her hair. She, too, was old; but the mass of her hair was still gold. I lay there, holding my breath, and, lying so, fell asleep.

The voices woke me again. The man and the woman stood on the canal bank above us. They were quite dressed. He wore a light grey business suit, clean collar and cuffs. Even as I looked he cocked his hat, jauntily. They talked in low tones to each other, looking down at our boat. Never have I seen such envy, regret, and such bitter knowledge as in those two gentle faces.[31]

The Farsons were bearing witness to a Germany in the throes of a post-war economic despair. Several years earlier, in 1923, the French began to occupy the Ruhr Valley, the beating heart of German industry, to force the Germans to make reparation payments. Far-left uprisings rocked central Germany; in Saxony and Thuringia radical governments assumed power; and separatists agitated in the Rhineland. Hyperinflation impoverished the German people. In January 1923 the exchange rate stood at 17,000 marks to one dollar; by December it stood at 4.2 billion marks to the dollar. Germany was on its knees.[32]

One of the Wandervögel stayed with the Farsons—a young man with a scar on his forehead who claimed to have flown in Baron von Richthofen's squadron, the Flying Circus. Several of his friends still flew; they had gone down to Morocco to help Abd al-Karim in his war against the Spanish and French colonial powers. The young man said he would be there too if an English pilot hadn't shot him—this explained the crease in his forehead. The young man stayed on the Farsons' boat during the day and sat in the cabin and drank schnapps until midnight, "talking about the next war without restraint."[33] He hated the French and declared that all the physical activity in Germany served a single purpose—to fit the nation to war. At night he went ashore to find a place to sleep. One day he left the boat and never returned.

After three weeks of hauling his boat uphill along the Ludwig Canal, Farson pulled it through the final lock and into the Altmuhl, a pleasant little stream that carried them straight into the upper Danube. From here, no more than 1,600 miles remained to the Black Sea. Vienna lay a mere 300 miles ahead.

But first *Flame* had to shoot through the arches of the eight-hundred-year-old bridge at Regensburg, or Ratisbon, and navigate the rocks and rapids where the Danube gushed through the gorge above Kelheim.

The Danube is motion personified. It is almost alarming, after the drowsy repose of the Ludwig's Canal and Altmuhl, to face the ice-gray flood rushing out from the gorge above Kelheim. It was a moment we had planned for years; yet we had no map, pilot, or chart, charts of the Danube being, apparently, non-existent. We would have to "go it blind," like the first savage going down on a log,—or the Crusaders, who swept past Ratisbon with 400 row-boats in the eleventh century. With a "here goes" sort of zest, we sent *Flame* out of the Altmuhl and were whirled away like a leaf.[34]

Here disaster nearly struck. Only one arch of the old bridge was navigable, and Farson was unsure which it was. He had removed the boat's mast to fit under the arch and had inquired at Kelheim about which arch to steer for. But as the boat raced down the river, carried by the increasingly wild waters, he realized at the last minute that the peasants had directed him to the wrong arch. It was filled with rocks and the white froth of rapids. He swung the boat sharply to the right in a desperate attempt to squeeze through a small arch by the town wall. *Flame* just made it through, nearly grazing the stone wall as it passed. Below the bridge, residents of Regensburg gaped with surprise to see such a tiny boat come from above. They waved to the Farsons as they passed.

But more danger loomed. "We swung into a black gorge, smoking with mist, raced along swirling, wind-twisted pines and shot into the open country beyond," Farson wrote in his dispatch to the newspaper. "There we got our first real taste of the Danube—the experience that was to warn us and let us know, once and for all, that this was no Mississippi, or Hudson, or Delaware—but a fierce, impatient and unkindly flood that seemed to feel it has a long way to go—and a short time to get there."[35]

At Vilshofen they hit a rock ledge just as they entered another rapids. The impact broke their keel. They managed to make it through more rough waters by racing under the castles of the Wachau Valley and anchoring one night below the castle of Durnstein, where Richard the Lionhearted was held prisoner, before sailing into Vienna. Here Farson took the boat to a shipyard for repairs. The Farsons checked into an old hotel, the Meissl und Schaden, to luxuriate in a hot bath. From Vienna, the trip became less of an ordeal, more of a slow float. Serious rapids lay far ahead of them, just above the Black Sea, but for hundreds of miles the great river drifted slowly through Hungary, Yugoslavia, Bulgaria, and Romania. The Farsons could worry less about the trip—the navigating and steering, finding food, and preparing it on the Primus stove. From here on they could savor the surrounding lands, dine in restaurants in little towns along the shore, and Farson could send off his dispatches via telegram or diplomatic pouch.

In Chicago, readers welcomed the dispatches, and since readers were paying customers, editors were delighted. The *Daily News* gave Farson's colorful articles prominent play and had syndicated them to thirty newspapers. Managing editor Charles Dennis smiled with content to find they had won a readership. "I am glad to say that your articles please me very much," he wrote Farson in Budapest, care of the American consulate there.

"The method of writing that you have employed seems to me admirable and I shall be glad if you continue in the same sketchy vein except when you have material that you think should stand alone instead of being part of the log of your voyage."[36] He followed up with another letter, addressed to Farson care of the American consulate in Belgrade: "I am glad to say that your articles are attracting a great deal of attention and I am sure they will make a real hit. Since your preliminary articles have gone so well, I have great hopes for those just received and for the rest of this very excellent series."[37] The praise must have buoyed Farson's hopes. His goal was to perform so well that awestruck editors would implore him to join its staff. So far, he was throwing strikes.

From Vienna, Farson continued to treat his readers to sketches of life in the Old World. When they arrived in Hungary, Admiral Horthy, the nation's regent, invited Farson out to shoot partridges at an old Hapsburg hunting lodge. He ended up shooting with five admirals, "not one of whom now had a ship."[38] Horthy and Farson managed to cover themselves in mud, and as Farson sat in a bathtub while staffers cleaned his clothes, Horthy entered the bathroom with a decanter of brandy and two glasses, filling one for Farson. When he told Farson he had shot very well, Farson "almost drowned from sheer pride."[39] Farson next traveled, over land, to the Rumanian frontier to shoot partridges. He ended up drinking red wine and singing songs with a group of Magyar cowboys out on the Hortobagy, the great Hungarian plain. Watching the cowboys through the campfire, Farson thought they hadn't changed much since the Mongol invasion.

Back on the Danube, the border guards of Bulgaria apparently mistook the Farsons for smugglers and opened fire on *Flame*. A few handshakes and pantomimed explanations patched things up, and the next night on top of a cliff overhanging the Danube, the Farsons were the guests of honor at a regimental dinner at which Eve danced the Hora with the regiment's colonel while a sergeant-major whisked Farson around the dance floor until they collapsed. After forcing Farson to make a drunken speech, the regiment carried him around the town square on their shoulders. But not all was mirth and amusement with the soldiers. The agreement reached at Versailles had reduced the Bulgarian army to thirty thousand, a humiliating cut to the country's military, so every soldier trained to become a noncommissioned officer—a necessary and preliminary step to build a stronger, more efficient fighting force for the next war.

The trip took a turn to the bizarre in Romania. They were greeted in the village of Coronini, above the rapids at the Gorge of Kazan, by a Father Bufanu, who insisted he had dreamed of Farson's arrival the night before. He then offered several pieces of advice: first, get a small dog "to give warning when the Bulgarians attack you";[40] second, make sure to bring a pilot on board *Flame* to navigate the treacherous rapids through the Gorge of Kazan; and third, when you arrive in Bucharest, make sure to visit the Queen. The Farsons ignored all three pieces of advice. They decided to shoot the gorge and the notorious "Iron Gates" without a pilot. The thought of trying to pass through the Iron Gates, a narrow gorge linking Romania and Serbia, had long been a concern for Farson even before they left the United States. Now, after passing under the massive stone bridge that the Roman emperor Trajan had built to cross the Danube during his first Dacian campaign eighteen centuries earlier, the Farsons experienced firsthand the rushing torrent known as the Iron Gates: "It takes a special towing-steamer two hours to climb this downpour of the Danube. We shot down it in precisely six minutes. All we lost were some cups and saucers that a lurch or sudden wind swept off the deck."[41]

A week of smooth sailing followed the harrowing trip through the Iron Gates, and the Farsons docked in Giurgiu. Finding little of interest in the small town, they boarded a train that carried them north across yellow plains for three hours and into Bucharest. Perhaps weary from their journey, they were not impressed with the city. Farson's dispatch to his Chicago readers conveyed the sense of a weary traveler:

> Bucharest is a false-face of Paris, or a great masquerade, or a gold-plated Ingersoll. Things are never as good as they look. At first you think you've found a real city,—then you know it is Hicktown,—painted up. There is only one hotel worthy of the name and that you can't get into, as the guests hold the rooms by the year.
>
> The other, almost-hotel, is an ornate, deceiving affair. The price for the rooms seems cheap. But as there is a tax for heat, a tax for light, and a tax for,—well, it is not so cheap. There is even a tax for each time you use the

elevator,—and when people come to your rooms. A government tax leaps on top of all that.

You shower tips like the rains of the spring. If you don't,—the people come up and ask for them. You tip the elevator man as you come down in the lift. If one porter brings in your bags another porter helps put them down on the floor, a third picks them up and a fourth brings them upstairs. Your floor-man then takes them from him and brings them into your room. Then they all stand holding out their hands,—to see whether it will rain or not.

The tips are not much, and after you get over your first revulsion of always shelling out even for asking the time,—you might be as tolerant about it as the Roumanians are. If only you got something from them! But rudeness seems the chief stock-in-trade of the menials of Bucharest.[42]

Back on the Danube, Farson discovered that the dramatic stretch of water through the Iron Gates had taken its toll on *Flame*. Just ninety-two miles from the finish line, the Black Sea, Farson had to beach the boat at Galatz: The keel had once again snapped. The boat's stern had also been smashed. Farson loathed Galatz. While shipyard workers tried to repair his boat, he walked around the town, a large grain port, and found it had only two distinctions: the first was a cadre of taxi drivers composed of a religious sect of Russian eunuchs; the second was the sign in his hotel, which read, LADIES AND GENTLEMENS WILL PLEASE RETURN TO THEIR OWN ROOM BY MIDNIGHT. Farson's distaste for the city and his hotel seems to have extended to the entire country, and perhaps with reason. On a side trip into Bessarabia, Farson watched Romanian soldiers threaten peasants with bayonets and shoot at them as they tried to escape across the river at Chisinau (now in Moldova). Every official demanded a bribe, and the Romanian Secret Service detained and interrogated him, noting that telegrams of his arrival had been crisscrossing the entire country. Farson had to explain that he wasn't a spy, but his interrogator let him go only reluctantly. Farson was not a spy, of course, but he had gained local residents' trust by fishing for sturgeon with them and then interviewed them about the deadly Tatarbunary uprising of 1924. The thought of Farson scribbling notes while residents babbled on about the death of three thousand people probably lay at the source of the authorities' consternation.

The repair work on *Flame* continued. Late December had arrived, forcing the Farsons to bundle up in every piece of clothing they owned while Farson fretted over the possibility that the river would freeze and leave him stranded just short of his goal. The thought devastated him: "I had crossed Europe nearly 3,000 miles, and on the very last lap of it I might lose my race. *Almost* to reach the Black Sea would be worse than never having started at all. I had no philosophy against defeats like that."[43]

Farson would suffer the same despair nearly five years later, at the height of the Caucasus Mountains as he dared to try to cross the Klukhor Pass alone in a blinding snowstorm. But now, on the banks of the Danube, Farson's situation wasn't really all that bad, for he had already achieved his ultimate goal, a job offer from the *Daily News*. In a letter dated December 10, managing editor Dennis praised Farson for the "exceptional literary quality" of his travel sketches and added that "an arrangement of permanency" was Farson's for the asking.[44] Farson had apparently already suggested a preference to be posted in Russia, but Dennis gently reminded him that the newspaper's current correspondent there was doing an excellent job. He hinted that the *Daily News* might be able to use Farson in the Near East. In any case, he suggested that the details could be worked out later. "You have done a very remarkable piece of work in your Danube voyage," he added in closing, "and I trust that the material thus obtained will achieve permanence in book form. I have instructed our Art Department to preserve for you all negatives received."[45] So Farson had a job lined up and permission to reuse his material to publish a book.

All that remained was to get *Flame* repaired and sail her through the Sulina Canal connecting the Danube to the Black Sea. With the ship at last in decent enough shape to continue, the Farsons tossed their duffels onboard at 2:30 p.m. one day and set off from Galatz, so eager to leave that they didn't bother to stow their stuff. They ran straight ahead until midnight, butting into chunks of ice in the water along the way, and only stopped to anchor when they had reached the island of Isaccea. The Farsons slept with all their clothes on. The next morning they found that the surface of their drinking water had hardened into ice. But their race to beat winter and avoid becoming frozen on the ice of the Danube was over. They steered into the Sulina Canal beneath a clump of willow trees, stopped briefly to enjoy cognac and jam with a Yugoslav canal tender, then continued. In the dispatch that ran in the February 17, 1926, edition of the *Chicago Daily News*, Farson could not hide his joy at being so near the sea:

> The world was an infinity of sky over a featureless marsh, and here, suddenly, we felt the sea—a "lift" in our senses. There was nothing to mark it—just the "feel." We knew it was there. Then like a dream, some fanciful port in a reverie of adventure, appeared the gold-crossed, fantastic red Russian towers, the lighthouses, the slant sailing rigs and the black hulls of the ocean tramps in Sulina. We ran down past a medley of foreign shipping, saw the snow-swept English lawns of the Danube Commission, faced the red and green lighthouses at the Danube mouth—and there, coffee-colored, pounding and white, raced the everlasting waves of the barbaric Black Sea.
>
> We had sailed across Europe.[46]

They had indeed. And Farson had learned several important things: He now knew for certain that he could handle a boat as well as he thought he could, and he knew that Eve's sense of adventure was a match for his wanderlust; and, perhaps more importantly, he now knew he could write well enough to earn a spot on one of the greatest foreign news desks in America. He could make a living and see the world as a foreign correspondent. His childhood dream was coming true.

2

→ • ←

The Old General

I am fevered with the senses,
I am fretful with the bay
For the wander-thirst is on me
And my soul is in Cathay.

There's a schooner in the offing
With her topsails shot with fire
And my heart has gone aboard her
For the Islands of Desire.

—Negley Farson, penned in a hospital bed

WHEN NEGLEY FARSON FINALLY sat down to take stock of his life, his memory first turned to his grandfather, former Civil War general James Scott Negley. In Farson's mind, the old general was the First Real Man—the original adventurer. Farson's parents, Enoch and Grace Farson, had essentially abandoned him when they "parked" him with the old man and, quite literally, sailed off.[1] General Negley, Grace's father, turned out to be just the role model that the young boy needed. The general was a tall man with a short temper, had been places and done things, and he still knew how to throw a punch.

Farson was born on May 14, 1890, and he spent his boyhood under the freewheeling care of the general and the watchful gaze of his two spinster aunts and three black servants. It is always difficult to say where any man's fate is sealed, where his feet are set upon his proper path, but the odd family at the general's house most definitely determined much of the young Farson's future. His lifelong love-hate affair with money, his disdain for an office job, his restlessness, all took shape at the general's modest house among the tall pines in Plainfield, New Jersey.

"My grandfather kept his three negro servants by the simple expedient of not paying them. They did not seem to mind."[2] So Farson began his 602-page autobiography, *The Way of a Transgessor,* which appeared in 1936. In Farson's telling, his turn-of-the-century childhood was at times idyllic, at times impoverished, due to the general's failed business schemes. This was the Gilded Age, when the so-called robber barons—Carnegie, Harriman, Rockefeller, Vanderbilt—dealt in railroads and oil and steel, amassed fortunes, smoked cigars with congressmen, and drank warm brandy from crystal goblets. An envious, impoverished public was gripped by money mania. The bolder among them engaged in get-rich shenanigans. It was the era of far-fetched plots and the flimflam man, of bold business undertakings. The general was firmly part of his time, struggling to seize a fortune as enthusiastically as he had fought to save the Union.

He limped around his land in a black alpaca coat, dreaming up money-making ventures. The result was a life of boom times quickly followed by lean spells: One year Farson's aunts would be laughing and cavorting on the lawn as they played hostess to tennis parties and served tea and cakes; the next year the racquets lay on a shelf, gathering dust. One year's new suit became the next year's patched duds. In the small wood-frame house with a mansard roof, Farson watched as his grandfather tried to fend off creditors, at times violently. Such dustups were bound to shape Farson's attitude toward work, money, and class. He recalled the butcher, the baker, the laundryman arriving on the front porch demanding payment. One creditor became so insistent that the general physically kicked him off the porch, resulting in a lawsuit. The general mollified other creditors with vegetables from his garden. At other times, the general's murky business schemes—sometimes

involving railroads, sometimes banana plantations—drew strange characters from far-off places like Mexico and Cuba, men who smoked cigars
in bed and burned holes in the sheets. At one point the general sailed off
to England for two years, scraping together all his money in a desperate
attempt to make more while his young wife tended to Farson and used her
charm and good manners to keep the creditors at bay.

For all the general's money woes, he still found the means to send
Farson to the state fair every year, once to New York to see Buffalo Bill.
Farson loved the general. The old man had earned his limp in battle, in the
war with Mexico, where a bullet pierced his hip. He had run away twice as
a young man to fight in the war, the second time with his cousin, who died
by his side during the twenty-day siege of Veracruz. But Negley was bul-
letproof. When the Civil War broke out fourteen years later, Negley, now
a gentleman-farmer who found his greatest joy in grafting plum branches
to peach trees and peaches to plums, returned to soldiering, raising his
own brigade to fight for the Union. He marched with Sherman through
Georgia to the sea. At the Battle of Stones River in Tennessee he won fame
when he rode up with reinforcements to save the Union's beleaguered left
flank, shouting, "Who will save the left?"[3] The cry became a popular Civil
War song that immortalized the Illinois regiment that took up Negley's
challenge. But war is fickle, and Negley was later court-martialed following
the Chickamauga campaign of 1863 and was never given another field com-
mand. The way Farson told the story, his grandfather was accused of refus-
ing to leave the battlefield and may have even shot some of his own men to
prevent them from fleeing. The reality was different: General Negley had
commanded fifty artillery pieces on Snodgrass Hill and withdrew them—
prematurely, according to his commanding officer—to support the Union
retreat to Chattanooga. Negley demanded the court-martial to clear his
name and was vindicated. He followed up his military career by serving
several terms as a Republican congressman but, unlike other congressmen
of the era, failed to turn his elected office into a moneymaking position.

General Negley was born, grew up, and lived much of his life in
Pittsburgh, but had moved to the small town of Plainfield under cloudy
circumstances. First, after his wife's death, he had scandalously married
a woman roughly the same age as his son, Jim. His second offense to the

senses of the local bluebloods involved a snow-white horse named Billy, which he had captured from a Confederate colonel. The general had given the warhorse to his young bride with instructions that the horse should never be put in harness. When Jim disobeyed and harnessed the horse, the general seized a whip and lashed his son across the face. Jim packed his bags. He never returned. Several years later, the family saw Jim's name on a list of passengers aboard a ship that had gone down off the coast of Buenos Aires. Pittsburgh society never forgave the general.

Despite the checkered past, Farson relished the way his grandfather bulled his way through the world and thought he "made other men around him look like mongrel dogs."[4] His grandfather, in turn, loved him, allowing the small boy to plunge his hands into his silvery curls, to tug on his goatee. He saw in Farson a surrogate son who he hoped would one day drop the name Farson and carry on the Negley name. Farson also loved the servants, Abner and his wife, Rhodie, from whom he learned respect for different classes of people. The third servant, Simms, spent his time reading law books instead of polishing the family silver. Farson admired him for going on to become a New York lawyer. And if Farson felt any shame that his grandfather occasionally could not afford to pay his faithful servants, he never owned up to it.

If the general taught Farson how to barrel through life with his chin out, it was Abner who gave him his love for the outdoor life, taught him how to keep chestnuts soft, to trap rabbits, to skin muskrats. They were vital lessons to a young boy who considered the outdoors his church. The outdoors nourished his soul and gave him a love for adventure and exploration. He noticed that the world of business made his grandfather miserable, that the old man only became truly alive in the natural landscape, strolling his land and discussing fruits, trees, the soil. The young boy resolved to side with nature, to hell with commerce. Even if he didn't realize it then, he was learning to rebel against the modernizing world around him, the ballyhooed progress that he saw purely as industrial encroachment on forests, fields, and creeks. Farson rambled through the meadows and thickets, memorizing the names of the different grapes that grew on his grandfather's land, toting the .22-caliber rifle that he paid for with the allowance he squirreled away in a cigar box with a nailed-down top. He learned to climb trees, swing on vines, tie knots, catch grasshoppers, set traps, and dig for worms. He built his own canoes, sailed, learned to fish for smallmouth bass in lakes and streams, for speckled trout and flounder in the nearby Sandy Hook Bay. He lived a life of boyhood adventure in an era when boys sparked their imaginations with the novels of Joseph Conrad and the stories of Jack London and Rudyard Kipling.

At age eleven, during a hunting trip, a friend accidentally shot him in the left leg. "I've murdered him!," Farson recalled his companion yelling.[5] Then the friend ran away. Bleeding, Farson crawled through the fields in search of help. Two farmers eventually found him and rushed him to the local hospital. There, after telling a little girl that he shot "bunnies," she responded, "I hope you'll die."[6]

In recounting the shooting accident and the little girl's criticism, Farson played it for laughs; but it would be the first in a long series of accidents, mishaps, and injuries that would bedevil him throughout his thistle-rich life.

3

→ • ←

Fish Mad

FOR ALL HIS LATER sophistication in dress and manner, Farson dubbed himself a "country bred" boy who learned to hunt and fish as part of the routine rite of passage in rural America.[1] He became "fish-mad for life" thanks to the heft and weight of a twelve-pound carp he once winched out of a small pond using corn as bait.[2] He roped the carp to the handlebars of his bike and pedaled home, where, to his astonishment, his grandfather ordered Abner to throw the fish on a brush pile. (Carp supposedly tasted like mud.) Undeterred, he went fishing with a friend who hooked a nesting two-and-a-half-pound smallmouth on a flashing spoon. The bass leapt into the air, then dove deep and hard, making the reel scream, before his friend landed the trophy on the bank for Farson to admire. This glorious achievement sealed his fate, he said, and fanned his desire to "fish and fish and fish" with a passion he would take to the far corners of the world's oceans and lakes and rivers.[3] The boy learned how to read the local water—whether that of the fecund Delaware Bay or the booming surf off the New Jersey coast—one of the finest skills of a good fisherman. He fished hard and free, partly driven, like most fishermen, by the atavistic impulse of the hunt, sometimes by the need to simply eat. At the age of twelve he spent time on the New Jersey coast, making friends with local fishermen, spending "marvelous nights with the ocean roaring and churning itself like a wild beast by our sides."[4]

One day, he convinced a brawny fisherman to take him out on his skiff to the banks where he could "pull up all sorts of wondrous things."[5] But the boy never got his chance. He waited on the pier for the skiff to show. It didn't. He learned later that one of his aunts had forbidden the fisherman from imperiling her nephew with such an adventure. The discovery hardened his runaway heart and gave him "another incentive to fish, fish, fish; and the further away from home it was, the better it would be."[6]

In 1901, when Abner, weeping openly, told him his grandfather—the "grand old man"—had died of complications from diabetes, young Farson was taken further under the wings of his protective aunts, who themselves had practically been held captive by the general's old-fashioned, patriarchal worldview.[7] One had aspired to be a doctor, the other a singer. The general forbade both dreams, cloistering them in his small home, which became their small world. While the general lived, the women had failed to escape their unfulfilled existence. Farson witnessed their empty indoor lives and bounded out the front door of the house as often as he could.

Drink came early in his life, and the initial encounter offered no hint that he would form a lasting relationship with alcohol. His first taste was offered by a town drunk named "Spieler" Welch. One misty night, Farson accompanied Welch to fish for catfish from a bridge overlooking a tiny stream that fed into a swamp. In addition to teaching Farson how to handle a fish, Spieler handed the boy a flask and told him, "Here, Kid—have some bait."[8] Farson foolishly took a long pull and found his lungs on fire. He spat out what he could of the burning liquid and nearly tumbled off the bridge. He later claimed he could not stand the taste of whisky again until he was twenty-four—a distaste he would overcome with a passion.

Following the general's death, his widow sought her pension as the wife of a Civil War veteran but ran into an obstacle straightaway. She had married the general at the end of the war, so she had not suffered "the full four years' agony" to merit a full pension.[9] The government offered her a sum that she considered insultingly small. Bureaucrats, able to bend only so much, agreed to increase the sum slightly, but when it came time for her to request that Farson receive an appointment to West Point, as the general had wished, she was still so angry at the government that she refused to ask. She spent the pension on educating the boy elsewhere—the private Phillips Academy at Andover. He was fourteen when he stepped onto the campus in 1905.

Farson's time at Andover ended in spectacular failure. Which is a shame, because of all the schools he attended, Andover was the only one he loved. Located in a small village in Massachusetts, the Phillips Academy, as it is more properly known, was the first prep school in America. In Farson's time, it was still the best. Other boarding schools had cropped up in recent years to serve the sons of those made rich by the nation's industrial prosperity, but none had yet caught up to Andover: its foreign language teachers were exotics from the Old World, its math teachers were published authors with reputations in the field, and its liberal arts department rivaled those of some colleges.

Doubtlessly what Farson most relished, though, was not the school's academic program but its insistence that all boys must participate in sports. Farson jumped in, managing a basketball team, pitching for his class baseball squad, taking part in gymnastics, and holding down the position of secretary of the gun club. Further chipping away at his study time, he spent many nights playing poker with the older students. In addition to all the frenetic sportsmanship and gambling, Farson worked as a "heeler" for the school's student newspaper, the oldest student-run publication in the nation. As a heeler, it was Farson's job to collect news items and announcements from various dormitories and deliver them to editors in time for the paper's next edition. It was Farson's first taste of the profession that would bring him acclaim and fulfill his burning desire to travel the world. It would also introduce him to the merciless demon of newspaper deadlines.

Farson lasted two years at Andover. The cause of his departure centered on his roommate and another boy, an athlete whom Farson respected so much that he stood up whenever he entered the room. The schoolmate's name was Kilpatrick, and he had hatched a plan to toss a local man into a pond on the Andover campus. Kilpatrick was convinced the man had squealed on Farson's roommate for kissing a local waitress, a violation of school rules. (Farson himself claimed to have had his first sexual experience while at Andover, picking up a girl on a merry-go-round and paddling her out to an island on a lake: "She did not know much more about these things than I did. But it wasn't the disappointment I had been told it would be.")[10] Farson considered Kilpatrick's plan "not only concise, but alluring, breath-taking, enchanting, daring, absolutely unrefusable."[11] In reality, it was simply a matter of gathering a mob of students who dragged the man from the front porch of an inn, carried him to the edge of a pond, and chucked him in.

Punishment was swift. The school closed for four days while administrators subjected students to interrogation. In the end, thirty were dismissed. Among them was Farson. His grandmother came up from Plainfield to plead his case, and though the head of the school, Al Stearns, brought up Farson's poker-playing, the tiny woman whom General Sherman had once hoisted aloft was too much for him. He agreed to give Farson the standard ten-week suspension. But Farson quit, unable to remain after so many of his friends had been thrown out. In leaving Andover, he made sure to shake the hand of the one student who had valiantly tried to stop the mob violence. Farson considered him "a hell of a fine fellow" and admitted that he "admired his guts."[12]

Following his departure from Andover, Farson was sent to Chester, Pennsylvania, to live with his father, Enoch S. Farson, whom he hardly knew. He knew that his father was about thirty-four years old in 1889, when he married the general's daughter, Grace Negley, who was a teenager at the time. Enoch had courted the much younger girl by showing up at her door with a banjo he could barely play, an act that prompted Farson to conclude that his father was an ass. His parents had drifted in and out of Farson's childhood and had never taken his education seriously, considering it less important than their need to winter aboard their boat in some new locale. They jerked him out of one school after another, nine in all, by his account. Farson had made sporadic trips from his grandfather's house to his father's, but his father had taken no interest in him until he was old enough to shoot, fish, and sail. Enoch Farson was, if not a failed businessman, then a failing one. He had inherited the Farson Manufacturing Company from his father, whom Farson knew as the hardest drinker along the Delaware. The company crafted refrigerators of fine wood. A rival firm in Grand Rapids, Michigan, had found a way to make them more cheaply, though, so Enoch Farson had switched over to making expensive, handmade furniture. The business didn't exactly thrive, and Enoch Farson, in his fifties when his son came to live with him, had become fretful and surly. Farson long remembered the shame he felt as richer men in the small town hushed his father at the dinner table. His passion was not business: it was the boats he had owned, starting with the *Juanita,* the one in which he had sailed away with Farson's mother after leaving the boy with the general. Since then he had owned a succession of other vessels, each one smaller than the last. Pictures of them hung on the walls of his small house in Chester.

The young Farson was miserable, hated Chester, and longed to run away. "That town frightened me," he recalled. "I never witnessed anything more disheartening than the morning rush of business men to catch the trolley at the end of the street. One morning I watched a boy walk out of it. He was going off to a salmon cannery up in Alaska. I leaned out of my window and cheered as he passed by. I was only sixteen then and did not have the nerve to escape."[13] A female friend named Theo Towe who had a crush on Farson wrote to him years later and recalled his teenage longing to break free: "I can remember you now saying, 'I have the wander lust. I want to see the world and write most of anything in this world!'"[14] The distaste for the humdrum working day, the longing to escape, were already there in Farson's character, commanding him onward, outward, away. His impulses were as strong as his grandfather's preference for botany over business, as powerful as his father's love of wind and wave above industry and success. Such yearning would always be Farson's compass.

He found momentary relief from his misery in the same place his father did—on the deck of a boat. His first winter in Chester, he managed to buy a secondhand Bridgeport gunning skiff for twenty-five dollars. He spent the winter caulking and patching it. In the spring, he and another boy dropped it in the Chesapeake Bay and spent weeks sailing, drifting south. They had no destination, only a desire to enjoy the pong of the bay, two boys free from all cares. They exhausted their money, lived on nothing but blue crabs for two weeks, and finally made it home by hauling the skiff aboard a larger boat heading north, paying for their passage by working as crewmen. All in all, Farson considered it grand. He had sought adventure to test his mettle and had found it. The taste was in his mouth now.

Back in public high school in Chester, he found salve for his restless spirit in sports. He played guard on the football team until he managed to break his shoulder. But when his shoulder healed, escape arrived from an unexpected quarter: Farson discovered that he was one of those freaks of nature who could, almost effortlessly, run fast, throw far, and endure much. He was, much to his own surprise, an athletic prodigy. On a whim, he entered Pennsylvania's Middle State interscholastic championships in the shot put. And won. From then on, he was hooked, traveling hundreds of miles for a chance to win a medal, which he would then give away to his current girl-friend. "This was the hey-day of many an American boy, this brief burst of athletic glory, before he settled down for life to rot in an office of some sort," Farson recalled. "And I resolved to cash in on it for all I could get."[15]

Farson's passion for sport—which, like fishing, he called his "madness"—paid off.[16] In his travels around the state to collect medals, he caught the attention of Michael C. Murphy, the University of Pennsylvania's athletic coach. Murphy, too, had been a sports enthusiast from his youth. By the age of twenty (he was born in 1861) he was traveling the country to participate in six-day foot races, which were then all the rage. He also played minor league baseball and did a bit of boxing, and his ability to spot raw talent led him to become a trainer. One of his trainees was the great boxer John L. Sullivan. Murphy had been athletic director at Yale (which Farson still hoped to attend) but arrived at the University of Pennsylvania in 1896 to take charge of training track athletes in the spring, footballers in the fall. In 1906, he began a rebuilding campaign that helped the school capture various athletic championships. His success led to his appointment as trainer of the U.S. Olympic teams in 1900. When Farson first came to his attention, Murphy was a trainer with a national reputation; Farson was a nobody, an unhappy teenager with a clutch of shot-putting medals. Murphy pushed Farson to give up his dreams of Yale and come to the University of Pennsylvania in Philadelphia. "I'll teach you more than these damned professors ever will," he told Farson.[17]

Farson heeded Murphy's advice and enrolled in the Pennsylvania school in 1910.

Though a passionate reader all his life, Farson was by his own admission a lousy college student, not prone to spend nights hunched over equations by lamplight. Part of the blame perhaps lies at the feet of his guardian, who, over a farewell lunch of lobster salad at the Bellevue Stratford, advised Farson not to work too hard, to instead invest his time in making friends and joining the right groups. Farson heeded the advice. His guardian was a Wall Street businessman whom Farson's grandfather had instructed in his will to look after the boy. Farson saw in the act a parting shot at his father—an effort to deny him a place in his son's life. But the guardian was, like the grandfather, an on-again, off-again, in-debt, out-of-debt Wall Street player perpetually scheming to win back his lost fortune. He was hardly the man to guide Farson on any moral path. In the books he later wrote Farson never revealed the name of his guardian, just as he rarely mentioned the name of his younger brother, Enoch S. Farson Jr.

Following his graduation from high school, Farson was single-minded in his motivation for attending the University of Pennsylvania: he would become an engineer and build railroads or bridges in South America (construction of the Panama Canal was underway, and Americans had turned their avaricious gaze to their southern neighbors), or anywhere that would keep him from toiling away his life in an office. However, he needed money, and during the summer break he took a job as a salesman, working on commission for one of the Standard Oil Company's subsidiaries in New York. He traveled the commercial and industrial neighborhoods of the city, where he was simultaneously aghast at the poverty he saw and admiring of the rich warmth of slum tenants' lives when compared to the "clerks" he saw along Broadway.[18] The experience hardened him in his already obsessive loathing of the life of his father, and he declared that he had never seen emptier lives "than those of the young men I saw sitting in offices waiting for the clock to strike five."[19]

For Farson, an engineering degree was a path away from that fate, a key to a life lived outdoors. As in high school, though, Farson spent his collegiate time avoiding textbooks. Sports remained his passion. He continued to win first- and second-place medals for the shot put and broad jump. He also joined the National Guard of Pennsylvania, commissioned as a second lieutenant in 1913 and earning qualification as a sharpshooter. But the highlight of his years at Penn were the boat races, for Farson had taken up rowing, and later in life, "when things all started to break the wrong way," he would urge himself to keep going, to keep fighting, with the words, "Just one more stroke."[20]

Years of training had given him the physique necessary for the sport. He stood six feet tall, weighed 186 pounds, and had a powerful forty-three-inch chest. With an impressive physique coupled with thick brown hair, good looks, and eyes the color of cornflowers, he had little trouble attracting young women. His college friends called him Big Swede.[21]

Away from campus, in New York, the wanton ways of the bachelor's life beckoned. He made two close friends: a red-headed real estate agent named Bob Rainy whose family had given him up as a "bad egg," and an employee of the Italian consulate named Caesar Guillimeti.[22] The trio plumbed the nightlife of New York to its depth, eating to excess, seeing shows, enjoying midnight dinners in a bordello whose madam was a good friend of Guillimeti's. But Farson's truest friend was Joe Graham, known as Jo-Jo, a gymnast whom Farson noticed on campus one day as he waited to train on the gym's rowing machines. After talking to each other for a few minutes, they discovered that they were both majoring in civil engineering, and for the same purpose—to escape the humdrum world of the work office. "We did not care how big the position might be, not even in a president's chair; neither of us wanted to sit in some office for fifty weeks out of every year—which was what was called 'making good' in the United States of our epoch," Farson recalled.[23] Making the relationship even sweeter, Jo-Jo owned a yacht he was obsessed with, the *Anna*. Learning of the boat, Farson resolved to cultivate a relationship with Jo-Jo. By the end of the year, they had determined to head for the west coast of South America as soon as they had their diplomas in hand. Railroads needed to be built over the Andes, and they would build those railroads.

But first they determined to take a summer cruise down the Chesapeake, so hours they should have spent working at their drawing boards they instead invested in fitting out the yacht and making it ready for the voyage. At last the day came, and they set out from the Corinthian Yacht Club. They had only sailed as far as Delaware City, however, before Jo-Jo decided to catch a train back to Philadelphia to run a mysterious errand. He returned the next day with his girlfriend, a showgirl named Toots. Farson seethed, but dutifully made the young couple breakfast in the mornings, dropping nine eggs to boil in the coffeepot, turning a loaf of bread into buttered toast, and slicing up cantaloupes. But eventually the lovebirds' cooing began to sound to Farson as unpleasant as squealing bicycle brakes, and when he could take it no more he gave Jo-Jo an ultimatum: either the girl would leave, or he would. Jo-Jo and Farson argued. Toots, however, was determined not to have her summer spoiled. She arranged for a girlfriend to come down from New York to join them. But the instant Farson saw Violette, he hated her. So she abandoned ship, and Toots went with her back to New York. Farson and Jo-Jo completed their journey, sailing peacefully along the shores of Tidewater Virginia and arriving back at college three days late.

One night in the fraternity house where he lived, Farson received a phone call from Jo-Jo's father: Jo-Jo and Toots had eloped. The old man wanted Farson to rush down to Philadelphia to break it up. Farson trekked to their apartment and tried, but seeing the two so content, he abandoned the mission. He rarely saw Jo-Jo after that. When he finally did see him again on campus, Jo-Jo had been crying. Toots had won a beauty contest by standing on a banquet table naked. Jo-Jo was devastated. Two weeks later he caught a boat for Panama, hoping to become a soldier of fortune in South America. Farson gave him his most prized rowing medal as a going-away present.

Meanwhile, a New York actress with one blue eye and one gray eye helped finish Farson's college life. He had met her at a party and fallen in love. But his mother and aunts disapproved of the relationship, presumably because his girlfriend was an actress. Into his junior year the couple kept up their romance, despite the rude behavior of his family toward Ann. But one day he received a letter from her describing how his family had "all cut her dead in the street" in front of a producer she had hoped to impress.[24] In anger, Farson decided to leave college that night. Before departing, he said goodbye to the engineering dean, Edgar Marburg, whom Farson idolized as the world's greatest bridge builder. Farson had studied civil engineering with the specific dream of building bridges in the high Andes of South America. In parting, Marburg smiled and said: "Negley, I wish you would make me a promise. Promise me—for the sake of humanity—that you will never build a bridge."[25] Farson left for New York, where the Standard Oil Company rehired him. Once again he was an oil salesman.

Trudging the squalid commercial streets of the metropolis in the oppressive heat and humidity, Farson quickly learned the centuries-old misery of the trader who can find no buyer for his wares. The recession of 1913–14 was on; business activity had declined nearly 26 percent across the United States, making it tough for Farson to find paying customers. He considered the salesman's life "a monotonous performance, based upon professional ingratiation, obsequiousness, and a hide like a crocodile."[26] He told Ann he couldn't go on, that he was desperate to make a break. Fortuitously, an envelope bearing a Canal Zone stamp arrived. It was from Jo-Jo, demanding that Farson hurry down to British Guyana to join him in prospecting for gold. Ann told him the idea was crazy.

"No more crazy than dying of dry rot here," he responded.[27] He talked her into it.

Before hopping a boat to gold and adventure, though, Farson decided to compete in the big New York Fall Games held at Travers Island, home of the New York Athletic Club. Farson won the javelin throw, so organizers allowed him three more attempts in the hope that he could break the American record. On his first fling, he tore the main tendon off a thigh bone. There would be no new record this day. Nor ever, as far as Farson was concerned. For his injuries were adding up: He had already been shot and had broken a shoulder bone and two fingers. He now suffered a tendon tear that, a doctor later discovered, had developed a deep, lingering infection. The dream of South America had snapped along with his tendon.

Downhearted, broke, aching to run away, he returned to his humdrum job, hobbling along on his daily sales calls. Farson looked across the street one day and saw a sign bearing the name of one of America's biggest steel companies. Its president was the father of a university friend who had crewed with him. Farson dropped in to say hello, and his friend promptly offered him an engineering job—in Manchester, England. Farson practically leapt at the chance.

Ann, the woman for whom he had abandoned college, balked. In the summer of 1914, he left her in a taxi two blocks from the dock where he boarded the *St. Paul*. He rejoiced in the knowledge that for the next ten days aboard the ship he would have no responsibilities. Ann drove off in the taxi without looking back.

4

→ • ←

England and War

THE VOYAGE ACROSS THE Atlantic was memorable, not because of the nightlife aboard the *St. Paul*, or any major storms at sea, but due to events then shaking the world. Even before the ship sailed, Austria-Hungary had declared war on Serbia. The date was July 28, 1914. Many voyagers intending to travel to Europe that summer suddenly canceled, giving up their berths on the *St. Paul*. They were immediately filled by young Englishmen living in the United States who were determined to rush home before war began. They were out of luck. On August 1, with the ship steaming along the Gulf Stream, Germany declared war on Russia. On August 3, Germany declared war on France and sent troops into Belgium. The following day, England declared war on Germany, marking the official beginning of World War I. Aboard ship, Farson joined a boisterous group of Englishmen in the smoking room to sing "Rule, Britannia." When they asked him to lead them in singing the "Star-Spangled Banner," he discovered that he didn't know the words.[1]

Farson arrived in Liverpool in early August, and already the country was on a war footing. Trains carried troops to training grounds and toward the front. Farson was bound for Manchester, where he was to take up a job in the engineering department of Hans Renold Ltd., a company that manufactured chains. Ultimately he became "Manager of the English Speaking Agencies," a preposterously important title for a twenty-four-year-old American in an English conglomerate.[2] He would remain in the job less than a year—taking responsibility for writing the company's advertisements—before his restless spirit carried him off to Russia, but his short stay in the British Isles would profoundly shape the rest of his life. And England would inevitably become the center of his life.

First, he fell in love with the place. On weekends he roved over the moors and downs, fished in the small brooks, shot game in the marshes. He marveled at how the British had managed to keep their land fresh, green, unspoiled. By comparison, he felt the Americans had swept over their continent like a host of locusts, attaching wires and paving over pastures with reckless disregard. Farson walked a mile and a half to work at the chain factory from the small home where he rented a room. He grew to love the morning mist and the evening damp of English weather, against which he fortified himself with a typical, leisurely English breakfast of tea, toast, eggs, and steamed tomatoes.

Second, he loved the pace of the average Englishman's life, for it confirmed his suspicions that the American way of doing things was wrongheaded. In college he had learned to compare world economies by the wages they paid. In Manchester, he saw a level of contentment among his colleagues that had nothing to do with the size of their paychecks. They weren't making much money, but they took immense pleasure in trying to produce the highest-quality chains in the world. In the United States, Farson thought, businessmen would be racking their brains trying to produce chains at the lowest possible cost. But here in the assembly lines of Manchester, he saw the lowliest workers genuinely interested in the quality of their product. They earned modest wages, lived in humble houses, and spent their free time in simple pleasures such as taking rambles through the woods and attending lectures on nature. The English lifestyle, or what Farson made of it, anyway, confirmed his notion that there was more to life than piling up money in a bank vault.

And third on his list of life alterations, in England he learned to drink, to *really* drink. He fell straightaway in love with the pubs, those cozy corners where men congregated to sip their pints and puff their pipes. The workers stampeded to the pubs after work; even the humblest among them achieved a sense of self-respect and decency with a pint of bitter in their hand, a mate at their elbow. Farson became a lover of whisky and soda, a combination he judged necessary to ward off the "marrow-drenching" yellow fogs of Manchester.[3] He drank whisky while walking across the moors on weekends with his landlord, he drank whisky while socializing with colleagues at the Manchester Engineers' Club, and he drank whisky on outings with a close friend in the company.

But, paradoxically, the calm, idyllic Englishman's life rattled Farson's nerves. In Manchester, he admitted to himself, he was only "playing at life."[4] Afraid of getting comfortable, numbed by routine, he had to get away. "I knew that I was not going to stay there any more than I could have remained an oil salesman in New York. Too much was going on 'outside.' Perhaps the war was the chief reason for my restlessness. So many of the men had gone off and come back to visit us in khaki."[5] Indeed, the war was calling, and Farson was being pulled into it in a very real way. Once, out on a date with a local girl to the movie theater, he was accosted by a recruiter, a tall Scot in full Highlander kit. The Scot asked Farson why a strong young man such as himself wasn't in uniform, and he did not relent in cajoling Farson to enlist even after Farson announced that he was an American. A crowd began to form, murmuring their displeasure. Farson heard someone mumble about the "bloody Americans."[6] He was mortified. He admitted to himself that it was humiliating to walk about Manchester, a healthy young man, and run into the fathers of those who had volunteered to fight.

Still, it was his old feelings about the nine-to-five life, his disdain for the clerk's life in New York, for his father's business worries in Chester, that pushed him to move on. He saw that the English way "was a dead end. There was something fatalistic about the way the English accepted the various given conditions of their lives and in the way they resolved to settle down happily in them. . . . They were dull. Therefore, when the chance came, I took it."[7]

The chance was a meeting with some American businessmen who had come to Manchester. Farson had orders to show them around the assembly lines and entertain them after hours. At dinner with them in the French restaurant of the Midland Hotel, they impressed him with their optimism; he allowed them to talk him into joining their venture. They were setting up an export shop in London with the express purpose of trying to win war contracts with the defense ministries of Britain, France, and Russia. After putting them aboard the train for London, he went straight to his boss and resigned.

A week later he was ensconced in the Americans' office in London, where he met his new boss, a Tasmanian whom Farson quickly recognized as little more than a con man with villainously handsome looks and a charming but completely untrustworthy sales pitch. The fledgling business, located in a flat in a building whose other tenants were prostitutes, worked through its connections with a couple of Danes in the hope of winning a contract to sell motorcycles to the Russian War Department. The corrupt Tasmanian had planned to sail to St. Petersburg to help seal the deal but decided to send Farson instead after reading about a ship sinking off the coast of Norway—its passengers froze to death in their lifeboats. Two days later, Farson sailed from Newcastle with 150 gold sovereigns. He counted them out piece by piece, so worried was he that his especially shifty boss would cheat him. He also carried what he assumed to be letters of introduction. But when he opened the envelope en route, he found only a note that read, "Good luck. Everything is left to your discretion."[8]

The ship first docked in Denmark, where Farson caught a train to Christiana to meet the two Danes who were supposed to be helping his enterprise make the necessary connections to sell the motorcycles. In Christiana, he came face to face with the corrupt, underhanded world of arms merchants. To his credit, his suspicions were aroused at once. He proceeded with caution. For starters, one of the two Danes, Heinrich, was a German, busy trying to work deals supposedly to help Russia defeat Germany. Second, neither of them (the other was a bushy-bearded lawyer named Hakonson) had made contact with a Russian middleman whom Farson's boss had explicitly told them to work through. Finally, they both used every argument they could to dissuade Farson from continuing his journey to Russia. They were close to making a deal, and they argued that his presence would only gum everything up. Farson recalled:

> From these two sinister creatures I learned that there were something like
> nine different men, representing that many factors in the negotiations,
> between my London principals and the Russian War Department. I also
> saw, when I began to insist upon proceeding there, how frantically anxious
> they were that I should not reach Russia. They predicted all sorts of ugly
> "accidents" that might happen to me. And the Dane so convinced me of the

duplicity and high-handedness of the Russian customs officials that I gave him my case of gold and silver athletic medals to keep. Mementos of an early life that I valued so much in my childish fashion that I would not even leave them with my supposed Tasmanian colleague in London.[9]

Eventually, when the two realized that Farson was too pigheaded to turn back, they welcomed him into the fraternity of shady arms dealers. All three went out and got drunk together. The following day, Farson was riding a train through Sweden above the Arctic Circle. Next stop: Russia.

5

→ • ←

Russia

A DECADE BEFORE HIS TRIUMPHANT boat trip across Europe, Farson's arrival in Russia marked the grand beginning of his adventurous trek through the world. He would spend three years there, perfect his skills at heavy drinking, woo and bed women, and socialize with czarist royalty. At first sight—though his first sight was little more than a sentry box in the middle of the frozen Torneo River—he fell in love with the country, vowing to die there. He nearly did.

The Russia that Farson encountered in 1915 was an inexorably unfolding disaster. While a revolutionary spirit was abroad in the land, the war was devastating the czarist government, the economy, and the morale of the people. The outbreak of hostilities with Germany had temporarily halted protests and tamped down discontent with the czarist regime as Russians united to face a common enemy. But the Russian war machine immediately met with reversals. The first major battle, at Tannenberg in 1914, was a calamity: more than thirty thousand Russian troops were killed or wounded; another ninety thousand were captured. By the end of the year, in less than six months of fighting, nearly four hundred thousand Russian soldiers were dead; a million had suffered injuries. Young men with almost no training were thrown into the meat grinder to add their names to the list of the dead. Czar Nicholas himself took charge of the army in 1915 as the populace grew increasingly irate with government corruption and the influence of Rasputin on Empress Alexandra. But the czar's personal involvement did little to improve conditions: After Germany turned its attention to the Eastern Front, the Russians were driven out of Galicia and Poland. Meanwhile, the army was now constantly short of rifles, ammunition, uniforms, food. By mid-1915, soldiers were arriving at the front without weapons. By the end of October 1916, Russia had lost up to 1.8 million soldiers, with two million more held prisoner, another million missing altogether. The conditions directly contributed to the mutinies, insurrections, and, ultimately, the revolution that Farson would witness.

All that lay ahead. After saying goodbye to his traveling companions, arriving in St. Petersburg, and disembarking in Finland Station, the young, inexperienced Farson managed, barely, to communicate to the driver of the horse-drawn carriage that he wished to go to the Hotel Europe. He planned to make the hotel his headquarters as he worked to plug himself into the Russian war machine to hawk arms and machinery. In the lobby, a swirl of lights, gypsy music, beautiful women, and officers bedecked with medals, Farson encountered the man the Danes were using as an intermediary in Russia, a Danishman named Frosch. Like the other Danes, the mysterious Frosch instructed Farson to stay as far away from the War Department as possible, promised that the conclusion of a big deal was imminent, and beseeched Farson to disappear and not throw a wrench into everything everyone had worked so long to achieve. Farson instantly sized him up as a swindler and almost immediately rushed out to cable London to ask for permission to "proceed independently."[1] By the time the answering cable arrived (permission granted), Farson had set up shop in a room of the Hotel Astoria, facing the great square in front of St. Isaac's Cathedral.

At the Astoria, with its French dining room constantly full of officers and diplomats and courtesans and arms dealers, Farson met the man he would only identify as Frumkin—the man the London office had been desperately entreating the Danes to meet with, and whom the Danes had energetically avoided. Acknowledged as the man who had all the right connections with corrupt Russian officials in the war office, Frumkin struck Farson as possibly the most devious human he had ever met. Frumkin looked and talked like an actor, had received an education in New York that only multiplied his skills for duplicity, and "could think twice as quickly and around ten times as many corners" as Farson: "He knew it. I knew it. And, when Frumkin knew that I knew it, we became quite friendly and frank with each other after a time. I really got to love the old rascal."[2] Frumkin was in actuality S. O. Ochs, the Curtiss Aeroplane Company's senior agent in Russia.[3] He worked with a partner in New York, Robert Pluym, to sell Curtiss planes to the Russians. The company also had a team of pilots and mechanics in the country to assemble the planes and show them off. Ochs's role was to deal directly with corrupt government officials, to grease their palms when necessary. Which was, according to Farson, nearly always. Somewhere in his time in Russia, Ochs had become not just an agent for Curtiss, but a go-between for many of the arms dealers who had flooded into the country with the outbreak of war. Ochs had apparently helped establish the rules of the game early on. Those who coveted contracts with Russia mustn't go to the War Department directly; they must find an intermediary—like Ochs. Ochs knew which officials to bribe, and how much cash was necessary. Farson, forced to play the game for his livelihood, quickly realized that the results of all the corruption was the death of innocent Russian soldiers. The war, he concluded, was not being lost at the front; it was being lost in St. Petersburg, in the dingy offices of corrupt bureaucrats. Farson watched as whole battalions marched off to slaughter, one with rifles, the next without, ordered to pick up the rifles of others once they had been killed.

As War Department officials delayed orders in an effort to squeeze higher bribes from the arms merchants, Farson became trapped in the monotonous routine of a salesman's life. Day after day he awoke before lunch, donned his suit and hat, and trudged over to the War Department, despite warnings that he must only work through intermediaries. The effort was a charade, and Farson struggled to contain his fury—an emotion made more intolerable by the arrival of letters that gleefully informed him that most of his friends back in the States were busy becoming millionaires thanks to generous war orders. Officials had long ago received his proposed contract. The price had been established and seemingly accepted. But it was all a ludicrously improbable situation, and no contract materialized.

The nightlife at St. Petersburg offered an orgy of consolations, however. Arms merchants like Farson spent their time dashing from one party to

another in a haze of increasing drunkenness. At one party Farson organized, a drunken friend ended up suspended out of a third-floor window,
and none of the revelers, not even the suspendee, could remember how
he got there; after another night of drinking, Farson accidentally boarded
a train that took him to Moscow in his shortsleeves.[4] Other nights were
spent at the Imperial Russian Ballet. Still others were spent in nightclubs
where nude girls sat at the piano, a sight so common Farson grew bored
of it. During his first summer in St. Petersburg, Farson could not remember ever going to bed before six in the morning. He spent long nights
in cabarets, surrounded by cigarette smoke, young women, "crazy laughter and gypsy songs."[5] The days he spent fucking—driving young girls
out to secluded spots, swimming naked in the rivers, sprawling out on a
hundred-year-old croquet lawn. He also shot pigeons, ate mountains of
fresh cucumbers, and played golf. Once he took part in a party that lasted
three days and woke up at the end of it in an open Daimler car, out of gas,
with no recollection of how he got there. He was spending his Tasmanian
boss's gold sovereigns as only a young man could. If a life of total dissipa-
tion was the target, Farson had proven himself an expert shot.

Business eventually took Farson and Ochs to Moscow, where they
holed up at the Hotel Metropole. There, while having tea, Farson met
Shura Alexandra Georgievna Tomachova, a runaway Cossack girl from
the Caucasus, perhaps seventeen or eighteen, with high cheekbones, a
pointed chin, and a firm neck. His attraction to her was instantaneous.
He convinced her to take a stroll around Moscow, and though they were
barely able to communicate, he managed to seduce her. Young men easily
tire of such romances, though, and Farson was glad to leave her behind
when he and Ochs returned to St. Petersburg days later.

But Shura was not to be dismissed so easily. The day after his return to
St. Petersburg, Farson received a summons to report to the lobby of the
Hotel Astoria. There stood Shura, surrounded by a pile of wooden boxes,
a country girl wearing a hideous red hat. Alarmed, Farson hustled her up
to his hotel room, from where, he thought, he could "handle this affair."[6]
He couldn't. She had come to stay: "Nothing could shift her. I gave it up.
Why try, anyway."[7] Farson planned to be in Archangel in seven or eight
days and determined to leave Shura behind once more in the hope that

she would find another man or her way back home. Days later, Farson was aboard a train rumbling out of St. Petersburg for Archangel, ensconced in the lower bunk of his carriage. As he prepared to turn out the light, he looked up and saw—Shura. Once again she had refused to be dismissed.

In Archangel, Farson saw firsthand why Russia was losing the war. It was the spring of 1915; the great port "lay smothered under layers of lead ingots, steel bars, rusting motor-cars, bales of soggy cotton and broken crates of machinery of every description."[8] Everywhere Russian officials scrambled to and fro. An avalanche of war matériel had poured into the city meant to feed Russia's mighty army, but it lay abandoned to rust and rot thanks to official corruption. The railway bed was literally sinking under the weight of the matériel. While Ochs scurried around in search of the right officials to bribe, Farson and Shura spent their days at the docks watching the frantic activity aboard the many ships that had successfully run the gauntlet of the German navy. They often sat on a crate containing a magnificent Rolls Royce that had been brought and left to rust. Eventually—after a week of pleas and arguments—he put her on a train home, and he and Ochs raced down to Crimea. Ochs, whom an increasingly cynical Farson described as a "vindictive slut," hoped to sell hydroplanes to the Russian navy.[9]

Spring was in full bloom when the two dropped their luggage in rooms facing the Black Sea, and they immediately got down to business. While Ochs practiced his dark art of oiling corrupt officials, Farson began flying with the Russian pilots. Every morning at seven, they flew over the ports and scoured the Black Sea for German submarines. Occasionally German ships shelled Sevastopol in an effort to hit the hydroplane base. Once Farson and a Russian pilot, both naked, flew an experimental Russian hydroplane out over the water and the German ships. In another adventure, Farson spent hours in jail, frog-marched to his cell by a stern guard waving a 9mm Luger, after authorities found he had a camera. Farson was released only when a pilot arrived to say Farson was needed to make up a foursome on the tennis court. Things didn't go as well for Ochs. Farson returned to St. Petersburg to learn that Russian secret police had tossed Ochs into prison. He had apparently double-crossed someone in one of his shadier deals; now, his victim was working behind the scenes to exact revenge, and Ochs faced charges of being a German spy. He also faced a possible appointment with a firing squad. One of Ochs's fellow wheeler-dealers, an American millionaire who lived in a suite of rooms at the Astoria, tried to get the American embassy involved by claiming Ochs was an American. When he asked Farson to vouch for Ochs's American citizenship, Farson refused. When the millionaire suggested Farson's unwillingness to help could lead to Ochs's execution, Farson merely replied, "I don't care a damn!"[10] Ochs eventually agreed to flee the country after Russian authorities agreed to seize his fortune. He and Farson would never work together again.

Just as Ochs's role in Farson's life neared its end, another exotic arrived in Russia to influence the young arms merchant. This was John Reed. The controversial journalist—heralded across the United States for his coverage of the Mexican Revolution, during which he spent four months sharing the travails of Pancho Villa—caught Farson's eye one evening as Reed sat in the dining room of the Hotel Astoria. With him sat an older man, Boardman Robinson, the Canadian American illustrator who, like Reed, worked for *Metropolitan* magazine. Following the outbreak of war in August 1914, *Metropolitan* sent Reed by boat to neutral Italy with instructions to find the war and write about it. The pair headed to Paris. France, however, frustrated Reed with its censorship—Reed was not sympathetic to any particular side in the war—so he traveled to London. The rest of 1914 he had spent in a drunken debauch, then headed to Berlin with a German lover. After a brief return to New York, he set out for central Europe, this time accompanied by Robinson. The two witnessed the ravages of war in Serbia, Bulgaria, and Romania before they finally traveled to St. Petersburg and fell under Farson's gaze in the hotel. In fact, Farson had met Reed several years earlier in Greenwich Village and admitted to being captivated by him. Reed was a mere three years older than Farson. But whether Farson knew it or not, Reed was exactly the kind of man Farson longed to be—fiercely independent, adventurous, and disdainful of the status quo, a man who could earn an honest buck with his pen.

With Ochs in jail, Farson and many other arms dealers were forced to reestablish connections with the Russian War Department; that is, to find bribe-worthy officials on their own. But Farson took a break from his duties to spend time with Reed and Robinson. The relationship would be a boon for all of them. "If they made that Russian summer a Nirvana for me, I was a goldmine for them," Farson recalled. "For about a week we did nothing but pick each other's brains all night over the open-air dinner-table in the courtyard of the Hotel Angleterre where they were living."[11] Their tête-à-têtes would have historic consequences: Farson gave Reed and Robinson the scoop on Russia's tottering war machine and detailed, step by infuriating step, his futile efforts in St. Petersburg, Ochs's shenanigans, the names of the numerous officials who moved only after a bribe was pushed into their pockets, and the sight of unarmed soldiers marching through the snow toward near certain slaughter at the front. He introduced Reed and Robinson to an Englishman who was the secret representative of the vast Vickers armament company, as well as to groups of Russians aflame with revolutionary spirit. The material that Farson gave Reed abundantly helped inform Reed's next book, *The War in Eastern Europe*. The corruption Farson laid out stoked Reed's anger, a class-conscious anger that became nearly animate within the pages of Reed's later masterpiece, *Ten Days That Shook the World*. In return, Farson received an education from Reed in real journalism. Afterward, when he was himself a world-famous foreign correspondent, he searched out sources that reminded him of himself in St. Petersburg, "someone naïve and fresh and full of rage and energy."[12]

Ultimately, everything that Farson shared with Reed, including a handwritten dossier on his dealings with various War Department officials, ended up in the hands of Russia's Secret Service. As Farson met and drank with the two journalists, the police kept them under constant watch. When Reed and Robinson left their room at the Angleterre, it was promptly searched. Czar Nicholas's government had been suspicious of the two as soon as they had entered Russia. Now, upon seeing the material they had gathered in St. Petersburg, the government gave them an ultimatum: get out of Russia, via Siberia, or face punishment, which included imprisonment or the firing squad. Reed appealed to the American ambassador but got nowhere. Only after the British ambassador, at Robinson's request, wrote a polite letter to Nicholas did the government consent to let them slip away through Sweden. They did.

With his two adventurous friends gone, Farson sank back into his monotonous routine of being shunted about by War Department bureaucrats out to hustle bribes. He returned to his regular social life of consorting with fellow arms dealers and young women, temporarily running afoul of a Cossack whose girlfriend and pistol he had made off with. But his business dealings reached a dead end—his association with Reed and Ochs, still in prison and facing the possibility of execution as a spy, had damaged his ability to make inroads with officials. Desperate, hoarding the few rubles that remained in his pocket, he formed a partnership with the representative of the Robert Dollar Company, a San Francisco–based shipping firm. Together, they decided to try to sell motorcycles to the War Department. They bolted a machine gun to a side car to entice the Russians to deal. But the day they were to test the big American motorcycle dawned cold and drizzly. Their Russian test driver failed to show up at the airfield where the machine was to undergo its trial runs in front of the potential buyers. Farson, who barely knew how to drive a car and had never in his life sat on a motorcycle, agreed to fill in for the test driver. Years later, he would remember the night before the motorcycle test as one of the last nights he was able to "walk about freely" on his own two legs.[13]

Wearing a blue double-vested suit, Farson jumped on the motorcycle. With a few kicks of the starter it roared to life and sped off, and a terrified Farson hung on for life. He took it halfway around the square in front of the Hotel Metropole before he felt confident enough to really put it to the test. First, he took it over a series of bumps, then down a ditch and up the steep bank on the other side; then he sped up to show off the machine's acceleration. A twisting, cobbled road ran along the edge of the airfield, bordered by a wooden fence. Farson rounded a turn in the road, sensed the wheels slip on the slick cobbles, then felt himself flying helplessly through the air as the motorcycle jumped a ditch and crashed through the fence. He awoke to hear someone remark, "It's still running!" as others pulled him torn and bleeding from beneath the slightly crumpled motorcycle.[14] In the days afterward, he developed an infection and underwent a ghastly operation to remove part of his left leg bone. His hotel bed served as the operating table, his old writing-pad was employed as a chloroform mask, and he wasn't quite sure if the surgeons were fully qualified. His friends took care of him and rolled him out to dinner parties in a wheelchair, but the combination of his lack of money—he was more skilled at cavorting than closing deals—and his poor physical condition forced him to consider a return to the United States for a proper operation. He wired his anonymous guardian for money, and one day his friends put him on a train at Finland Station in St. Petersburg. A Russian nurse named Anna Goertz accompanied him. Three days later, in Gothenberg, Sweden, he was carried aboard the *Stockholm,* a ship on her maiden voyage to America.

The voyage was not without mini-adventure. A foreign correspondent was aboard ship, and Farson took a dislike to him, appalled at the journalist's pretensions of knowing everything. It was too much for Farson to bear. So Farson and Anna chatted up the correspondent, a man identified only as Dunham, and fabricated an entire front of the world war, recounting the nonexistent battle of Stakan Chai in which General Moroshnie swam an entire regiment of Cossack Oodkas across the Lena River, where every last one of them was killed by the Austrians. What Dunham didn't know was that Stakan Chai roughly meant "glass of tea," General Moroshnie was "General Ice Cream," and Oodkas were "ducks." Farson assured him that the censors didn't want news of the battle to reach the papers, so if Dunham could get the story into print, he would have a tremendous scoop. Dunham, practically salivating in anticipation, filled his notebook with Farson's fantastical details.

As the ship neared American shores, though, Farson began to doubt the wisdom of his prank. If the correspondent printed the story, his career would be so much smoldering wreckage. So Farson called the correspondent down to his cabin and confessed. The correspondent reacted less than graciously. The next morning a small card appeared on every table in the dining saloon. It read: "Miss Anna Goertz & Mr. Negley Farson Beg to Announce Their Engagement."[15] The joke devastated Anna, who had a fiancé waiting for her in Philadelphia. The ship's captain invited the couple to dine with him that evening, and the two felt compelled to keep up the charade. But it didn't end aboard ship; somehow the wounded correspondent got word to the press corps in New York, and a throng of reporters met Farson at the dock, snapped pictures, and asked pointed questions in order to flesh out their story of shipboard romance. Farson's guardian was also dockside, and he was appalled—he wept to see the decline in Farson's health as they carried him off the ship. Farson had shrunk from his athletic 182 pounds to 140. The next day, as Farson lay in a hospital bed awaiting an operation on his shattered left leg, an orderly handed him a New York newspaper, the *Bulletin*. On the front page was a picture of him and Anna. Her fiancé saw the story and immediately broke off their engagement, until Farson wrote an apologetic, explanatory letter. In the end, the fiancé greeted her with open arms. But Farson suffered as the butt of the ghastly joke for years to come. Nearly a decade later, the Alumni Register of the University of Pennsylvania reprinted an engagement announcement that claimed that Farson "was badly wounded and nursed back to life by Miss Goertz."[16]

Farson spent the next several months in a New York hospital, strapped to a board as the traffic roared in the streets below. John Reed brought books and tried to persuade him to become a Communist. Eventually Farson felt well enough to move, so his guardian transferred him to his estate in upstate New York, where in the mornings a nurse wheeled him down to the dock and he went out in a canoe to fish for bass. Despite the isolation, Farson became aware of what he called the increasing "war order madness" sweeping the United States.[17] The nation's exports to Europe were trebling—from about $1.5 billion before the war to an eventual $4.3 billion. Companies big and small could not move fast enough to hire export managers to send overseas to win contracts for their products. The belligerent countries were buying in bulk, and the Americans wanted in on the action. Feeling as if his contemporaries had bolted out of the starting blocks to claim a pile of money while he was left at the starting line, Farson formed a partnership with a Swede named Torsten Landby whom he and Anna had met in the train station in Sweden on their way from Russia to the United States. Torsten had seen the strenuous effort it took Anna to shift Farson about, so Torsten, well over six feet six inches tall, simply picked Farson up and carried him in his arms. The two had struck up a friendship aboard the *Stockholm* (Torsten had even served as Farson's best man at the dinner the captain held in honor of the young couple he presumed were engaged), so back in New York they agreed to form an export business, Landby & Farson Company, and return to Russia. Their plan was to sell engineering supplies, a line of products that Farson thought would last well beyond the war years. Farson bought a portable typewriter and began to fire off letters to manufacturers, offering his company's services in representing them in Scandinavia and Russia. With companies yearning to profit from the war, he had no trouble lining up eager clients.

In 1916, Farson set sail back to Russia aboard the *Danske Fly*. The trip was risky: German U-boats patrolled the Atlantic and were sinking roughly a thousand ships each year, and merchant shippers had developed no reliable way to avoid the attacks. Whereas his first boat across the Atlantic two years earlier had been filled with young men eager to get to the fight, this boat brimmed with war profiteers who had vowed to make their fortunes. Though Farson was now one of them, he found their company tedious. So he formed an exclusive club of just a dozen members who paid dues and adhered to a set of bylaws, the first of which was, "The chief object of this Corporation is the total corruption of the ship."[18] As president, Farson lived up to the Corporation's ideals and took a young Norwegian girl into his cabin with caviar and two bottles of champagne. Sometime during the voyage, an impoverished couple gave birth to a baby girl in steerage. Farson's Corporation agreed to "buy" the girl, each member giving the parents ten dollars so that the Corporation could claim to be the child's godfather during the journey. The Corporation also gave the newborn girl her name—Atlanta Flyvia. The young mother wept in gratitude.[19]

Farson's attempt to reenter Russia collided with the czar's hostile border guards. No doubt due to his association with John Reed, officials refused his passport. Their refusal threw his business plans into disarray. But a member of the U.S. legation in Stockholm issued Farson a new passport, appointed him a diplomatic courier, and gave him a diplomatic pass. The Russians scrutinized the paperwork, then grudgingly let him enter their crumbling country.

For crumbling it was. Farson immediately noticed the difference upon his arrival in St. Petersburg. In fact, the first words he heard from an English expat there were, "Nobody expects Russia to win the war now!"[20] Everywhere Farson witnessed doom, gloom, and a defeatist atmosphere. Crippled soldiers stood in the street and begged for money. Healthy soldiers openly boasted that they had deserted. Rasputin had been killed, and factory workers and peasants warily recalled his prophecy that the Romanov empire would topple if anything happened to him. Food scarcity had begun to plague St. Petersburg and Moscow as the agricultural system started to collapse: The harvests were ample, but the peasants became more reluctant to sell their grain. Meanwhile, the government had been printing rubles willy-nilly to pay for the war, so prices had climbed dramatically. The runaway inflation prompted workers who worked ten hours a day and six days a week while living in the unsanitary conditions of overcrowded cities to strike and protest for wage increases. Workers' committees formed—egged on by German propaganda—and throughout the country an unhappiness with the czar began to spread. The revolution was coming.

Farson launched his business in a ground-floor room on the corner of St. Isaac's Square and moved into the large home of a rich Englishman along the Neva River, where every day he witnessed signs of the pending revolutions. Lines outside stores ran around entire blocks. Conversations with friends concerned relatives who had been killed at the front, the sullen attitude of the returning soldiers, the increase in executions of corrupt officials, and the difficulty of finding food and clothing. Soon came reports that war supplies were piling up and wasting in the great ports of Archangel and Vladivostok thanks to venal officials and a railroad system straining under the weight of the war.

"With its two mouths—Archangel and Vladivostok—choking with the food of war, Russia lay like a prostrate Mars, starving to death," Farson recalled. "It was a process of wastage that one could witness on every side. As plain as watching a man die from phthisis in a hospital ward. A man who was becoming rotten inside."[21]

Realizing that goods were not getting into Russia, Farson and Torsten halted their efforts to make deals to sell American products to the War Department. They would no doubt just sit and rot at the ports. Instead, they decided to devote themselves to trade inside Russia and met with some success in selling black dye, chemicals, and wool. But coming upheavals would strangle their newborn accomplishment in the cradle.

In March 1917 Farson witnessed a murder and what would come to be known as the Kerensky Revolution, in which a provisional government was set up (to be later swept away by Lenin's October Revolution and the ascendancy of the Communist Party). Farson had become accustomed to the menacing crowds that congregated in front of the Cathedral of the Virgin of Kazan, but one morning he noticed an additional feature—the Cossacks, normally so ruthless as they trampled the mobs under the hooves of their horses to restore order, were doing their work half-heartedly. They laughed and jostled with the crowds. When a policeman tried to clear protestors to make way for a tram, they merely jeered at him. Farson stood alongside North Winthrop, the American consul in St. Petersburg, and watched as a mob of several thousand made their way down the Nevsky. Shopkeepers rushed out of their stores to pull down their steel shutters.

Farson lunched at the Hotel de France, where he grabbed five bottles of White Horse whisky to steel himself for hard times ahead. Outside, he found a servant of his English host waiting for him in a sleigh. Farson and a friend hopped in, and the servant drove the sleigh through streets crowded with an angry mob. More than once the servant used his whip to slash at protestors who tried to stop them. At the intersection where the broad Letaney crossed the Nevsky, they stopped. A detachment of mounted Russian Uhlans, their lances pointed straight at Farson, flew down the boulevard in full gallop amid a storm of snow kicked up by their horses' hooves. Farson watched as the Uhlans swept past him and charged directly into the crowds. They pulled up their lances at the last second but now used the lance butts to bash the heads of the protestors. At that moment a tram conductor attempted to drive his tram through the crowds. In seconds, a crowd of shrieking protestors was upon him. Farson watched as they dragged him from his tram and beat him to death with his own brake bar. "I believe he was the first person killed in the Kerensky Revolution," Farson would later write.[22]

More deaths followed. For the next week, mobs organized by students and factory workers hunted down the czar's policemen and killed them wherever they found them. At one point a crowd of some four thousand angry protestors approached the Englishman's house where Farson had holed up, and he temporarily armed himself with a Browning pistol he found in a closet. He continued to do business in the city, but the sound of gunshots erupted around every corner. One night at the theater he watched as Kerensky stood up and gave a speech that roused the crowd, only to be followed by a burly sailor who stood and cursed Kerensky and the war. Another day, once again in the company of Winthrop, Farson was strolling across the grass in front of the statue to the Virgin of Kazan when he witnessed the droshky drivers whipping their stallions furiously as all of them raced off in the same direction. Behind them a sea of up to thirty thousand protestors, red banners aloft, choked the streets.

Shopkeepers once again raced out to pull down their steel shutters. A small group of soldiers stood in the middle of the Nevsky and cursed the swarming protestors. Alarmed, Winthrop beseeched Farson to return with him to the Singer Building, where he had his office. Shooting would soon start, he told Farson. Farson, who thought he knew the Russians by now, replied, "Never!"[23] Impressed by the guardsmen who stood erect in the Nevsky, Farson walked over to join them, slapped one of them on the back, and praised him for his forceful language. The guardsman smiled back at Farson, "his broad face beaded with sweat from his emotions, and then he began cursing the procession again. His enthusiasm was contagious. I caught it, and turned to call Winthrop, only to see him at that instant diving into the Singer building. I still had my hand on the big guardsman's back."[24] As Farson turned to enthuse with the guardsman again, he found himself staring down the barrels of about forty rifles. His heart stopped. Time also stopped as he waited for the shots, and at last they came. "The big soldier fell away from my hand. I was still holding it up—where his back had been—when I saw his arms go up, and then he lay sprawled at my feet."[25] The guardsman, Farson realized, "was quite dead: a neat little hole under his curly blond hair told its own story, and I felt a black rage stir within me. Also I felt a sudden desire to get out of that absurd street before I, too, should join the guardsman in the Never-Never Land."[26] Other soldiers also fell as Farson made his way to the Singer Building amid the pandemonium of shouts and shots.

Across the Neva, Lenin himself had begun his regular open-air harangues. Farson saw him on a raised platform, "a short, dumpy figure, with an enormous dome of a head, high cheekbones giving a sinister contemptuousness to his Tartar eyes. The great Lenin! But he was not 'great' to any but a very few people then. He was just this undersized new agitator in an old double-breasted blue suit, his hands in his pockets, speaking with an entire absence of that hysterical arm-waving that so characterized all his fellow countrymen."[27] The authorities failed to appreciate Lenin's abilities, Farson noted, so they allowed him to continue his diatribe.

For much of the historic summer of 1917, though, Farson's life was once again confined to the narrow dimensions of a hospital bed. His leg wounds had "broke[n] open" again, so he underwent yet another surgery and convalesced in a little log hospital on William Island, spending days lying beneath the birch trees.[28] With revolution in the air, danger was never far. One evening a group of Bolsheviks mounted a machine gun on the roof of the Stock Exchange and began spraying bullets about, starting with the Winter Palace, and then turning their aim to a group of women meeting on a bridge across the lower Neva. And then they turned the machine gun on the hospital. One of the nurses entered Farson's room and said, simply, "Goodbye." Alarmed, Farson asked if she was abandoning him. "My God," she exclaimed, turning red. "Of course not. I say good-by because we shall all soon be dead." The machine gunners soon turned their fire elsewhere, and everyone survived. Everyone, that is, except a Chinese immigrant who was found shot dead outside the hospital the next morning.[29]

Farson had started to hate Russia, so he decided, at last, to leave. He spent a final night with John Reed, who had returned to Russia and instantly became mesmerized by Lenin. Farson put Reed and his wife, Louise Bryant, in a droshky and stood on a pier as a barge ferried it across the Neva. Reed called out good luck, and Farson called back that Reed would need it more than he. Those were the last words he spoke to Reed, who would die of typhus three years later.

As for Farson, he was done with Russia. What had he learned from three years in the country? That people could be more greedy than patriotic. That they could be corrupt and oblivious to the suffering around them. That business was a slippery affair, with grifters everywhere and no guarantee of success. And that hawking war goods was not the life he had dreamed of as a young boy.

He envisioned himself in a pilot's uniform.

6

➔ • ◄

Crash Landing in Egypt

A MERICA DECLARED WAR ON Germany on April 6, 1917, allying itself with Britain, France, Italy, and Russia. Major General John J. Pershing would lead more than two million U.S. soldiers to the fight on France's battlefields. It was not to be, as Europeans came to call it, "the war to end all wars," but it did end the lives of about sixteen million men and women.

Farson, nearly twenty-seven, had tasted the joy of flight in Crimea and longed to be a pilot, a dangerously exotic ambition considering that the Wright Brothers' twelve-second flight over the sand dunes of Kitty Hawk had occurred just one decade earlier. "I would join some flying corps, and I really didn't give a damn which," he said of his inchoate plan.[1] He didn't give a damn about the danger either. Pilots required such a cavalier attitude considering that they flew planes powered by a single rotary engine and were held together by wire and canvas. A mangled death proved common. France, for example, built about sixty-eight thousand aircraft during the war, and more than three-quarters of them crashed or were lost in battle, and a flyer was four times more likely to be killed than an infantryman. In Britain's Royal Flying Corps (RFC) in 1916 and 1917, the average life expectancy of a pilot was, astoundingly, no more than two weeks. For much of the war, the average age of a pilot was twenty, while the average age of a dead pilot was twenty-one.

But as one RFC veteran later put it, pilots of that era were "adventurous spirits, devil-may-care youth, fast livers, furious drivers, and risk-takers."[2]

Though death was close enough to whisper in their ear, they were not to be deterred; men like Farson rushed to sign up.

He returned to England, where he feigned Canadian citizenship to join the RFC, listing his residence as Montreal (a third of RFC flyers were Canadians). When he took his physical in December 1917, he was still recovering from his motorcycle crash in Russia, so he pleaded for special permission to wear shorts during training. He ended up in training camp with a commission, a split-tail flying tunic, and orders to report to Egypt as a scout—he would be flying reconnaissance missions. A short train trip through France and a boat ride across the Mediterranean placed him in Egypt. Now he was once again where he wanted to be—someplace different, someplace exotic, the fabled land of the pharaohs. The ancient country spoke to him: "Shades of everything I had ever read! Here was I, a British soldier, going into Egypt. I was astonished to find myself shivering with emotion."[3] In Egypt with the RFC's Thirty-Eighth Training Wing, Farson flew the SE-5, an experimental one-seater that clocked up to 138 mph and carried a synchronized .303-inch Vickers machine gun and a wing-mounted Lewis gun that allowed the pilot to fire at an enemy below as well as ahead. The scout planes, however, were mainly used to coordinate field artillery and to take reconnaissance photos. Flying seemed intimate to Farson as he sat in an open cockpit, garbed in leather boots, fur-trimmed goggles, and shorts slick with oil thrown from the rotary engine. He marveled aloud at how he seemed to stand "just on the edge of a perfect life I dreamed of as a boy."[4]

Flying a French Nieuport Scout on a whim cracked that boyish dream. At his billet in Cairo on October 15, 1918, he decided to escape the oppressive heat of the morning, so he cranked up the Nieuport's engine, eased the plane into the sky, then turned and climbed to four hundred feet. A sudden slew wrenched him in his seat. The little plane abruptly began to spin violently. Farson hurtled toward his next brush with death:

> It all happened so quickly that I did not have time to think over my past life, as people are supposed to do when facing death; I did not have time enough even to be frightened. I simply knew that this was IT! And it was happening to ME! I could end up with a crankshaft through my chest as many of my friends had done.

"Your engine has failed!" my brain roared to my heart. "Open her up wide and dive for it!"

So I opened the bus up full wide and tried to dive out of it. It was a futile attempt, because I couldn't have been a hundred feet up. But that was the thing that saved me. Just as the sands swirled into my face, I heard a crash like the sound of a peach-crate smashing before I passed into the darkness. I went clean through the bus, the crank shaft passing under my arm, to end up against the sharp fins of the rotary cylinders.

It was with a feeling of the utmost astonishment that I woke up.[5]

Rescuers worked seventeen minutes to cut him free. Farson sustained a concussion, a broken right foot, and a shattered shinbone on his left leg, which also sported a cavernous hole in the bone—one that would never heal.

Sent to Ras El Tin hospital, a British army hospital that overlooked Alexandria harbor, he conversed from his bed with a strange visitor who turned out to be Fuad I, the sultan of Egypt. Fuad, who bore a scar on his throat from a gunshot he received during a dispute with his first wife's brother, approached Farson's bed to offer words of comfort. Farson summoned his dubious skills with the French language to speak with the sultan, but only managed to call him "Your Altitude" instead of "Your Highness" as senior British officers looked on in horror.[6] Sent back to England, Farson was appointed a flying instructor as the Allies attempted to aid General Anton I. Denikin, the chief general of the White forces in southern Russia, who had resolved to launch an offensive toward Moscow as Russia descended into civil war.

His life, as it always seemed to do, changed course quickly. A Russian love he had left behind now beckoned to marry him, and he felt obligated to resign his commission, though he was humiliated at the thought of abandoning the RFC after such a short stint. (Why did he feel obligated? Was she pregnant? Farson never explained.) But the engagement fizzled, leaving him penniless and with few friends. Surgeons removed bone from his broken right foot, but his injured left leg worsened. Farson underwent a series of gruesome surgeries in London—in one, the skin of his leg was pulled across his open shinbone and tacked down with gramophone needles—none of which were successful. He returned to the United States for more surgery and recuperation. His family met his boat at the dock in Philadelphia.

Before and after his surgery in a New York hospital, he filled his hours writing mushy missives to Enid Eveleen Stoker, a nurse to whom a friend had introduced him as he recuperated in his bed in London. Eve, as she called herself, was three years Farson's junior, born on March 28, 1893, in Moradabad, India. Her father, Thomas Stoker, had served Queen Victoria as chief secretary to the government of the North West Provinces until his retirement in 1899, and he and Eve's mother, Enid, now lived in the tony Egerton Crescent neighborhood of London. They had raised Eve in posh surroundings in India, surrounded by servants, and had sent her to finishing school in Germany. Her relatives were ambitious and success-ful: Uncle Bram Stoker, a red-bearded eccentric, wrote the classic horror novel *Dracula;* another uncle, Sir Thornley Stoker, was a royal surgeon; a third, Richard Stoker, was an army surgeon and fought in several battles in Afghanistan, where he once survived an attack by bow and arrow.

Eve inherited the same pluck as her father and uncles. She loved to travel, sought out new experiences, and spoke her mind freely. She had trained as a nurse and served in the Voluntary Aid Detachment in the Anglo-Russian Hospital in St. Petersburg during the war. She and Farson did not meet in Russia, but both were certain they must have passed each other on the streets of St. Petersburg.[7] Physically, Eve was a strong woman, stout and athletic, and she offered those she met a friendly face beneath short brown hair. Journalist Kenneth Alsop once described her as "dumpy and fat" but loaded with charm and given to laughter.[8] Decades later her son, Daniel, would defend his mother as "nice-looking."[9] He fur-ther described her as a gentle woman who expected the worst from life, though she wielded a sharp sense of humor and a desperation for travel and thrills.

In his letters to Eve from New York, Farson confessed the depth of his love for her and promised her a life of adventure—a promise he would make good on. "I love you; am miles away from you; and I am quite mad with the thought of it," he wrote on March 12, 1920. After acknowledging that doctors had strapped him down to limit the movement of his leg, he added:

> But I somehow never feel the confinement of things. I just sort of liberate my soul and go off on cruises of imagination and memory.
>
> Yesterday we went to Egypt, you and I, and we entered Port Said and we saw that mosaic crowd and—smelt the East again. And at night a big silver moon hung outside our window—and kissed you lying there—and your eyes made little dark pools.
>
> Then we rode into the Sahara on camels and you laughed at their pompous glares. And I opened my shirt at the throat and my arms were bronzed and I felt husky and cave-mannish. Then a violet night came on and we made camp, you and I.
>
> A cool wind came from out of the east. Scents of Arabs, mud walled towns, and lives of a thousand years ago.
>
> The camels grunted contentedly. The little fire cast dancing shadows and the stars swung lower and lower.
>
> You yawned prettily and remarked that there was a red glare in my eyes.
>
> And I laughed and picked you up in my arms and held you up to the crescent moon.
>
> "Allah! Allah! Look what I bring thee!" Ah Eve! We will live life won't we?
>
> And don't worry about me while I am lying here. They can tie down my old flesh and chop into me but my spirit will find yours and we will have hunting together. That is real life. When *that* feeling dies within us, dear, then we *are* dead—and not before.[10]

In a follow-up letter, written on March 24, 1920, he expressed his joy at receiving a Corona typewriter (the same as President Wilson!) and mentioned that an associate editor at the *New York Sun and Herald* had dropped by to tell him he was a good writer. For Farson had begun his writing career while in the hospital, banging out two articles on Russia—one about the machinations of Lenin—for the newspaper. But the writing he most cared about was his correspondence to Eve. The import of the March 24 letter to Eve came in the final three paragraphs, where their courtship by correspondence blossomed into a proposal:

The more pain I get in life; the more time I spend in vain rage against Fate; the more I see that life without love is merely vegetable growth.

So love me, my little Walrus, and hold your arms around me. If you are always true and fine, as you are, I'll make my life everything that you want it to be. You can't know how everything I hold dear in life now rests in your hands.[11]

7

➤ • ⬅

Life in the Wilds

FTER MONTHS OF RECUPERATION and similar letters, Farson
sailed back to England later that year determined to marry her.
Eve was his equal in determination. They wed at the Chapel
Royal of the Savoy Hotel on September 22, 1920, with the minister blessing
them as an Anglo-American alliance. Farson promised Eve's mother that
he would "keep your Eve free from harm and the sordid things of life."[1]
Decades later, Daniel described the sense his mother had that her life was
just beginning: "Everything lay before her: adventure, romance, disaster
and triumph, and ultimately 'the sordid things of life' he had vowed to
protect her from and which nearly broke her."[2] But all that was still to
come. The couple sailed for the United States from Southampton with just
one hundred British pounds sterling in their pockets and a promise of a
job for Farson in South America.

Then disaster struck: halfway across the Atlantic, the ship's radio
received news that the South American market had collapsed, along with
Farson's job prospects. The steward brought them the bulletin with tea.
"Well," Farson said, ruefully. "It looks as if we start from here at zero again!"
To which Eve laughed and suggested that they enjoy a big breakfast.[3]

And so, with both ready to throw themselves into whatever awaited
them, Farson brought his bride to New York City. Though Farson and
his father were emotionally distant, they were never estranged, so it was
no surprise that his father invited the newlyweds to spend their honey-
moon aboard his yacht. Afterward, the couple moved to Chicago, where
Eve taught herself to cook—Farson claimed he had a gastric ulcer after

six weeks of her cooking—and he took a job selling Mack trucks. Or trying to, anyway. Some days he knocked on thirty doors only to be thrown
out of as many offices. He sold a single truck, impotent as a salesman in
the face of the deflationary recession of 1920–21, when wholesale prices
across the country plummeted more than 36 percent. He limped up and
down Chicago's streets, angry at the heat of summer and bitter from the
cold of winter. He and Eve took an apartment in a poor neighborhood,
but when they arrived expecting to find it had been put in shape, they
discovered the place was a wreck. The landlord only agreed to give them
their deposit back after Eve called the landlord a swindler to his face and
began to abuse him with phrases that Farson said he "could never have
imagined."[4] They found another apartment on Everett Avenue, but the
rent ate up every bit of Farson's monthly paycheck except ten dollars.
To make ends meet they took on a boarder, a young man who studied
law at night. Still their finances were tight; Farson occasionally had to
go without cigarettes. The bandages on Farson's leg had to be changed
daily, so he would hobble down to the American Veteran's Hospital on
Biddle Avenue. An intern there told him the bone in his leg was deteri-
orating once again. So he traveled to Montreal and prepared to lie upon
yet another operating table.

Abruptly, he and Eve decided to end their eight-month ordeal in
Chicago—they would remain in Canada. They had only thirty dollars to
their name, but Farson was again ready to leap into some fresh unknown,
to start something new, something other than pounding the pavement
to make a buck. Possibly, like other veterans of the war and members of
the Lost Generation, he sought a respite away from the United States
and the throng of humanity, a salve for any psychic wounds he carried
from his brush with death in Egypt. As one historian later said of the Lost
Generation, "it was easy for the young men to take the next logical step—
active, conscious revolt and self-exile from a country which was neither
gay enough nor cultured enough to deserve their presence."[5]

As for Eve, she proved over and over that she was game for anything. The
two set out on a new adventure—to live in the wilds of British Columbia.
Both their families were scandalized. One family member opined that
people didn't just run off to live in the wilderness.

To which Eve starchily replied, "Some do."[6] Farson explained that he hoped to prove wrong the popular notion "that life was business and business was life."[7]

The Farsons, newlyweds with more courage than capital, escaped to a remote lake on Vancouver Island, a wilderness 290 miles long and 62 miles wide, located just off the coast of mainland Canada in the Pacific Ocean. Eve's uncle Dick Stoker—a man Eve's father considered mad because he lived "in a hut like a Red Indian"[8]—welcomed them to the island he had made his home years before. Tanned dark by the subcontinental sun of India, rugged from a life of simple soldiering, Uncle Dick and his Irish wife, Sue, had arrived in Canada by accident: They had left their remote home in Ladakh, in the Indian Kashmir, and abandoned plans to retire in Tasmania after falling in love with Vancouver Island. The couple built a rough bungalow of peeled logs—accented with an odd assortment of Indian architectural elements—in a forest cathedral of majestic trees on the most remote shore of Cowichan Lake. They spent only the warmer months in the house. In winter, the couple migrated thirty miles south to a more conventional house Dick had built amid a colony of English retired officers. Every Christmas the old soldier grew sentimental and wrote letters to urge his extended family to visit. None of his relatives took him up on his plea, penned every year, until Farson and Eve telegrammed him to say they were on the way.

Astonished and delighted, Dick and Sue welcomed Eve (a niece they barely knew) and her husband, showed them around their backwoods property and then simply handed over the bungalow—built so rustically that on cold nights water on the table froze ten feet from the fire. Cowichan Lake was twenty miles long, bordered by some of the oldest, largest pine and fir trees in the world. Some of the trees had been saplings when Columbus arrived in the Americas, and the forest was so thick that few ventured into it alone; a skeleton found in a tree hollow with a flintlock rifle and a broken leg served as a caution. But in clearings around the lake, a tiny colony of misfits, crazies, curmudgeons, and criminals had gathered in a spirit of bohemian weirdness. Among them lived "Old Tread," whom Farson described as the only bona fide settler in the region. Tread came from Canterbury; rumor had it that he was kin to the archbishop himself. Ostensibly the first white man to settle on the lake, Tread built a houseboat by felling huge cedar trees so they pitched into the water—an example that subsequent settlers followed. Another resident was Struthers, a former captain in the Royal Flying Corps "who had been flying booze for the whisky ring in Vancouver" before a crash nudged him out of the game.[9] Other inhabitants included Captain von Hauptmann, a German who wore a beard to his navel and a Basque beret on his shaven head; Ken, a local trapper and dangerous poker player; and Algy Cunwell, an English gentlemen whose entire knowledge, according to Farson, was limited to horses, hounds, and pheasants.[10] Then there was the "Remittance Man," whose family in Ireland paid him two dollars per day on the condition that he never come home, a dark family drama no one ever explained to the Farsons. But he had been found dead in his blankets, black from dirt, two years before the Farsons arrived. Hundreds of whisky bottles lined the path to his tiny apple orchard.

Farson and Eve determined to live on the lake surrounded by the motley crew of eccentrics. Their friends mailed new novels from London and New York, and he subscribed to the *New York Times Literary Supplement* and the *London Weekly Times,* rowing six miles downstream to pick them up with his mail at the general store. Everybody on the lake shared scraps of random reading material, which created a unique lending library. Farson read more at night than he ever had before.

But lake life demanded that they work to survive, and Farson had come equipped with shotgun, fly rods, and typewriter—for here he vowed to teach himself to write between chores. First, though, Farson faced down his daily tasks: He had to cut firewood, fell trees with ax and crosscut saw, and swing a heavy maul to split the cut wood to dry. In the winter, their iron kitchen range burned all day long, its metal ticking from the heat. Farson cooked breakfast every morning, a bitter task in the winter. He put coffee on to boil and fried bacon before banging out prose on his Corona. He could only earn cash by selling stories—an iffy proposition, as all freelance writers know well. After a stint at the typewriter, he would pole his skiff out on the lake to hunt ducks and to fish for the big rainbow trout that swam deep, or for salmon when they ran up from the sea. Twice a week he would row down to the Hudson Bay Company's general store on his mail run to buy coffee, tea, salt, and sugar. Rowing down to the store, he trolled lures behind his boat and almost always caught a few rainbow or cutthroat trout for dinner. In season he hunted from his skiff for golden-eye ducks and widgeons and flushed mallards from pools behind the trees. Near Bear Lake, a small pond connected to Cowichan by a creek, he shot a Canada goose—a bounty of food. "Put plenty of wood on, make a good fire; for tonight we eat," he announced to Eve as he entered their cabin, clutching the goose triumphantly by its legs.[11] They ate the whole bird in one sitting.

Finally, the writing career he had determined to launch began to blossom. One day, instead of the usual rejection slips he had been opening at an "alarming rate,"[12] he found instead a check for $150 for an adventure yarn he had written—"The Wells of Ibrahim." The pulp story, set in wartime Egypt and centered on the search for a military camel gone AWOL, ran in the January 1921 issue of *Munsey's* magazine. Farson now fancied himself an up-and-coming fiction writer. The $150 was a grand amount, enough to put three months of food on the shelf. Their general store bill for a year was only eighty-five dollars. The same day he hooked three salmon, one of which weighed in at more than twelve pounds. Life in the woods was suddenly all feast and banquet. With the hard cash as a morale booster, they decided to move out of Uncle Dick's bungalow, to find a houseboat and truly live unfettered on wild Lake Cowichan. Meanwhile, bolstered by his literary success, Farson sat diligently at his Corona and cranked out a series of short stories, convinced that he was on his way.

He was wrong. The second story he sent *Munsey's* crashed and burned. The editor, Bob Davis, wrote Farson, "This is more pitiful than a schoolgirl's graduation thesis."[13] Rejection slips piled up. Farson and various editors exchanged his manuscripts "as if I had been playing tennis with them."[14] Efforts to sell feature articles to the *New York Sun and Herald*'s Sunday section also stalled, with one editor chiding him for imposing his education on his stories: "You sometimes take too much for granted in your readers. They have not too much intelligence."[15] With each failed story, Farson's desperation deepened. At last he received sage advice from an old friend and former newspaperman in New York who did not disguise his disgust with the dreck that Farson was writing: "Look here, why the hell don't you write what *you* want to—what you see right before your eyes. Are you *blind?*"[16] The shock treatment worked: Farson wrote a series of articles about the salmon run, the logging camps, and the rustic lives of his neighbors. The *Sun and Herald* snatched them up. He sold more fiction as well, placing a short story in the November 20, 1922, issue of *Adventure* magazine, which he had read since its first publication in 1910. In a short note to readers on the occasion of his first story in the pulp magazine, Farson saluted his dead friend Jo-Jo, a kindred spirit with a "wanderlust, restless foot, love o' life, whatever it was."[17]

Farson had come to the wilderness hoping to teach himself to write fiction, and he had succeeded to some degree; but more importantly, he laid the groundwork for a successful career as a journalist.

The Farsons found their houseboat thanks to Swanson, the Swedish foreman of a five-man logging crew that employed a steam-powered winch to drag logs down to the lake to float them to sea. Swanson, who had fled to Cowichan Lake after stabbing a man in San Francisco,[18] lived on a fine little houseboat on the lake next to another houseboat abandoned by two other Swedes who had caught gold fever and run off to Peace River country in Canada's interior. Farson eyed the forty-foot raft of huge cedar logs as the perfect home. As winter approached, he claimed the abandoned houseboat for ten dollars a month in rent. Farson planned to float it to a remote area of the lake—into an elbow of water in the woods—where their nearest neighbor would be five miles away. The isolation lured them: The newlyweds had grown to love solitude so much that they never felt lonely at Uncle Dick's bungalow. Conversation with others proved a strain, so tuned to silence was the tempo of their lives. Sometimes, when they spied visitors approaching the bungalow by skiff or boat, they ran and hid in the woods.

Their new home would be even more splendidly isolated. They called it Mole End, the fanciful home of Mole, the character from the children's book *The Wind in the Willows*. Eve stained the houseboat's bare wood doors, floor, and window sills with a warm oak color. She made curtains of checked gingham, planted sweet peas and nasturtiums in boxes that hung from the sills. The two-room shack boasted several large windows. A cougar-skin rug warmed their bedroom floor. (Cougars abounded on the island.) The other room was a combination kitchen and living room in which books lined the shelves of one wall. Oil lamps—"the most comfortable light to read by on long winter nights," Farson claimed—beat back the gloom of darkness.[19] Farson built most of their furniture, including one sumptuous chest of drawers hammered together from old coal-oil crates. He rigged a fishing line that hung from the houseboat at night so that almost every morning he could pull in fat rainbow trout for breakfast. Often he boiled them and ate them cold. Sometimes Eve would serve the trout with mayonnaise or stuff it with a parsley dressing and bake it in butter, or grill it with strips of bacon tucked inside.

As Farson convalesced from his war injuries, he and his wife slowly lost touch with the outside world. Months passed, time became hazy, marked more by nature, by a sullen rainy season that spat against the cedar shake roof of the houseboat, or by the bright sun on a spring morning. In the fall, he hunted deer. Once on a moonlit night he shot a deer in a glade, and the mortally wounded animal leapt up into the moonlight, a majestic sight that Farson found as lovely as a "heraldic tapestry."[20] He set traps baited with dead ducks and caught two enormous racoons one winter. He fashioned their tanned skins into a fur collar for Eve.

Spring excited Farson the most. "The snow would drop from the trees. The sun would be hot and fresh in our faces as we walked outside our door in the mornings," Farson observed. "The mountain across from us would be beginning to lose its hard, blue stare and take on deep shadows. Instead of that melancholy black of open water in dead winter, the lake would be almost a blinding blue, shimmering in the heat haze. The woods would begin to fill with trilliums and dogwoods and little wild pink lilies."[21]

Millions of blood-red salmon fought their way inland from the sea, up strong mountain streams, seeking the riffles of their birth home. Farson, the former javelin champion, hurled spears at them and once struck a fifteen-pound dog salmon as it swam in the shallows. The big hens flicked their tails in the riffles to clear out a nest on the bottom and laid thousands of pea-sized eggs in the redd for the bucks to fertilize. Then the salmon, mission accomplished, died by the millions, filling the woods and the Farsons' nostrils with a foul stench.

After two years, Farson had learned to expertly swing an axe, hammer nails, repair floorboards, carve furniture, handle boats in the dead of night, forage for wild fruit, and hunt and fish for food. He had also found some success in his freelance writing for newspapers and magazines: the couple had saved an astounding $1,800. But doubt about his life's course began to well up. He felt guilty at hiding from a world he was inexplicably driven to see. "My conscience had lain dormant," he said. "What was life, anyway? Weren't we living a good life out here? Weren't we both making good at it? Wasn't I getting pretty sure now that I would sell a short story or an article when I wrote it? Well, then—why these qualms?"[22]

Two years seemed enough to Farson, though Eve wept when he suggested it was time to leave. Inexplicably, he chose to return from the wilderness to big-city business—the very thing he had sought to escape on Cowichan Lake. He stepped firmly back into civilization and met his former Mack truck manager as soon as he disembarked from the train in Chicago. To Farson's surprise, he was chosen as a manager of salesmen in the chaotic Milwaukee territory. He immediately ordered Tony, the secondhand truck salesman, to slash prices on every truck. (Tony, a tough salesman who carried a revolver in case he met a former customer, protested the price cut.) After he had whipped Milwaukee into shape, his bosses gave him the plum job—Chicago. "It was a pretty tall jump from the houseboat in British Columbia to this job," he said.[23] But he threw himself into it and picked out twenty of the largest accounts the company had never won against bigger competitors. Researching one of the accounts—a company that needed to replace its entire fleet of trucks—Farson met with its president and somehow wrangled a high-dollar contract. He called it the most dramatic day of his short business life. Farson could hardly keep from yelling with joy when the president signed the document.

As he walked out, a rival salesman waiting in an outer office asked, "No use of me going up?"

"No, not a bit," Farson replied.[24]

He had suddenly become a successful businessman and was leading a life he had so earnestly detested in his youth. It would not—it could not—last.

8

→ • ←

The Exotic Life of a Foreign Correspondent

AFTER ABANDONING THEIR LIFE in Chicago and sailing across Europe aboard *Flame,* Farson and his wife spent the next three months in Constantinople, where Farson learned the ropes of the foreign correspondent's trade. He and *Daily News* editor Charles Dennis had agreed that he would be the newspaper's roving foreign correspondent, based in London, but available for dispatch to any corner of the globe at a moment's notice. It was an arrangement ideally suited to Farson's wanderlust. Dennis saw the urgency of placing Farson in Turkey due to the international crisis brewing there—the Mosul question. The Mosul region had belonged to the Ottoman Empire until Great Britain seized it after World War I. But after the Turkish War of Independence ended in 1923, the Turkish government claimed ownership. Meanwhile, Faysal ibn Husayn, the Hashemite ruler of Iraq, petitioned England to give the oil-rich land to him. Tempers flared, diplomats were at wits' end, and by the time Farson arrived, some observers had concluded that Turkey was ready to go to war for the oil fields. At the same time, domestic politics roiled the country: Mustapha Kemal Pasha was modernizing the nation. He had abolished the fez, stripped the mosques of their role in the education system, and hanged enough Turks to keep others from open revolt.

Farson's first dispatch from Turkey in 1926 captured the violent campaign of repression then underway:

> Constantinople, Turkey, Jan. 20—Seven reactionaries from Marache were hanged in Angora today, making the official total of such executions

thirty-eight since Dec. 1. Eighty-five other reactionaries have been sentenced to from two to twenty years' penal servitude. These are from the disaffected districts in Trebizond, Erzerum and Rizah and include preachers, former deputies, newspaper men and muezzins. This unrelenting campaign shows the determination of the Kemal government to crush the opposition into line for "legislative progress."[1]

When Farson arrived in Constantinople, all he knew of the city was what he had read in the exotic adventure novels of French naval officer Pierre Loti, but he threw himself into his work and paid calls on Turkish bureaucrats, the Greek ambassador, British and French diplomats, and the American commissioner, all in an attempt to make sense of the sundry behind-the-scene schemes in the works. He didn't neglect the nightlife. The Farsons visited the three hottest nightclubs—the Turquoise, where Russian princesses supposedly served drinks and offered themselves to patrons; the Rose Noir, the scene of sinful debauch; and Maxim's, an all-night cabaret run by an American from Mississippi, Frederick Thomas. Maxim's, according to Farson, adroitly played to the expectations of American tourists. When the Americans arrived from their tour boats, the cabaret's Russian waitresses would all dress up in Turkish "bloomers," and Thomas himself put on a fez, threw down a prayer rug, and prayed toward Mecca—all to give the tourists a little faux local color.[2]

After three months in Turkey, and with the Mosul question put in the hands of the League of Nations, the Farsons determined to set out on another adventurous trek. With his editor's approval, they would travel by car over ancient trade routes across Kurdistan and Persia all the way to India. But it was not to be. One day in Bursa, the former capital of ancient Turkey, Farson found himself weaving in the street, his bum leg on the fritz once more. The Farsons boarded the Orient Express and dashed back to London, where Farson underwent yet another operation, this one at St. George's Hospital. His doctor, the preposterously named Giddy Colquhoun, warned Farson that the damage was so extensive he would most likely find himself back in the hospital. Eve, meanwhile, set up house in south London, making sure when she went out to wear the raccoon collar that Farson had fashioned for her: She wore it as a badge of honor, proof to her family that she had been able to live rough in British Colombia.

After several weeks abed, Farson limped out of St. George's with a black felt boot wrapped like a python around his left foot. He and Eve flew to Paris in May 1926 to meet an old friend, Chicago socialite Janet Fairbank. But while there, Farson's editors cabled him to return to London, where the *Daily News* had set up an office in Trafalgar Square, close to Whitehall, the center of British power. His editors warned that British workers were preparing to strike. Industrial laborers and workers on Britain's critical railroad system united with Welsh miners in their fight to prevent wage cuts and worsening work conditions. One million miners had been locked out of the mines; a half million other workers lay down their tools in support. Farson arrived in London in time to throw himself into the throng of agitated workers and Communists as police charged the crowds with batons drawn. But the heart of the strike beat in Wales. Unable to drive because of the pain in his foot, and with trains at a standstill, he rented a Daimler limousine and drove across England to Cardiff. From there, Farson rode a motorcycle across the mining valleys of Wales, rushing from coal tip to coal tip to hear labor leaders plead with angry miners to remain peaceful, worried that British officials would use any violence as an excuse to crush the strike. The reporting work was dangerous. Miners distrusted Farson as an outsider and a newspaperman. Occasionally, he had to plead his case to the strikers, arguing that he was merely a fair-minded American journalist with no stake in the outcome. At one rally, hard-faced miners mistook him for the coal mine owner's agent and approached him angrily. A labor leader stepped in to rescue him before fists flew. But after ten days, the unions gave up in defeat. The Great Strike of 1926 was over. Farson had experienced it firsthand.

The threat of a duel in Italy next called Farson to Rome. The *Daily News'* correspondent there, Hiram Motherwell, had run afoul of Benito Mussolini's fascist government due to his honest reporting on the 1924 assassination of Socialist deputy Giacomo Matteotti. An upset fascist and former *Daily News* employee approached Motherwell one night at a dance and slapped him across the face. Motherwell was too stunned to react and had the wife of a colleague on his arm. He led her to a chair and left without attempting to defend his insulted honor. Breaking news in Romania forced Motherwell to rush to Bucharest. Tales of Motherwell's "cowardice" blazed across Rome—he had been slapped in the face but had done nothing in response. Foreign correspondents across Europe gossiped endlessly about it, and when Motherwell returned to Rome, some friends suggested he must fight a duel to defend his honor. One friend in Paris volunteered to come to Rome to school Motherwell in the art of fencing. Eschewing the more gentlemanly Code Duello in favor of an American solution, Motherwell walked over to the Press Club, found the fascist, and knocked him to the floor with a single punch. "My honor is still officially, as well as morally, unblemished," Motherwell later said of the incident.[3]

Motherwell's situation was now untenable, and his time was up. Farson took over the Rome bureau. For the next months, he struggled against the antipathy of the fascist government, overcoming bureaucratic intransigence to write about the stern hand of fascism, or what he called Mussolini's "castor oil treatment."[4] Farson wrote about Mussolini's skill in invigorating the economy, while at the same time managing to mock him. One day, Farson interviewed the great Indian poet Rabindranath Tagore, who was then in Rome, and he followed up the interview with an account of a speech Tagore gave on "the meaning of art," with Mussolini in the audience:

> In spite of the extraordinary courtesy of the Italians, the Indian poet was up against a tough job. To talk for two hours to an audience in a language which you are perfectly certain must be only half understood is a true test of courage—to try and expound at the same time the most delicate theories is not only courage—it is sacrifice. And perhaps that is why Sir Rabindranath started singing when he felt things growing "cold." At any rate he must have been inspired by the fine courtesy of Mussolini (who does not understand English) sitting there for three hours with all the apparent interest of a man who is listening to the speech of a lifetime.[5]

Farson was glad to leave Rome, later recalling:

> Mussolini's jaw!
> I saw that everywhere I went in Italy. My paper was distinctly not popular with the Fascists, and they kept me waiting an hour and a quarter in the

Foreign Office, when a colleague took me over to Palazzo Chigi to present
my credentials. The Party man, the man the Fascists had put in to break the
Press, stamped up and down like a mad Mickey Mouse when he did consent
to see me—all the time pounding a copy of the *Chicago Daily News* that lay
on his impressive desk.

"Imperialism! Imperialism!" he kept shouting at me. "That's what you
say about us! We mean to fight! We mean to make war! Imperialism!
Imperialism!"[6]

His editors rewarded Farson for his performance in Rome by letting
him choose his next assignment. Naturally, he suggested an arduous trek.
Farson proposed to drive a car north of the Arctic Circle—the kind of des-
ultory stunt that his editors appreciated. He planned to drive due north
through Sweden all the way to the coast of Norway where he would put
the car on a whaling boat and ship it south to where roads began again.
His editors agreed, and the Farsons sailed for Sweden. In Stockholm,
Farson and Eve, who was now pregnant, stepped into a specially outfitted
Ford. They had prepared the car with extra gas tanks on each of its running boards and four extra tires lashed to the rear bumper. They tied tents
and duffel bags to the hood and set out into the deep forests of Sweden.
Though his medical boot still hobbled his gait, Farson was glad to be
adventuring once more; his sailing trip across Europe must have seemed
like a distant memory to his restless mind. "Our hearts sang with the joy
of being alive in that lovely land," he recalled.[7] In Dalecarlia, Farson's powerful physique grew stronger. He swam in the cold waters and let the sun
bronze his face.

Five hundred miles lay between Stockholm and the Arctic Circle, yet
the Farsons had covered only about two hundred when calamity struck.
Outside Lake Siljan, the couple got lost in the woods, and as they hiked in
the dark in search of help, Farson felt something in his left foot snap. The
old injury had returned. They eventually found an inn, but at dinner that
night Farson fainted, crashed across the table, and upended his coffee
cup. The next morning the staff carried him through the forest and loaded
him onto a passing train. He underwent an operation in Stockholm the
following day. A surgeon cut a hole through the large bone of his left foot

and plugged it with gauze. The surgeon left, after instructing nurses not to touch Farson.

The wound became infected, however, and in the following days his temperature soared to 105 degrees. Despite Eve's pleas, none of the other doctors and nurses dared touch Farson. Exasperated at last, she called in a brilliant surgeon, a Communist named Silversjold, who operated again that evening. He bored the hole completely through Farson's foot and elevated it to drain through the night. Farson, who had begun to beg surgeons to amputate his leg, lay abed and read *Beau Geste*—if he couldn't adventure, he could at least read about it. Now a long recuperative period began. By the end of it, he had spent a total of three years in bed, beginning with his hospitalization in Egypt due to his plane crash. His injuries had landed him on surgical tables around the globe—Cairo, Alexandria, Chatham, London, Moscow, New York, Montreal, Vancouver, Stockholm. Yet he kept pushing forward. Eve transported him to their London home in South Kensington where he lay for six months, his leg wrapped in an iron surgical boot. (Interestingly, Farson's friend Frank Morley wrote a completely different account for *Brooklyn Life,* claiming that a car had knocked Farson down in Sweden and crushed his left foot, adding: "The Swedish surgeons were ruthlessly determined to amputate. Farson fought against them, enduring three partial operations in quick succession, till he was almost done in. Then his wife, an extremely capable woman, kidnapped him from the hospital and brought him on a stretcher across to Berlin, thence to London.")[8]

In the meantime, in Great Britain, Hutchinson & Co. Ltd. in 1926 had published Farson's dispatches from *Flame* as a book titled *Sailing across Europe,* and in the United States, the *New York Times* heralded the book's pending U.S. publication by the Century Company in the same article that it announced the forthcoming publication of Hemingway's *The Sun Also Rises.*[9] While Hemingway's book would endure as one of his greatest achievements and cement his role as a leading voice of the Lost Generation, Farson's book merely served as a stepping-stone to his later fame. Still, the book received unqualified praise from some critics. *Time* magazine's reviewer wrote: "Traveler Farson is a cheery, seaworthy person and a first-rate reporter. He saw a great deal that was significant as well as colorful and tells it very well."[10] The reviewer for the *Morning News* of Wilmington, Delaware, called it a "happy chronicle," praised Farson's eye for color and personalities, and opined that the "record of his amusing months on the island waters can be compared to Robert Louis Stevenson's 'An Inland Voyage' for intimate pictorial interest."[11] On the other side of the Atlantic, reviews were equally positive. The *Westminster Gazette*'s review was typical, hailing the book as "unusual and interesting" and complimenting the writer's "breezy style."[12] In an April 1926 *Travel* magazine review that turned into a five-page summary of the voyage, reviewer R. J. Hart asserted that it "would be difficult to plan a more exhilarating European trip than the inland voyage taken by Negley Farson in his twenty-six-foot yawl, the Flame." *Sailing across Europe,* he added, was "a log book that captures all the thrills of his thoroughly delightful and unconventional trip."[13] (In an exchange with Hart before the review appeared, Farson was modest and claimed that "Any yachtsman with courage, patience and a good supply of cigarettes can do it.")[14]

Farson, recuperating from his Swedish misadventure, continued to file occasional dispatches from his bed as the year wore on, prompting his editor, Charles Dennis, to write to say the editors "admire your grit in not giving up in the difficulties," but more to the point, Dennis began to persuade Farson to try his hand at writing fiction.[15] The newspaper had managed to make circulation gains among female readers with serialized "romance-for-the-modern-girl" type tales in which plucky heroines fended off the advances of coercive mashers, and fought, connived, and schemed their way to true love. By December 1926, Dennis's flattery and cajolery had persuaded Farson to try his hand at it. Dennis was delighted at the opportunity to keep Farson writing, since he was, after all, still drawing a regular paycheck: "Knowing as I do your preference for the writing of adventure stories, I realize that the task outlined must be uncongenial to you," Dennis wrote in one letter. "I have been, however, so much impressed by the high quality of your articles that I feel hopeful you will become interested in working out some such serial as The Daily News would particularly like to have."[16] Dennis called Farson's attention to two serialized stories that had been successful, "Sonia" and "Sonia's Married Life," and advised Farson that the formula for successful newspaper fiction included familiar Chicago landmarks and "every-day adventures of joy and disappointment, love and hatred and revenge amid ordinary city scenes."[17]

Weeks later, Dennis wrote to congratulate Farson on the birth of his son, Daniel, who arrived in the world on January 8, 1927, in the Farsons' home. While Eve struggled to give birth, Farson was two floors below, typing the last chapter of "that abysmal love story" for the *Daily News*.[18] Eve vowed she would never forgive him for continuing his work on the story while she suffered. The novel, titled "East of the Garden" by Farson but renamed *Daphne's in Love* by his editors, ran in thirty-one installments over five weeks. Farson, working night and day on it as he lay recuperating in his boot, had vowed—for no particular reason—to write the entire thing in a month, and he succeeded.

The story, later published as a book by Grosset and Dunlap of New York, reads as if it were written by a first-time fiction author in extreme pain, under tight deadline, while his wife screamed in birthing agony nearby. The book was a limp imitation of Anita Loos's *Gentlemen Prefer Blondes*, which was a top seller of the era. Publishers were rifling through manuscripts in a desperate attempt to find a tale with the same winning formula, and Farson's, presumably, was close enough.

The story Farson worked out centered around two young roommates, Daphne and Ivy, as they searched for true love in false-hearted Chicago. Daphne falls for a young cad named Taffy Ledoux but is eventually wooed by her boss at the Eureka Motor Truck Company. Ivy, meanwhile, helps her boyfriend steal the designs for an air brake from the trucking company, and they run off together. But when the blame for the theft shifts to Daphne, Ivy confesses her guilt, Daphne is restored to the good graces of her colleagues, and she ends up in the arms of her boss, an older man who had survived World War I with a bayonet wound in his chest. Farson plumped his tale full of flapper-era slang such as "flivvers" for automobiles, "he really knows his onions," and references to Mary Pickford. Per Dennis's instructions, Farson also filled the thin plot chockablock with Chicago landmarks—the Randolph Street Market, Michigan Avenue, the Oak Street beach, Lexington Avenue traffic, and well-known restaurants and nightclubs.

More interestingly, and almost certainly inadvertently, vague hints of sexual frustration peeped through Farson's prose. Farson's unmet desires found expression in his frequent descriptions of his heroines in their small apartment. Sentences such as "They lolled around on their beds in their pajamas," and "Mrs. Woodbottle looked suspiciously at Daphne's transparent pajamas, at Daphne's heaving breast . . . her white skin," appear with noticeable frequency.[19]

The book was a jerry-rigged assemblage of tawdry working-girl romance and clichéd sentimentality, and Farson himself had no regard for it. Yet, though the plot was tired, Farson's writing skills were enough to make it an enjoyable read. Each day's installment ended with a cliffhanger that lured readers into coming back for more. His editors evinced not only contentment, but pleasure. Dennis wrote to congratulate Farson on succeeding "wonderfully well in producing the kind of story that we feel would be useful for our purposes."[20]

Yet writing tawdry, subpar romances for young Chicago women was not Farson's dream, and he could no doubt see that somewhere his life had taken a disappointing turn. He had started out well as a foreign correspondent, traveling across Europe and filing dispatches from glittering capitals. He had taught himself to be a first-rate newspaperman, and he knew he could do the job well. But now he lay confined to a bed, a new father facing down the routines of domestic life. It was enough to make a man go crazy—or plot another escape.

9

→ • ←

Whaling Adventure

FARSON HAD PROVEN THAT he could remain productive from a bed, but as his health returned so did his itch to wander. He didn't know where he wanted to go, exactly; he knew only that it was time to once again put his prodigious energies to the test. His destination was settled thanks to Frank Morley, a friend and photographer who had been with the Southern Whaling and Sealing Company in the Falklands. Morley had coauthored a book titled *Whaling North and South*, and he gave a copy to Farson, who promptly decided that he must head to the far-flung Shetland Islands, the cold, bitter, northernmost point of Great Britain and the center of the empire's whaling industry. The remoteness of the islands called to him. Farson admitted that the only thing he knew of the Shetlands was that as a boy he had once owned a Shetland pony, so he bought train tickets for Aberdeen, Scotland, left his infant son with Eve's mother in London, and he and Eve set off to see what the Shetlands were really like. It was the summer of 1927, and Farson's leg was still in a cast.

"Whatever it was I had expected the Shetlands to be—they weren't," he wrote in one of his first dispatches back to the *Chicago Daily News*. "Instead of two islands I found more than a hundred. Instead of Scotch I found a language even more unintelligible, where people called whales quails and quails whales—which was very confusing. I found the people were Scotch, but that they were mostly descended from Vikings, Picts and some amorous gentlemen of the Spanish Armada. I found people who had never seen a railway train, or a street car—or even a street."[1] Farson claimed to have met people on the island of Foula who had never seen a tree, having lived their entire life on the windblown Shetlands.

Farson came to the islands in the hope of boarding a whaler and chasing a whale, an adventure he began to organize as soon as he arrived. But first he traveled through the island chain. He made a base camp in a hovel in the town of Lerwick, a gray little fishing village where the population shrank from eight thousand to four thousand with the arrival of winter's ice, snow, and bitter winds. In summer, though, up to six hundred fishing trawlers lay in the harbor, and a "jostling mob" of Dutch, German, Scottish, and English fishermen crowded into the narrow, twisting streets. The hardscrabble life of the Shetlanders stunned him. Only a tiny fraction of the total land was under cultivation, perhaps less than 5 percent, and most of the island residents lived in tiny stone cottages near the crooked shores. The men were fishermen who chased herring across the North Sea with gargantuan nets. The women spent their days knitting the wool of the sheep that roamed across the hillsides. The knitting more than the fishing kept starvation at bay, Farson observed. It was a full-time occupation for many of the women. One day Farson watched as an elderly lady carrying a backpack full of peat trudged across the moors. Her hands were busy with something at her waist. Farson realized at last that she was knitting as she labored along the slopes.

As for the landscape, he found it bleak, monotonous. The islands themselves struck Farson as battered mountain ranges at war with the ice. He made a note of the black peat bogs and desolate moors that formed the islands' interiors, where water flowed into lochs that lay as black as coffee. The surrounding hills were bare of trees, given over to grass and the roughly 160,000 sheep that sustained the Shetlands.

On Fair Isle, population 127, he watched weathered Shetlanders spin wool and make tweed, as well as do their own dyeing, using formulas handed down through generations. "There are hand looms in some of the old crofts where the whole family make tweeds," Farson wrote in his eighth dispatch to Chicago:

I have watched them at work. The boy, serving his five years' apprenticeship, sits on a perch before the taut warp, working four bars with his feet, to shift the changing combinations for the woof, and with his right hand he jerks a string tied to the end of two springy pieces of wood. These are the "trips," which have buffalo-hide butts that stop the sharp-pointed bobbin and shoot it back and forth through the warp. . . . A daughter fills the spools. And the old man, the master craftsman, sets the warp on a set of studs like hat pegs in a fashion which, with the boy's footwork on the four bars, results in a sporty tweed pattern. A skillful family will make a yard of tweed per hour—and sell it for $1.50.[2]

On Shetland Island, the Farsons visited the Hillswick Fair and watched as the residents pulled their prize sheep and bulls through the town and carried their worldly goods in little red-wheeled, blue-painted peat carts. Everyone looked poor, Farson thought—the young boys wore their brothers' hand-me-down shoes, the girls tied their handkerchiefs to their sashes lest they lose them, the old men wore wrinkled tweeds, their Sunday best. On the island of Foula—"a fantastic rock sticking out of the empty Atlantic"—he traveled to the 1,370-foot cliff that forms the island's eastern edge.[3] For generations, the people of the island had taken their dead to the top of the cliff and tossed them into the sea below. They could not waste precious land on graves. One hundred and forty-nine people lived on the island when the Farsons visited; Farson found them tight-lipped and inhospitable.

"Is there anywhere here," his wife asked one native, "where we can get a cup of tea?"

"No," came the answer.[4]

As usual on his trips, Farson made time to go fishing, pulling thirty small trout from a lake during a four-hour period. It was, he said, the finest day of fishing he had ever experienced, despite a full day of harsh weather. "I was wet and hungry," he told his readers in Chicago, "but at 9 o'clock I was sitting by a cozy peat fire—and thirty red-spotted trout."[5]

But he had come to the Shetlands to catch a whale. His friend Morley had arranged for Farson to accompany a whaling outfit, a crew of eleven Norwegians, including their fabled gunner, Olaf Olafsen, who had recorded 2,600 whale kills. Around midnight on August 19, 1927, Farson limped along the deserted wharf at Olna Firth and climbed down to the steel deck of the

Skeena, a ship designed specifically to chase whales. The ship was 105 feet long, built for speed and quick maneuvering. Her back half had no keel, allowing her to turn quickly. Built the year before, in 1926, she weighed 188 gross tons and, driven by 600-horsepower steam engines, could run at 12 knots an hour, or 240 miles a day. She carried a harpoon gun on her bow. The harpoons were essentially bombs, with two and a half pounds of gunpowder on their tips. Tethered to the harpoons was a third of a mile of line that ran to giant springs behind the mast, which served as a sort of fishing reel. The ship, Farson observed, was a "regular shark among ships, a mean, ugly, evil-nosed little killer. And everything in her, including the men, is dedicated to this pursuit."[6]

For days the *Skeena* trawled the North Atlantic while the crew searched for fin whales, but they seemed to have no luck. Farson wrote frankly that he was desperate to kill one. Even Olafsen, the great gunner, despaired of ever seeing a whale again. In the meantime, Farson got to know the crew, spending days in conversation with the Norwegian sailors like Neilsen, who had a voluptuous woman tattooed on his right forearm. Beneath her were the words "true love." On Neilsen's wrist, where the name of his girlfriend had been, there was now tattooed a snake. Farson also chatted with the mate, Pederson, the oldest man on the boat at sixty-three. He was known to his shipmates as a bit of a Bolshevik because of his grousing that the forecastle should have its own mess with hot food like that served in the messroom below deck. Farson enjoyed one of the younger sailors, Gunnarsen, after observing that whenever Gunnarsen met the second engineer on deck, he playfully kicked him in the ass. But the man Farson admired the most was Olafsen. With silver hair and hands as hard as a turtle shell, he appeared to Farson like a rock. Sixty years old, he had been at sea since he was fourteen; his skin had deepened into the color of meerschaum, setting off his blue eyes. Unspoken circumstances had taken a finger from one hand. And, Farson noticed, before Olafsen drank his coffee he first put a spoonful of sugar in his mouth. Given a cigarette, he would light it, then set it down and forget it so that it often burned holes in charts and blankets. Meanwhile, as the sun sank into the ocean day after day, Farson had given up his hopes. "I would never get a whale," he lamented. "The season was ending, the station would close, the world probably would do something to prohibit whaling and the epoch would end. I would go to my grave whaleless."[7]

At last, on the day Olafsen had decided to turn the ship back toward land, the luck of the *Skeena*'s crew turned. As Farson lay in a coil of rope in the stern sheets and Olafsen steered for home, a whale spout appeared on the distant horizon. The lookout man spied it and shouted "Blast!" For the next two hours, the little gray ship zigged and zagged across the ocean as smoke belched from her red funnel. The ship's sudden twists and turns in pursuit of the great whale reminded Farson of a polo pony. As the hours ticked away, Farson realized they were chasing two whales. First they would appear directly in front of the ship. Then to the right. Farson watched in awe as the creatures broke the surface and curved back to the depths. Olafsen tried to guess where they would next surface and barked orders to bring the ship close enough for him to fire the harpoon gun. For Farson, the hunt was agony; he had never known such intense suspense:

> There was something epic about the scope of that chase. The world's greatest game. Our field, if you wish to call it that, was a shifting patch of the stormy Atlantic—about a mile wide—for it was a long time before we got any nearer to them than that. The Skeena wheeled, turned, and darted like a polo pony following the ball. And the ball, in this game, was the "blow"—that quick puff of pale vapor—which might appear anywhere among the splashing disorder of those waves.[8]

Olafsen proved to be too experienced for the whales to escape. When they eventually rolled up out of the water directly in front of the ship, Olafsen fired a harpoon at one of them. Then silence. The whales slipped beneath the sea's surface. The crew killed the ship's engines. Olafsen dropped to his knees and peered over the bow. Then Farson heard the harpoon line whiz wildly. Like any trout or salmon on a hook, the harpooned whale was making its run, struggling vainly to free itself from the five-foot steel shaft. Farson watched as the whale broke the surface and charged forward, leaving a "bright crimson wake" of blood.[9] Now Farson witnessed the whale thrash through the water as it desperately tried to survive. It rose up out of the water and dived in again, always turning back on itself to switch direction. Farson found it exasperating to watch the whale in its death throes. Apparently Olafsen did too: twice he abandoned his gun to return to the mess and drink coffee. But the dying whale emerged too close to the ship just as Olafsen returned to the deck. He jumped to his gun and fired another harpoon. Streams of dark red blood shot straight into the air. "I was horrified by the sight of those thick heavy jets," Farson admitted to his readers:

> The whale shot off on his death rush, failed, and stopped to blow a low, labored jet. He was dying. That great bulk rolled on its side, gray as a battleship (and it seemed quite as large) and then the whale stiffened. A strange head emerged from the waves, as if for a last gasp of air, and, across other waves, a delicate tail curved out—beautiful as a butterfly's wing. They stayed there, the strange head and that beautiful black and white tail and then they slowly slipped back into the waters. We had killed our whale.[10]

If Farson summoned the spirit of Herman Melville to write about the death of the whale, he called upon the skills of Upton Sinclair to describe its dismemberment on shore. As he watched, the crew carved into the beast lying lifeless and open-eyed on the flensing platform. The four-inch-thick sheath of blubber was hard as gristle, Farson was amazed to discover, and it crackled as the men hacked into it and ripped it off the whale. The men then cleaved into the stomach, and Farson realized that the gurgling sound he took for a mountain stream was the blood pouring from the carcass. Then the entrails spilled out, steaming and looking like "twisting blue pipes."[11] Vertebrae large as chairs were lugged to crushers, and steam-powered saws further split them into tiny pieces. Farson watched as the crew fed strip after strip of the blubber, still crackling, into a chopper, then hauled it in buckets to cauldrons where it boiled. About fifty barrels of whale oil, each worth twenty dollars, was all that remained of the whale. "I was ashamed," Farson admitted. "There was something about our desecration, that man should be so greedy for money that he couldn't let the whale be."[12]

Later, back on the bridge of the ship, Anderson, the mate, informed Farson that the whale was a female, and pregnant. That, Anderson said, was why she fought so hard.

For Farson, the adventure was an unqualified success, despite his qualms about killing the whale. The trek across the Shetlands and the endless hours in the cold spray of the North Atlantic were exactly the kind of living he wanted to do. Once more he had proven his mettle. He had resumed his traveling ways.

10

$\rightarrow \cdot \leftarrow$

Among the Spaniards

M EANWHILE, FARSON HAD ANOTHER tawdry serial novel ready to inflict on the public. He had first mentioned it to his editors in the spring of 1927, toward the end of his eight-month bed rest, just as *Daphne's in Love* was beginning to appear. Titled *Fugitive in Love,* the serialized novel created some friction between the writer and his editor, Charles Dennis, at the *Daily News*. Dennis concluded that the physical attraction between the main characters—one of whom he dismissed as "just a two-fisted mechanic in greasy overhauls"—was slightly unseemly.[1] He insisted that Farson rework the novel and demanded an "additional 15 to 20 percent atmosphere" to soften the harshness of the tale.[2] The fact that the male protagonist was an accused murderer further alarmed him. Presumably Farson heeded Dennis's advice, for the story finally ran in the newspaper, appearing regularly from January 31 to February 24, 1928. Set in 1920s Chicago, the story once again revolved around a young woman, this one a nineteen-year-old named Jenny Cain who struggles to break free from the control of her father, a corrupt building contractor in the city. Jenny falls in love with her father's supervisor, who had murdered a man in San Francisco. Or so it seemed. After various escapes and brushes with violence, it all works out in the end.

While *Daphne's in Love* showcased the nightlife, fashion, sights, and sounds of Chicago, *Fugitive in Love* characterized it as polluted, corrupt, and overcrowded. Farson eventually sold the book to the Century Company publishers for a five-hundred-dollar advance, 10 percent on the first 2,500 sales, and 15 percent on every sale thereafter. The book,

apparently, flopped. For the rest of his life, Farson would never say anything good about his burst of fiction writing or the two novels that he had
penned while lying in bed for eight months.

Even before the book's serial run, while Farson, in fact, still lay in bed
recuperating as his wife struggled to give birth to their son, Farson had
conjured an idea for another travel adventure. Having braved the rains
and gales of the Shetlands, he now turned his attention to sunnier climes:
Spain. In particular, the Pyrenees. He told his editors (who he knew hated
the thought of their world correspondents renting expensive cars) that
he would travel as much as possible by mule, make his way up and over
the mountain chain, and stop at the smallest, dirtiest little villages he
could find before taking a train to the country's Mediterranean coast.
From there he would once again take up a mule and travel from pueblo
to pueblo. As usual, his editors agreed to his itinerary, and shortly before
Christmas 1927 he set off for the land of the Basques.

Why Farson chose Spain is a mystery, but perhaps he had been inspired
by Hemingway's *The Sun Also Rises*. He had been to Italy and Turkey, so
there was no need to return; and he may have ruled Greece out due to the
massive outbreak of dengue fever in that country in 1927. He may have
chosen Spain because he liked the idea that the Pyrenees formed a wall
that cut off the country from the rest of Europe. Spain, he remarked, "is
neither included in its ambitions nor entangled in its politics."[3] In any
case, he landed there shortly before Christmas at an interesting time. The
era of the Bourbon Restoration was nearing its finale: Alfonso XIII was
still on the throne, but he had turned from liberal-minded ruler to a man
increasingly irritated by constitutional government, and more and more
supportive of the reactionary pillars of the Spanish world—the church,
the landowners, and the army. The army, in fact, had staged a coup in
1923 and brought General Primo de Rivera to power, and de Rivera had
kept Alfonso on as king, but more as a figurehead than a ruler. But de
Rivera's government, just four years old when Farson arrived in Spain,
was already losing its grip on power: Liberalism was spreading among
the masses, even priests called themselves liberals, and opposition to the
regime intensified. His government would last another three years, col-
lapsing at last when the global depression hit in 1930. But as Farson made

his way into Spain, the question of the nation's direction had not yet been decided, and everywhere he met a people torn between the country's ancient traditions and the demands of progress.

Farson's itinerary was helter-skelter, seemingly improvised on the go. He arrived in the country bearing two letters of introduction; when he presented them, the first recipient promptly left the country and the second took to his bed. Farson started his trip with no one and nothing to rely on except his own grit. Traveling by car, atop buses, astride mules, in the third-class compartments of trains, he crisscrossed the country and stayed nights in shabby hotels, in the impoverished homes of peasants, and under the stars. At one point in the journey Eve joined him, and the two rode out of the town of Loja toward Elche while villagers gawked to see an English gentlewoman on a mule. By the time their trip ended, Farson had limped up and down the streets of San Sebastian, Ujue, Olito, Pamplona, Burgos, Saragossa, Madrid, Alicante, Cadiz, Elche, Murcia, Seville, and Archidona. It is impossible to arrange the names in any order and draw a straight line between them. From the Basque country of Navarre to the plains of Pamplona, from Aragon to Castile, with side trips that engendered other side trips, Farson was happy merely to wander like Don Quixote across the landscape. He also spent a few days in Andorra, where he interviewed the president, more properly known as the Sindic General de les Valls d'Andorra. The only awkward moment there occurred when Farson spied a pile of Andorran passports on the table and asked for one as a souvenir; the syndic had to decline, fearful that Farson would try to claim Andorran citizenship, which was not easy to obtain.

Though he became enamored of the scenery, the bronze, jagged mountains of Navarre, the terraced fields, the "inevitable" Moorish castles perched atop the little hills, Farson seemed to take more delight in the people, and he took pains to describe them for his readers. His twenty-seven dispatches appeared in the *Daily News* every Tuesday and Friday for several months. The Spaniards he found to be a vexatious people, generous but reluctant to invite outsiders into their homes, lazy, still undecided about the proper use of technology. "Spain is not a practical country," he lamented to his readers in his first dispatch. "The Moors brought in bathtubs, and the Spaniards won't use them. The British gave them locomotives and express trains and the Spaniards run them at nineteen miles an hour. The Americans gave them motor busses and the Spaniards use them as cuspidors."[4]

The old ways still prevailed: women drew water from wells while the men worked vast fields with nothing but hoes and shovels; clothes were washed in streams; and every conceivable kind of cargo was carried on the backs of mules. Farson loved it—he grew especially fond of food cooked over hearth fires and the sound of the bells tinkling around the necks of mules—and shuddered to think that modernity would one day catch up to Spain. In the Basque lands of the Pyrenees, he watched men perform totem dances as they impersonated bears and horses. The Basque men all wore berets, and they lived in tiny mountain villages of stone chalets with wooden balconies and overhanging eaves. They meandered over to the local café after their dinner and left their wives and children behind, along with their goats, cows, burros, and mules, all of which lived in the house. By the time Farson arrived in the winter, the Basques had sent their sheep—a well-to-do family could own as many as two thousand, Farson was told—down to the plateaus to graze until spring.

In one Basque village Farson met Jesus Basiano, an artist who had studied in Rome, sought fame, and come up short. Basiano clung to Farson for no reason that Farson could fathom—Farson spoke almost no Spanish, and Basiano spoke no English. But Basiano followed Farson everywhere, and when Farson tried to shake him—by surreptitiously maneuvering to catch an early-morning bus out of town—Basiano showed up at the bus stop ready to go. Farson dined in his hotel, where two waitresses, one a red-headed beauty, the other older and dark, snatched up any sketch that Basiano did and promptly criticized it. When Farson pulled out his notebook to jot down a few lines, they grabbed it and tried to read his notes. In one home, he stayed with a family that gathered around the hearth each night with their cats and dogs. At breakfast, Farson sat on a stool as the senora kicked the cats and poured him some coffee. When the proprietor offered him bread that he had sliced with a bloody knife—he had just killed a lamb—Farson's stomach recoiled. He went hungry.

Basiano figured in several of Farson's dispatches as the Spaniard refused to let Farson out of his sight, even as Farson schemed to shake

loose of his admirer. The dynamic gave Farson's dispatches a certain far-
cical thread, as he portrayed Basiano as a tenacious but tedious sidekick
he could not dodge. Farson eventually rented mules, and, when Basiano
insisted on accompanying him up the steep slopes of the Pyrenees, Farson
pushed ahead so vigorously that Basiano at last gave up, turned around,
and went home without even saying goodbye. High atop the mountains,
Farson looked down the slopes far below to see Basiano in retreat, a slowly
disappearing speck on the landscape.

Through cold winds and torrential rain Farson rode up into the mountains, where he lodged briefly with Augusto Labryu, a young Basque with
a tremendous mop of hair who had helped him negotiate for the mules.
Labryu accompanied Farson to various Basque villages, using his flawless
French to serve as interpreter for Farson, who could make himself understood in *la langue de Molière,* though he had never mastered the tongue. In
the Basque highlands, Farson found that every family owned its own borda,
or cabin, in which they kept their pigs and chickens. The families lived in
their bordas during the summers, watched their flocks of sheep, and gathered snails. Young girls who worked in the sandal factories in nearby cities
came up to the mountains to find husbands, who, soon after marriage,
picked up the habit of leaving their wives at home every night as they wandered off to the local cafés. Farson met plenty of Basques who talked politics; he was shocked to discover that some conservatives frowned upon the
building of roads, since roads meant that young people could go out to the
cities and grow discontent with life in the villages. On the final day of 1927,
Farson found himself in the ancient land of Castile, in the city of Burgos.
There, in keeping with the custom, he ate twelve grapes as the clock in the
Plaza Mayor struck midnight, a ritual the locals assured him would bring
him good luck in the coming year. In the local hotel, Farson asked for a
room with a bath. The proprietor put him in a room with a bathtub next
to the bed. Farson, worried that he would fall out of bed and into the tub,
found it to be one of the most precarious nights of sleep in his life, though
he had previously slept on a dining room table on the boat trip back from
Egypt to France, in a chicken coop, and on top of a Bessarabian clay stove.

Farson jumped aboard a train and rolled south from the Pyrenees. He
relished the Spaniards' way of traveling: small families boarded with saddle

bags in which they carried packages stuffed with whole meals of sausage, huge slabs of bread, and bottles of wine. "I traveled more than 1,000 miles third class in Spain," Farson informed his readers. "For diversity I know nothing that can beat it. I traveled all one night with a nun, a Spanish traveling salesman and a guardia civil. The salesman told stories."[5] Farson couldn't understand a word, of course, but judged the salesman a fine fellow by the way he used his vaudevillian charm to make the demure nun choke with laughter. Farson rode into Cadiz with a group of peasants on their way to a carnival—they were dressed in medieval costumes and tried to help him buy some oranges as the train passed through the vast orange groves of Murcia. The train always chugged off before the peasants managed to negotiate a transaction, but, once, Farson looked out the window of the train as it left a station and saw a small Spanish boy running to keep up, carrying an armload of oranges.

In Loja, Farson and Eve—he never said where exactly she joined him in Spain—rented mules for a trip across the mountains to the city of Elche, a town of some notable history because the Moors defended their possession of it until the thirteenth century. Farson's mule was named Ferdinand. Eve's was Isabella. The ride across the mountains of Andalusia was difficult, and one night the Farsons found themselves far from any village. It was cold. They had no blankets, no fire, no idea where they were. At a dim crossroads, they began to argue bitterly. Farson wanted to ride all night; Eve wanted to stay put. At last, Don Pedro Moleno Garcia emerged from a clot of peasants and offered them hospitality. As they waited for dinner at his hacienda that night, he teased them mercilessly by taking Eve's English-Spanish dictionary, flipping through it and calling out the English names of succulent foods—shrimp, lobster, asparagus, partridge. The Farsons greeted the mention of each dish with a hearty "sí!"— delighted that their host would offer them such fine food. But in response he merely said "No tengo"—I don't have it. The wicked humor amused Farson immensely. "This Spaniard was a ghastly joker," he summed up. "He was an imp. He had picked us off the road to amuse himself."[6] In the end, the sausage he served them was inedible.

From Don Garcia's hacienda, the road to Elche once again became pleasant. "The road is blinding white," Farson noted.[7] The hills were bare and appeared as giant piles of sand. The almond trees were mere puffs of pink and white blossoms. The landscape was cut by irrigation canals, through which brown water flowed. Date palm trees towered over the landscape, and thick clusters of yellow dates hung "like lanterns."[8] The date palms eventually became a forest. When the forest ended—Elche appeared. Farson immediately loved the village. Wires ran over the small streets so that, in the heat of the day, large canvas shades could be pulled to cover the entire street and the café tables on the sidewalks. Men dozed outside the old yellow church, while others played sleepy games of dominoes and sipped vermouth. The men wore black suits. The girls, Farson noticed, seemed to be thinner than elsewhere in Spain; they also looked him in the eye—provocatively, he thought.

Later, when he took stock of his trip and prepared his dispatches for the newspaper, Farson concluded that the glory of Spain resided in its rustic heart: Unlike the rest of western Europe, it had not yet modernized. It was not, as he put it, "a nation of factories and shopkeepers."[9] The hotels and restaurants of Spain were grubbier than elsewhere, he conceded, but that shouldn't bother anyone with spirit. Farson was glad he had come. Decades later, after the Spanish Civil War and World War II, he was still convinced that the Spanish were the most wondrously simple people on the face of the earth.

11

✥ • ✥

Russia Again

THE YEAR 1928 TESTED the durability of the Farsons' luggage and was a busy one for the Farsons, beginning with the trip across Spain and their return to England. Then the Olympics took place in Amsterdam, and the *Daily News* dispatched Farson to the Netherlands to provide stories on the American athletes. As Farson watched, the Americans dominated the games, winning twenty-two gold medals and fifty-six medals in all. Among the standout American competitors was Johnny Weissmuller, who won gold as a swimmer and followed up his success by starring as Tarzan in a dozen films.

For Farson, though, the games were memorable for the fact that during them he received word of his father's death. Enoch Farson Sr. was in his seventy-second year when he died of a stroke. Farson could not attend the funeral, but he expressed pleasure in knowing that the obituary that ran in the *New York Times* was written the way his father would have wanted it. Leaving Enoch Farson's business title to the final sentence, the obituary opened instead with the announcement of the death of "one of the best-known yachtsmen on the Delaware River."[1] Boating, not business, was his father's passion.

Following the Olympics, Farson returned to Russia for an assignment of indefinite duration, where he would replace the colorful Junius B. Wood, known for smoking cheap Russian tobacco in a corncob pipe and fixing his own vodka with a lemon peel.[2] Stalin and the Communists were making massive changes to the economy, and Farson's editors wanted to take a closer look. This time he was accompanied by Eve and their one-year-old son,

Daniel. How exquisite it must have seemed to Farson when he received the cable from the Chicago office telling him to head immediately to Moscow. Fourteen years earlier, he had arrived in Russia and fallen instantly in love, even expressing the wish to die in the land of the czars. Returning now would be a homecoming of sorts. But the country that Farson returned to was far different from the one he left: it was now the Soviet Union, and the czar was long gone, executed along with his family in Ekaterinburg by the unforgiving Bolsheviks. In Moscow and St. Petersburg, where he had once attended glittering all-night parties with Russian royalty and dined deep into the evenings with his fellow arms merchants, there was now the hum and clang of industrialization. Peasants had swarmed to the cities in search of jobs in the new factories. Soviet bureaucrats were busy pushing people around. Instead of arms dealers as companions, Farson found himself in the company of some of the English-speaking world's grand foreign correspondents; Moscow had become an aquarium full of sharks. There was Eugene Lyons, for instance, an overt Communist sympathizer who had jumped from the Russian news agency TASS to work for United Press International. Also in Moscow already was Walter Duranty, the *New York Times*' Moscow bureau chief who would go on to win the Pulitzer Prize, then be denounced by his employer for failing to cover the 1932–33 famine in the Ukraine that resulted from Joseph Stalin's forced collectivization. But in 1928, when Farson arrived, Duranty was still the preeminent reporter covering the Moscow beat. Farson's colleague at the *Daily News,* John Gunther, was also dashing around the capital with his notebook open. Among such journalistic luminaries, Farson was still a cub learning to tip his fedora at the proper angle.

Still, with his ability to make friends fast, he soon found himself in the company of his colleagues, competing for scoops against them by day, drinking hard at diplomatic parties with them at night, always scheming to seduce some foreign diplomat to betray his true feelings about the Soviet experiment with Communism. When future journalist Rhea Clyman showed up in December 1928 with only fifteen British pounds in her purse and no place to stay, the Farsons allowed her to hole up with them in the Grand Hotel, where they were living. She slept in the bathtub. Several days later she landed a job as Duranty's assistant, and over the next nine months he trained her to be a reporter. (While Duranty ignored the Ukrainian famine in 1932, Clyman traveled to the Soviet republic and filed eyewitness reports, to which the Soviets responded by throwing her out of the country.)

Though Farson may have gotten into Duranty's good graces by supplying him with an able assistant, life wasn't all smooth fellowship for him among his colleagues. In one notable instance, Farson reported on a lively party attended by the foreign press corps in Moscow to honor the arrival of a group of American businessmen. During the party the correspondents anxiously awaited a phone call that would tell them that the Chinese had responded to an ultimatum they had received from the Soviet Union as the two nations prepared to go to war in Manchuria. But while they were partying, China bypassed the Moscow correspondents, and Beijing's representative gave the Chinese statement to TASS, which splashed the scoop around the world. When editors back in the United States saw Farson's detail-packed story about the party and noted that their correspondents had been scooped, they bawled the reporters out for negligence, assuming that they had missed the story due to the drunken revelry. "I heard from my home office on the matter, as did others," Lyons recalled.[3]

In another episode, Farson won both the respect and envy of his colleagues when he and Lyons broke the story that Stalin was exiling his rival, Leon Trotsky, to Turkey. Farson picked up a tip on the exile first and shared it with Lyons, with whom he had formed a secret alliance in the hope of beating their rivals, including Duranty. For days Farson and Lyons were unable to get the scoop past the watchful eyes of the state censors. Exasperated at last, Farson delivered his story to the U.S. embassy and asked officials to put it in the diplomatic pouch to a neighboring capital, where the news was flashed to Chicago. That same day, Lyons sent his dispatch as a private letter—an end-run around the censors—to his wife in New York. United Press International published the story under a London dateline to keep Lyons from being expelled.[4]

Farson, a competent Russian speaker, threw himself into his new assignment and wore out his shoe leather visiting diplomats and Soviet officials, collective farms, and new factories, where he recorded the harsh conditions under which Stalin was trying to build a new world. Though later criticized by Ayn Rand for being a little too "pink,"[5] Farson was openly skeptical of the achievements of Communism thus far and plumped his stories with the wearisome diatribes of officious, petty commissars, and descriptions of the overcrowded conditions in which the new Soviet man lived. In one Moscow neighborhood Farson found "seven families—twenty-two persons—living in eight rooms of a big apartment formerly occupied by a single family consisting of husband, wife, and child."[6] The kitchen held seven tables where each family prepared its meals on one of thirteen Primus stoves. In another story he wrote of finding a dozen people living in a single room. Still another story noted: "Most of the rooms in these congested apartments are so stuffed with furniture that you cannot cross them in a straight line in any one direction. The family has very often moved all its belongings, usually the contents of a former entire apartment, into their one cell."[7] Other stories described the monotonous propaganda that had appeared in the textbooks of schoolchildren, the communal kitchens where eight or nine families cooked their meals on two stoves that were heated just twice a week, and impoverished factory foremen who still dreamed of a Communist paradise as they watched their party bosses grow rich.

Farson also escaped the city to visit the collective farms and the peasants. His dispatches centered on the ordinary citizen, the mechanic, the farmer, and the shopkeeper. Just as he had promised the *Daily News'* owner before he sailed across Europe, Farson gave his readers a glimpse of the common life. In Ukraine and the southern Urals he saw arrogant young Communists jeer at religion while the peasants, openly defiant, went to church and lamented the loss of the czar. Farson also wrote detailed dispatches on the bread shortages that had spread through the countryside, the sight of starving cattle standing in the fields, the schoolchildren who received a single meal a day and the violence of the kulaks, that group of slightly wealthier peasants who had learned to exploit Communism to extort money from their fellow peasants. According to Farson, the kulaks viewed newspaper correspondents as informers for the state and had killed 172 of them in one year. Everywhere Farson looked, he saw a populace struggling under the demands of a merciless form of government. He estimated that he wrote more than a hundred articles in an effort to show the "real Russia."

One dispatch began:

In Soviet Russia a mother can take her baby to prison with her if she wants to. She can keep it there until it is four years old, after which the State will take charge of it, place it in some children's home and return it to the mother after she has done her time. And as both prison and nursery are usually much superior to the baby's own squalid home, a Russian baby in prison has as much fun as Russian babies outside, if not more.[8]

Another dispatch began:

About 15 miles outside Kiev in the heart of a silent oak forest lies the old Feofany monastery—a Byzantine creation of turbaned domes, cupolas, and sharp spires like witches' hats; colored bright green, white, and red; popping up out of the dark forest. Once it was the home of the Black monks. But they are dispossessed now; you can see them working like ordinary peasants in the wooded rolling fields, an angry look in their eyes; bearded men in skirts and strange bee-hive hats, greasy hair hanging down their bent backs. Never, almost, since the beginning of history have priests been treated like this; for not only have they been driven from their home, but their home is actually practicing what they once preached. It offers a refuge to homeless children.[9]

Back in the United States, readers loved Farson's dispatches, showering the *Chicago Daily News* with letters praising its intrepid foreign correspondent. One writer, who identified himself as W. J. Tallman of Chicago, wrote: "Mr. Farson obviously is not afflicted with an inferiority complex and hence does not resort to ponderous prophecies and mournful moralizations to justify his contributions. He gives us the result of ocular and auricular investigation, neatly and cogently phrased."[10] Other enthusiastic readers simply called Farson's work "full of humorous, tragic and realistic material."[11]

As for Farson, after seeing the sensational headlines that often ran above his stories, he wondered why Russian authorities hadn't summoned him for a bawling out. Or perhaps he hoped that they would drag him from his bed and throw him out of the country, for Farson had grown weary.

Following months of reporting from Moscow and other Soviet cities, months of covering proletarian poverty and the foolish arrogance of the

Bolsheviks and their Soviet commissars, the urge to move, to strap on his boots and go exploring, was upon Farson once more. One night during the winter of 1928–29, while sitting on the bed in the tenement flat of his friend Alexander Wicksteed, his vague wanderlust shaped itself into a more definite plan to visit the Caucasus. Wicksteed had been there: the romantic scene he painted of the mountain vistas, verdant slopes, swift, icy streams, and vast glaciers was too much for Farson to resist. The next morning he wired his editors a request to journey across the remote mountain chain on horseback, from where he would wire the newspaper stories about "Strange people in strange places."[12] He received an immediate reply: "EXCELLENT YOUR SUGGESTION HAS GREAT SYNDICATION VALUE PROCEED."[13]

In what proved to be a stroke of genius, Farson invited Wicksteed along. His role would not be that of a guide but of a foil, someone Farson could use to add eccentric flavor to the travel book he would eventually write. The book, now a classic of the travel genre, is chock-full of Wicksteed, whose ability to irritate Farson became one of its best recurring themes. Farson would eventually sum him up simply as "the most whimsical, witty, dirty, unpredictable man I ever travelled with."[14] Wicksteed was indeed a character, cantankerous and eccentric, a loner in Moscow because he was welcomed neither by the Diplomatic Corps nor by the group of foreign correspondents who essentially formed the entirety of the expat community. A former missionary in Africa, he had come to the Soviet Union during the great Volga famine of 1921–22, helping to dispense Quaker Relief aid. He had embraced Communism and walked about Russia in his gray beard and shaven head, wearing a peasant's blouse, or *rubashka,* and sandals. A scholar of Dante and Shakespeare, he lived alone in a flat crowded by bits of errant furniture he had hammered together himself. A giant samovar sat in the middle of the room. Wicksteed earned his money by teaching English at the university—his method was grounded on a refusal to learn any Russian—and every May when classes ended he would light out for the Caucasus. There, he would find a tree along the banks of the Teberda River, stretch out beneath its canopy, open a book of sonnets, and spend the summer.

Farson's plans for their joint journey were more energetic. He set themselves a challenge—an arbitrary one, but nonetheless daunting: he vowed to cross the Klukhor Pass, a narrow, snow-clad notch at 9,400 feet in the Caucasus. A Moscow engineer had shown Farson a map with a long-forgotten path across the mountain chain; the Klukhor Pass was the key. Farson's plan called for the duo to travel east to west, clinging to the northern slopes of the mountain chain from the Caspian Sea to the pass, where they would cross to the southern slopes. From there they would follow the River Kodor to the Black Sea. Crossing the pass and making it from the Caspian to the Black Sea would constitute success; anything less would be failure. Their utter lack of preparation put them at an immediate disadvantage. "We did not think this would require any mountain work of much consequence, or knowledge of snow faces: that education was to come," Farson recalled. "Nor did we know that the spring is the worst of the rainy seasons in the western Caucasus, and that for a large portion of our ride we should be lashed by hailstorms, say up at 8,000 feet, which would only turn into pelting rain when we sought shelter lower down."[15] But those black clouds were still to come.

First, they needed supplies, and as luck would have it, Farson had cowritten a play scheduled to open in London in the spring of 1929. His newspaper had generously given him permission to return to London, all expenses paid, to attend the opening night at the Globe Theatre. While back in London he could plunder Fortnum & Mason and other stores for all the supplies they needed.

As for the play itself, it was so bad, such a perfect illustration of Farson's limitations as a fiction writer, that he would rarely speak of it later in life. The play, bankrolled by theater owner Sir Alfred Butt, was titled *The Black Ace* and uncomfortably touched on the theme of eugenics and the notion shared by many people of the era that superior humans could be created. Farson had collaborated with a playwright named Dorothy Brandon to create it. Raymond Massey played the lead role. Farson had apparently worked with Brandon on the play sometime between his recuperation in the hospital and his move to Moscow. If their work was hurried, it showed in the final product.

The play opened on May 9, and critics were instantly disdainful, if not openly aghast. The plot ran thusly: A French professor, through some unexplained pigment-altering technique, manages to turn a "Gold Coast negro" into a white man, who subsequently travels to an Alabama plantation in the company of a British man whose life he had saved. The Black man now speaks with a British accent and has a knowledge of Shakespeare. While the two men are at the plantation, the French professor arrives looking for the subject of his experiment to let him know that he has discovered that the pigment alteration is only temporary. But the professor then dies of a heart attack. He has said enough, however, to throw suspicion on the two travelers. The Ku Klux Klan, having heard that a Black man is about, arrives and lays siege to the house. The Black man gives himself up but, after shots and a scuffle, manages to escape across the river.

Critics yawned in near unanimity. The *Daily Mirror* wrote the play off as a "disappointing evening," though the critic singled Massey out for praise.[16] The *Sunday Graphic*, in a review of a single paragraph, said it was "a well-intentioned play, but on the dull side" and added maliciously that it "left us wondering who on earth The Black Ace was and where he had come from."[17] The critic for the *Era* wrote simply, "There are limits, and surely this pretentious melodrama oversteps the ordinary theatrical conventions."[18] The play closed on May 18. Farson himself walked out in the middle of the second act on the night of the play's second performance. He later blamed the disaster on Brandon and claimed that the plot was entirely her invention; he had only supplied the dialogue, which she had subsequently changed without his knowledge. "Of the play I have nothing more to say, other than that I do not wish it robbed of its one distinction: it was, without a doubt, not only the worst play that has ever been produced but that has ever been written," he said.[19]

Farson set about gathering supplies for the Caucasus trip. At Fortnum & Mason he picked up two bed rolls with rubberized groundsheets from which he intended to erect a pup tent. Because he planned to survive by purchasing sheep from shepherds, he also bought wax-cloth bags large enough to hold a leg of lamb. Smaller waxed bags were bought for other foodstuffs. Final purchases included a fold-up cooking outfit with aluminum utensils, a duffel bag full of tea, coffee, cans of jam, and twenty tins containing one thousand Gold Flake cigarettes. He also picked up his favorite fishing rod from his house in South Kensington. The bill he sent to the *Daily News*. "Embittered by my flop as a playwright," Farson wrote,

"I resolved that the Caucasian journey was going to be a success, even if my expense account made our foreign editor howl."[20]

Back in Moscow in his rooms in the Grand Hotel, Farson was perched on his windowsill watching Chinese jugglers outside when Wicksteed called to say he had procured boat tickets to begin their journey to the Caucasus. It was late May. Farson, still wearing a surgical boot while recovering from the 1927 operation on his foot, boarded a small paddleboat below the Kremlin and set off on his Caucasian journey. He and Wicksteed would spend the next weeks afloat. First, they traveled 115 miles down the Moscow to Ryazan. From there the currents carried them 550 miles farther down the River Oka to Nizhny Novgorod, giving Farson a panoramic view of the fabled Russian steppes: "Complete peace. The ship seemed to paddle on forever under its great bowl of blue sky. The ice had gone, and the steppes, which had lain locked in snow for the six winter months, were now sweeps of green to the far horizon."[21]

All was not tranquility aboard ship, however, or between Farson and Wicksteed, whose habits wore on Farson's nerves. The older man immediately began throwing eggshells (from their omelettes) under his bunk below deck. There they piled up along with a few fish heads. Furthermore, the handkerchief Wicksteed used to blow his nose also doubled as the covering for their supply of butter. Farson lashed out at his friend so vehemently that Wicksteed immediately dropped to his knees and began to sweep up the floor with his hands. Farson went on deck, ashamed at his loss of temper. When he returned, the two patched things up—but not before Wicksteed complained that Farson had liberally dropped his cigarette ash all over their table and the floor. The pair had turned into an old married couple.

The two finally went ashore at Stalingrad, where they waited nearly two weeks for a train before beginning their long journey by rail, four hundred miles, to reach the starting point for their journey by horseback. Once aboard, they slept on hard shelves and woke in the morning to watch an old camel plod through a wheat field. At Rostov-on-Don they saw men that Farson described simply as Turco-Tartars with ammunition cartridges on their chests and silver-handled daggers in their belts. They bowed ceremoniously to Farson when they weren't sharing a decanter of vodka. At

Mineralnye Vody (Mineral Waters), they changed to a smaller train. This one traveled an hour through the land of the Don Cossacks before beginning its climb into the land of the Kuban Cossacks. At last a giant white cone rose up in the sky—Mount Elbruz, still sixty miles away but terrible in its majestic height. At noon they reached their destination, Kislovodsk.

Here began the real journey across the Caucasus. But first, the two travelers needed horses. The search required two weeks. The time allowed Wicksteed to enjoy a bath in the area's fabled mineral waters—until he learned that two of his fellow bathers were using the waters in the hope of curing their venereal disease. After that, Wicksteed was more circumspect about dipping into the healing waters. In their second week of traipsing about the town in an unsuccessful search for horses, they were told that their best bet was to catch a ride on a wagon to Khassaut. The village was a harrowing twenty-four-mile trip up the slopes of the Caucasus and along the edges of sheer cliffs, but the tribesmen who lived in Khassaut were known as great horse traders. On the recommendation of a local, they sought out Uncle Yeroshka, an elderly, hard-drinking Kuban Cossack in black billowing pants who had shaved his gray head and instantly delighted Farson by cursing Soviet police officers as sons of bitches. Yeroshka offered the two a ride to Khassaut on a creaky cart pulled by two small horses, and after stopping to pick up a huge porcelain flask of vodka, the three set out for the mountain village.

The bumpy journey lasted two days; along the way Farson began to catch glimpses of the Caucasus he had hoped to see. The cart traveled upland among intensely green hills and fields as smooth as a lawn. In the distance loomed jagged peaks. They saw horsemen in black burkhas wearing silver daggers. They passed by what Farson described as a stone igloo—flat stones piled atop one another, without plaster, with no sod roof and no chimney to let out the smoke of the fire within. As night fell they began to freeze—Farson was too numb to light a cigarette—and the cliffside paths became so narrow that they had to walk behind the cart as Uncle Yeroshka encouraged the horses to keep moving.

Just as Farson began demanding that Uncle Yeroshka admit that Khassaut did not exist, they arrived in the town. The elderly Cossack banged on the door of the local schoolteacher and was embarrassed when the teacher defied custom and refused to put the guests up for the night. So they went to the local council chamber, where the secretary greeted them hospitably and brought them birch logs to burn in the stove, a pail of sparkling water to drink, a glass of butter to serve as dinner, and his only lamp. They slept on a hard floor, which was so cold that Farson had to admit that he had not properly prepared for the journey.

Uncle Yeroshka woke Farson before dawn and rapped noisily on the window to say goodbye. Upset at being awakened so early—he had purposely paid off Uncle Yeroshka and said his goodbyes the night before expressly so the old "hedgehog" *would not* wake him to say farewell—Farson boiled himself a cup of coffee and watched as a group of what he called Mongolians in fur hats began to assemble in the doorway. At length a leader emerged from among them—a tall man with a red beard in soft leather boots carrying a long, silver dagger. A veritable d'Artagnan, in Farson's mind; the man was a pure-blooded Circassian. He wore his fur hat cocked to the side and had a swagger about him. His name was Djhohn-hote. "There was a sort of an odour of honest simplicity about Djhohn-hote, sometimes very strong: he asked no more than to be allowed to live with horses, love them, and have a free life with them. He was the very spirit of the wild Caucasus. He looked on every Russian as a natural enemy of this free life in the mountains; which, of course, was precisely what they were."[22] Despite opposition from his fellow tribesmen, Djhohn-hote agreed to supply Farson and Wicksteed with their first pair of horses—a black stallion named Kolya and a packhorse named Marusha—and he also agreed to accompany them on their journey.

For the next weeks, their daily routine was an unbroken series of long climbs up the slopes of the Caucasus in wind, rain, and hail, followed by an evening of trying to dry out in whatever *kosh*, or stone igloo, they happened upon. Wicksteed bathed in the icy streams they crossed; Farson preferred sponge baths. The bandages on his left leg—they were practically a permanent part of his life now—were often sopping wet and in need of changing. Inside the kosh, they choked on the rolling black smoke of the fire. Then there was the ritual of haggling over the price of a sheep for dinner. Farson and Wicksteed had agreed never to pay more than seven rubles for a sheep, and they never did. In the mornings they stretched the kinks out of their muscles and headed back to the trail, always moving upward. "During that time I found that the soft Caucasian saddle is soft only in appearance," Farson noted. "It is built over wood, ridged like a sharp roof; and just in the most inconvenient place there is a hard rawhide knot which gouged out an open sore in my behind before that very first day was over. It bothered me greatly."[23]

The two continued on their upward trek through pine forests and along the mountainsides. The weather remained brutal, wet, and cold, though they occasionally enjoyed a string of starry nights in which they idly smoked cigarettes and waited for the campfire to steam the sogginess from their clothes. Farson kept two books in his pouch, Tolstoy's *The Cossacks* and Lermontov's *A Hero of Our Time*. These he read nightly by the light of the campfire. He also kept his notebook close at hand and filled it with the sights and smells of the Caucasus. The notes he turned into handwritten stories for the *Daily News* that he somehow—he never said how—managed to send to his editors. Wicksteed figured prominently in the stories, in which Farson had ungenerously but accurately dubbed him Doolittle, a nod to the older man's resolve to do as little as possible in the way of work. Farson was enamored by the minarets they passed along the way, the mud huts, the graceful way that passing Karachite horsemen leaned from their mounts to pick flowers from the grass, the sparkling streams where he occasionally put his two fishing rods to use, and the beautiful young Caucasian girls who shyly served him meals of corn pone and sour cream. All of it he described for his readers back in Chicago, and in the nearly one hundred other cities where newspapers were receiving his syndicated stories. Djhohn-hote, meanwhile, introduced Farson to passing tribesmen and curious villagers as "Negley Farson Chicago Daily News," which he had taken to be Farson's full name.[24]

One day an event occurred that Farson was seemingly never able to stop writing about. In the various books that he wrote, he interwove bits of his biography with current events, history, and geography, mixing and matching the bits and pieces as circumstances required. Rarely did he repeat himself. But one fish story has the distinction of being the only one to appear in three of his popular works—*Caucasian Journey, Way of a Transgressor,* and *Going Fishing.* In all three tellings, the story is one of triumph turned to tragedy due to rancid sunflower seed oil. The version from *Transgressor* is the most succinct:

> The next day I got thirty-five trout in the upper emerald stream. I do not think a fly had ever been put over those amazingly swift reaches of water before. Two Circassian horsemen who came down to the rocks couldn't believe it when they saw me snatching fish out of the stream with those tiny feathered things—not until I let them prick their fingers on the hooks. Then they appointed themselves my ghillies, and they and their horses went along with me until we reached a gorge down which even their cat-like little horses could not get.
>
> An instructor in Communism, a Don Cossack, whom Moscow had sent down to Utch Khalan to teach the backward Turco-Tatars the values of Communism, had laughed at me before I started fishing the previous day. Flies! He smiled, sneering at what he thought were my trinkets—no!— anyone who knew anything about fishing knew that one used worms. He was a conceited ass. I could not argue with him then—but I could now.
>
> Just as the entire slope of Mt Elbruz—whose two breasts of snow are a mile apart—was turning a light flamingo pink against the sky, I started back for Utch Khalan. I had ten miles to make through the woods. It was long after dark when I got there. But I looked up the Instructor in Communism and invited him to dinner. I brought two bottles of Naperouli, that dark purple wine of the Caucasus, to celebrate the occasion. Then Wicker and I took a swim, holding on to a rock and letting the icy stream wave over us, to get ourselves in shape for the dinner of our lives.
>
> "I'm a poor man," said Wicker. "I've never in my life had enough trout. But to-night—"
>
> He stopped. He made a horrible look at his plate. He spit out his trout. I tasted my trout—and choked.
>
> That horrible Cossack girl had cooked them all in sunflower seed oil.
>
> "I told her to do it," said the conceited Instructor in Communism. "Don't you know that that is the only way to cook trout?"[25]

He had the last of the argument—and the rest of the thirty-five trout.

The story did not appear in the *Chicago Daily News,* either due to Communist censorship or restraint on Farson's part—which seems unlikely, given his combative temperament. But Farson had his revenge on the instructor, of sorts: the story immortalizing him as a pompous ass appeared in three different Farson books.

For the following two days, Farson and Wicksteed rode with a tribe of Tartars as they cajoled their flocks across the mountain passes. To Farson, the tribe hailed from the time of Ghengis Khan. Elderly men rode along with their bawling babies tied with thongs to their saddles. In Teberda, a little Karachaite village in a bend of the Sukhuum Military Road, Wicksteed and Farson accepted the hospitality of a family with whom Wicksteed had stayed two years before. They treated the elderly eccentric with deep respect, and Farson surmised that the old English professor was probably the greatest man they had ever met. The family's son, Yusef, followed Wicksteed around like a puppy. Farson knew that he and Wicksteed were to part company in Teberda: the wild strawberries were simply too much for Wicksteed to resist, and he would spend his days picking them while Farson essayed the dreaded Klukhor Pass. They made their plans. Wicksteed would spend the rest of the spring of 1929 lazing beneath a tree, while Farson would cross the Klukhor, follow the trail down to Sukhuum on the Black Sea, spend a few days gorging himself on melons, then catch a boat across the Black Sea to Crimea, which he still remembered from his first days in Russia as a springtime paradise.

But failure threatened.

Yusef warned Farson that the pass was filled with snow, as was the valley that led up to it. Villagers also told him that an "idiot" had tried to cross the pass in May; he had not been seen or heard from since. But, after a few days in Teberda, Farson's wanderlust was raging—he had to move. He rented two more horses and set off on the 209-mile military road, taking young Yusef as a guide. Wicksteed, in his red and orange pajamas, waved goodbye. The road had not been repaired since 1913. As for the Klukhor Pass, it was only free of snow for two and a half months per year, beginning in August. It was now only late June. If he and Yusef could get over the pass, Farson calculated, they would be the first to successfully cross it this year:

This was enticing but not too encouraging. And the very road up from Teberda seemed to have a mysterious, ill-omened quality to it. To begin with, it heads at once into a deep pine forest. A dark trail—with strange holes in the bank from which come gusts of ice-cold air. The breath of the mountains. The Ganatchkir, a glacier river, thunders down this dark valley and is the colour of milk-ice. The mountainsides are strewn with amazing boulders and broken scraps made by ancient glaciers which once filled the whole valley of the Teberda. This is one of the most picturesque and wildest spots in the Caucasus.[26]

As they made their way up the valley floor, an impoverished Karachaite crawled out of his kosh long enough to offer the travelers a bowl of sour milk and warn them that it would be impossible to get the two horses over the pass. But Farson was nevertheless hopeful and determined: the only way to know for sure whether the pass was open or not was to keep climbing. When the valley became a gorge, they made their way up through the rocks along zigzagging trails, scrambling through a dank, dark pine forest. Giant boulders, loosened by heavy rains, had cut huge swaths through the woods, leaving trees strewn about like matchsticks.

They spent the night in a crude log cabin, invited in by an elderly woman who fed them sour milk and showed them what might have been her greatest treasure—a necklace made of old czarist coins, an illustration that Communism was still a relatively new experiment that had not completely taken root in the wild Caucasus Mountains. The next morning Farson awoke at six thirty and headed to a mountain lake to fish for trout. The lake water, however, was so pure and clear that the fish watched Farson on the banks and warily stayed away from his fly. After a quick swim in the icy water and a breakfast of tea and boiled eggs, corn pone, and his last tin of sardines, Farson set out with Yusef for the Klukhor Pass. Today would be the day he reached the top.

They left the valley where the cabin was located and began to climb up through the rocks and pine forests. Occasionally through the trees they spied the snowy peaks that were their destination. In the middle of the forest they came upon two men and a woman working to build a log cabin. In answer to their questions, the Russians told them the snow in the pass was hard enough to support their packhorses. In other words, the Klukhor Pass was traversable. When they left the forest, though, they weren't so sure. The military road that climbed in switchbacks along the steep slopes had broken off the sides of the cliffs in places. In other places, sections of the road were buried under deep snowdrifts. Climbing to seven thousand feet, they encountered vast snowfields. The horses' hooves began to punch through the snow, warmed by the Caucasus sun, and soon they were sinking into the snow up to their bellies. At times they became stuck. Farson and Yusef would tip the horses onto their sides, then help them to regain their footing, only to repeat the process a few yards farther on. So went most of the afternoon. At the end of one snowfield, they found the remains of a cow, apparently eaten by a bear. As the sun dropped toward the horizon, they at last reached the rocky trail that led up the gorge to the pass. It was steep, but clear of snow. The going became much easier. Farson could almost taste victory.

But the end of his journey was closer than he hoped. They had climbed the last thousand feet of the trail to reach a glacial lake, the high rim of which they had to skirt to climb through the Klukhor Pass. At a critical stretch of the rim, four hundred feet below the pass, water had broken through the ice and poured over the edge of the mountain in a drop of a thousand feet. The rushing water was a river only twenty feet wide, but it could not be crossed. The ice over which the water flowed could possibly hold Farson and Yusef, but not the horses weighed down with all their supplies. Four hundred feet below the Klukhor Pass, they could go no farther. Yet Farson did not recognize defeat. He unpacked bits of gear, resigned himself to spend the night alone on the steep, snowy slope, then dispatched Yusef and the horses to the valley below. He gave Yusef two instructions: first, find the Russians who had told them the pass was clear and curse them; second, find another Karachaite and come back in the morning with a load of firewood. Farson's plan was simple: the three men would set out the next morning to cross the treacherous torrent without the horses, each man carrying a heavy load.

As the evening turned to night, Farson, wet and sweating from the day's climb, sat on his bed roll in the snow and listened as the cooling ice made the mountains sound as if they were cracking apart. Occasionally the buzz of the torrent rushing nearby was interrupted by the sound of rocks as they broke free from the mountains and tumbled down the cliffs. As the hours passed, Farson cleared off a section of snow to better shield himself from the biting wind. Underneath, he unexpectedly found a small plank of wood. It was a miracle. Using a few pages from his notebook and shaving part of the plank into splinters, he was able to start a fire with which he made a whole pot of tea. Sitting alone atop the Caucasus with an endless supply of cigarettes, he leaned back and relaxed. Then, from out of the darkness, Yusef appeared, accompanied by a tribesman from the valley with a load of firewood. He had somehow made it down to the valley floor and back in a matter of hours.

The next morning, however, Farson's luck scuttled away at last. The three tried to cross the narrow rim and the gushing water, but everywhere the ice was too thin and soft. Farson nearly tumbled over the cliff at one point. As they debated whether to turn back, Yusef said simply, "It is better to live."[27] It was a bitter moment for Farson; if they could just move forward another fifty yards without dying, the worst would be behind them and they could make it through the pass. "There is no use dwelling on the disgust and humiliation of having to turn back, the gloom that almost made me sick, and the feeling of doubt and uncertainty that plagued me when we got down, once more, to the snowfields below the pass," he later recalled. "Better to live? I have often wondered since that day if Yusef was right; though we had no doubts on that sunny morning."[28]

On their way down, defeated, they passed a party of three men heading up to the pass. Their elderly leader sneered at Farson and Yusef and boasted that he would find a way to succeed. The thought gnawed at Farson and horrified Yusef, whose fellow tribesmen would look down on him if they discovered that someone else had succeeded where he had failed. But at dusk, down in the village in the valley, the three men came trooping down the slope, as defeated as Farson. Yusef's face brightened, but the elderly leader said he was soon going back up to make another attempt. Farson rested uneasy until, two weeks later back in Moscow, he received a letter from Wicksteed reporting that Farson's rival had once again been stymied by the mountain. The gist of the letter was this: "He is here in the village now, making all kinds of excuses. A Sukhuum mountaineering doctor who came over the Klukhor in dead winter, when he said it was easy with the deep snow, is also back here in Teberda. So is a so-called alpine party of twenty-four Leningraders, who came down here to 'do' the Caucasus. . . . Cheer up; it was the trip of a lifetime, yours and mine; I will never forget it."[29]

It was a grand adventure. And it had been an intense learning experience for Farson. His reporting skills shone in his incisive criticism of the Communist life. He was now a seasoned foreign correspondent. He knew where to go, who to talk to, and what to write.

12

→ • ←

Meeting Gandhi

IN 1930, INDIA WAS a boiling pot the British were struggling to keep a lid on. In March, Mahatma Gandhi led followers on a 240-mile, twenty-four-day march to the sea from his base in Ahmedabad to produce salt from seawater in the coastal village of Dandi. The act was in defiance of the British introduction of a tax on salt. Gandhi had been agitating for Indian independence since his return from South Africa in 1915, and his salt march spurred nationwide civil disobedience to the British Raj and turned the world's attention to India. As Gandhi urged his followers to passively accept British brutality with the goal of shaming the British, the American and British newspapers hurried their correspondents to the subcontinent.

The Farsons were back in London, and Farson was covering an international naval conference when he received a cable from the *Daily News,* "WILL YOU RUSH INDIA?"[1] Farson wired back "RUSHING,"[2] and twenty-four hours later, on April 12, he was aboard an Imperial Airways airplane bound for Karachi. The flight would take seven days; Farson maintained he slept only thirteen and a half hours the entire trip. The aircraft, a three-engine Heracles with a 105-foot wingspan, stopped in Brussels, Nuremberg, Budapest, Zemun outside Belgrade, Salonika, Athens, Crete, Alexandria, Cairo, Gaza, Fort Rutba in Iraq, Baghdad, Basra, Bushire (Bushehr) and Jask in Iran, Muscat, and finally Karachi. The flight kindled some nostalgia. Flying over Germany he looked down on the Ludwig Canal, where five years earlier he had heroically towed his boat more than one hundred miles; in Egypt, he looked upon the sandy hill where he had crashed his small plane and nearly died; and he also gazed on Ras el Tin, where he had lain in a hospital bed for months.

But more importantly, the stops along the way exposed Farson to the uglier side of British rule abroad:

The flight itself was a panorama of British power and prestige; the British Imperial Airways yacht, rusting complacently at anchor on Mirabella Bay, in the island of Crete, whose staff spoke of the entire inhabitants of the Mediterranean shores under the generic term of "dagos"; Cairo, theoretically Egyptian, but with a garrison of British Tommies playing snakes-and-ladders in the Citadel; Palestine, with the Arabs being pushed about by a lot of British policemen; Ft. Rutba, in the desert of Iraq, where the Englishman in charge complained that some camel bandits had just ambushed the convoy bringing his lettuce salad; Bushire, on the Persian Gulf, where we landed at night and had to taxi the plane inside a guarded barbed-wire enclosure, where at that same moment were five Arab sheiks the British were holding as hostages to stop a war between them; Jask, with one lonely Englishman, who had been watching one end of a cable line for twenty-seven years.

When he landed in Karachi, he noticed the Indians standing around submissively as the British officials ushered him from the airport.

Farson once claimed that his first day in India was one of the few days in his life that lived up to all his expectations. There had been a riot in Karachi the day before in which British soldiers had killed up to ten Indians, and the soldiers now warily patrolled the bazaar, unsure how the Indians would react. Undaunted, Farson threw himself into the buzzing marketplace. With the wide-open eyes of a Eurocentric Westerner, he marveled at the crowds: the sailors who had left their dhows in the harbor to visit the many brothels, the old men who wore nothing but loincloths and red turbans, the Hindu women with diamond studs in their nostrils or the ones who wore orange robes, the naked fakir who rubbed ashes on himself in the middle of the street, Muslim women in their black veils, the many merchants in their white robes, on top of which they wore European jackets. That night he dined at the Imperial Delhi Gymkhana Club, one of India's oldest such establishments.

The following day it was down to business: He was set to interview Gandhi. Farson traveled up to Karadi, in Baroda State, where he found the world-famous leader of India's passive resistance movement sitting under a mango tree, naked except for his loincloth, a pair of silver-rimmed spectacles, and two hats. Farson estimated Gandhi's weight at ninety-eight pounds. As the two talked, partially surrounded by the students of Gandhi's ashram, who squatted on their haunches, Gandhi spun cotton on his takli. Farson claimed that whenever he asked Gandhi a particularly thorny question, Gandhi would snap the cotton string, spend time to repair it, then move on to a completely different subject. The interview lasted two hours and forty minutes, during which Farson reached a simple conclusion—Gandhi wanted the English to physically beat the Indians. And Gandhi wanted the world to condemn the British as brutes, to shame them into leaving India.

Farson didn't know how it would end but concluded that blood would eventually flow. Gandhi could not control the Bengal terrorists, for instance, and Jawaharlal Nehru led a left-wing movement that advocated violence to overthrow the British. The Muslims in Punjab, meanwhile, didn't share the Gujerat Hindus' views on nonviolence. The residents in the Northwest Frontier could also turn violent. Gandhi himself told Farson he was afraid to enter Bombay for fear of causing riots. The British, too, understood that the situation could spiral out of control, that something must be done. When Farson later met with the viceroy of India, Lord Irwin, he concluded that the British were planning to arrest Gandhi, even though such an act could prove to be explosive. The date and place of the arrest were unknown, but Farson's accumulated experience as a foreign correspondent convinced him it would occur. He determined to get the scoop, which would be the greatest of his journalistic career. Meanwhile, Farson and the other American and British correspondents who had rushed to India spent the spring of 1930 sending back dispatches on the regular riots and beatings.

For the correspondents, the work was becoming dangerous, as Farson shortly discovered in Sholapur. He hurried to the city after British soldiers had killed as many as a dozen Indians. The Indians had supposedly tried to murder a British police captain. When Farson's train rolled into the station, Sholapur was in a state of siege. Farson put himself in the middle of it. A handful of Europeans with machine guns held the station, anticipating that as many as seventy thousand Indians were only waiting for the cover of darkness to attack them. The white women had been evacuated from the city—except for the "husky" Irish wife of a mill foreman. She sat with a rifle across her lap at the railway platform. "The rest of the Europeans were sitting about armed with shotguns, sporting rifles, or what have you," Farson wrote. "A hundred Dogras of the Bombay Grenadiers were posted around the railway station and out along the road leading to the bazaar, with machine-guns to absorb the first shock and try and shatter the expected attack."[3] Indians had already set fire to and destroyed a police substation inside the bazaar. They had also killed several native police officers and reportedly poured gasoline over one, setting fire to him while he was still alive. The ashes were piled yards from the train station. Two disguised police officers had agreed to stay in the city to raise the alarm when the attack began.

At two in the morning the alarm came. A Dogra raced in to wake the police captain, who was trying to sleep in a train carriage. He grabbed his revolver and rushed past Farson. Someone pushed a shotgun into Farson's hands. He told his servant, Abdul, to stay close to his side when the shooting began. It was a false alarm.

But they were not out of danger yet. As a show of force, the next morning the captain sent two buses from the railway station into the bazaar, each bus carrying fourteen armed Dogras. Farson boarded one of the buses. The route to the bazaar stretched one mile. As the buses slowly rolled along, Farson sensed a thousand eyes staring at them from the windows of the buildings along the road. When they reached the demolished police station, the street suddenly filled with a mob. As if on cue, Farson's bus broke down. The radiator cap blew off just as the bus turned into the "worst, narrowest street" in the bazaar.[4]

When the driver poured a can of water into the radiator, the engine cracked. They were now at the mercy of the mob. The crowd pushed within ten feet of the first bus. Farson noticed thousands of natives filling the streets behind them. Among them he spotted sinister-looking men who appeared to be professional thugs.

The situation had become alarming. Unsure of what to do, the Indians on the bus looked to Farson for a plan. Farson suggested the other bus tow their disabled bus with a rope. Happily, beneath a seat they found a piece of clothesline. But it snapped as soon as the first bus rolled forward. The crowd jeered loudly, then moved closer. At this point the driver of the first bus drove off, abandoning those left behind, including Farson, to an uncertain fate.

Farson took charge. He ordered some of the Dogras to fix bayonets and surround the bus while the remaining soldiers pushed it to safety. Farson called the moment the "worst ten minutes of my life. I've never been so frightened—before or since. Trying not to show it, by casually lighting a cigarette, I knew that while my hands looked steady my tongue was sticking to the roof of my mouth." He added, "I wanted a drink so badly I could hardly see."[5]

Throughout the following months, riots roiled India, including one protest in Bombay that drew two hundred thousand people. In his June 23, 1930, dispatch, Farson described the troops beating the peaceful protestors as a "bewildering, brutal and stupid yet heroic spectacle."[6] He described the scene in gory detail:

> Heroic, bearded Sikhs, several with blood dripping from their mouths, refusing to move or even to draw their "kirpans" (sacred swords) to defend themselves from the shower of lathi blows.
>
> Hindu women and girls dressed in orange robes of sacrifice, flinging themselves on the bridles of horses and imploring mounted police not to strike male Congress volunteers, as they were Hindus themselves.
>
> Stretcher-bearers waiting beside little islands of prostrate unflinching, immovable Satyagrahis, who had flung themselves on the ground grouped about their women upholding the flag of Swaraj (home-rule).[7]

Such dispatches from Farson shocked the world, which was paying close attention to events shaking India. Meanwhile, one of his colleagues, Ellis Ashmead-Bartlett, of the London *Daily Telegraph*, had also concluded with Farson that Gandhi's arrest was imminent. Ashmead-Bartlett, who had earned his reputation with his prescient reporting from Gallipoli during the war, conspired with Farson to determine when and where Gandhi would be seized in the hope of beating their fellow correspondents on a world-class scoop.

As luck, and journalistic pluck, would have it, Farson regularly sailed with a British official, and one day the official tipped him to the date and time of the arrest. But Farson didn't know *where* the arrest would take place. He immediately shared the explosive information with Ashmead-Bartlett. With only hours to go, Ashmead-Bartlett used his wiles to learn from a second official that the arrest would take place in Surat, as Gandhi slept. He would then be secretly put on board the Bombay-Baroda express train and taken off and formally arrested at Borivli. The two reporters schemed to be at trackside when Gandhi would be taken into custody. Farson met Ashmead-Bartlett at the Bombay Yacht Club, where they shared a drink with fellow reporters and ascertained that their competitors remained clueless. They chuckled when they learned they still had the story to themselves.

When they left the yacht club, they jumped into a rented car where Ashmead-Bartlett had placed their typewriters. They also looked to arm themselves. Finding no firearms handy, they settled on golf clubs. Ashmead-Bartlett, preferring finesse, selected a putter. Farson chose an iron, something he could put his powerful swing into. They filled their two thermos flasks with hot coffee. As they thought of their world scoop and relished their colleagues' pending discomfort, Ashmead-Bartlett could not resist quoting Shakespeare's *Henry V:* "Gentlemen in England now a-bed Shall think themselves accursed they were not here."[8]

Farson recalled the journey:

Racing through the dark, hot streets of Bombay, city of dreadful night, Indians sleeping half naked by the roadside, past the sultry sea and out through sleeping wattled huts and villages, past the "towers of silence" where obscene vultures were already circling in their loathesome flight before descending to pick the bones and eat the corpses of Parsee dead.

Through deadly silent groves of towering coconut palms and then, as dawn began to redden the hot sky, the tiny breakfast fires in native huts, bullock carts jogging along the dusty road—and the town of Borivli.[9]

When the car reached the Borivli station, the stationmaster informed them that the express train never stopped there. Farson intuited in horror that the train would stop above or below the station to avoid the town crowds. They were in the wrong spot. Their scoop was slipping away. Now the two journalists faced a quandary—should they go above or below the town? They gambled on above. They sped along the road; where it crossed the tracks, they saw two British police officers standing by lowered gates. They had guessed correctly.

They stepped from the car and made peace with the officious policemen by sharing their coffee. An American car, a Buick, sat hidden in a clump of palms near the road. Farson, in a later essay, reveled in what happened next: "Above the railway crossing was a deep red cut where the tracks curved through a large hill. And we watched it. I think one of the supreme excitements of my life was when I saw the great red and yellow Bombay and Baroda express roar round that cut, throw on all her brakes, and grind to a stop precisely where we were standing."[10] While hundreds of passengers poked their heads from the train windows to watch silently, Gandhi stepped from a purportedly empty restaurant car into the custody of a police officer who doffed his helmet to him. Gandhi recognized Farson and Ashmead-Bartlett. Farson's breathless dispatch read:

> Bombay, India, May 5—The most dramatic scene in the whole world at 6:30 o'clock this morning was when the Ahmedadad, fast flying Indian mail train, suddenly slowed down at a country roadside crossing fifteen miles north of Bombay, and before the eyes of half a thousand Hindu and Mohammedan passengers the half-naked figure of Mahatma Gandhi suddenly appeared from behind the closed blinds of a supposedly empty restaurant car and was assisted to alight by a polite English policeman.
>
> "Good morning, Mr. Gandhi."
>
> "Good morning."
>
> A little dazed, the holy man, naked except for his loin cloth, stared at the two ununiformed British political policemen waiting in shorts and solar topees—at the yellow American touring car, now shrouded in pink curtains, waiting to receive him—at the calm English officer of the Indian medical

service standing with a Red Cross bag ready to accompany him—and then the holy man smiled and sighed philosophically.

Gandhi had been secretly arrested five hours before, in the dead of night, at his home in Surat, 150 miles north of Bombay. He was now to be rushed under secrecy across country to Poona, where he would be detained in a prison awaiting his majesty's pleasure under ordinance 25 of the year 1827, whereby one disturbing the peace or likely to cause civil commotion may be imprisoned without trial.

Waiting patiently during the short interval while the great yellow express train lay halted in the open countryside and other taciturn British political officers dressed in shorts and golf stockings passed down his meager belongings, Gandhi recognized Ashmead Bartlett, veteran British war correspondent, and myself, whom he had met before, and who, aside from a handful of police and startled staring heads of Hindus and Mohammedans hanging out of the train windows, were the only other witnesses of this secret rendezvous.

He put out his sinewy little brown arm and shook hands with us.

"Have you any farewell message, Mr. Gandhi?' I asked.

"Shall I say it now or shall I wait?" he replied.

"You had better say it now," I urged.

"Then tell the people of America to study the issues clearly and to judge them on their merits."

"You have no bitterness or ill feeling toward anyone?"

"No, none whatever," answered the holy man. "I have long expected to be arrested."

"Do you think your arrest will lead to great disturbances throughout India?"

"No, I do not. In any case, I can say that I have taken every precaution to avert disturbances."[11]

The police officers helped Gandhi into the waiting Buick and drove away, and Farson and his colleague dashed back to Bombay with "the greatest story to come out of India."[12] They composed their stories on their typewriters as the car zipped through town after town. In Bombay, they cabled their stories to their newspapers, then headed to the Yacht Club, where they ordered a quart of Veuve Clicquot champagne, ice, and two pewter mugs. They poured the foaming champagne into the mugs and drank deep. "I have never enjoyed a drink so much," Farson wrote.[13] Ashmead-Bartlett was not as sanguine. He worked for the *Daily Telegraph*, a morning newspaper in London. Farson worked for a morning newspaper in Chicago. Farson's story would appear in that day's edition, whereas Ashmead-Bartlett's story would have to wait a full day. Farson could savor the taste of his champagne: he had a world scoop to himself.

13

→ • ←

Covering Hitler and the World

OLLOWING HIS BIG GANDHI scoop, congratulatory telegrams poured into the offices of the *Daily News,* which the editors graciously passed on to Farson. In London, Eve received a confidential letter from Farson's publisher, Walter Strong, informing her that he planned to submit Farson's work for a Pulitzer Prize—at the request of the Pulitzer Committee itself.[1] Farson did not win—his good friend H. R. Knickerbocker of the *New York Evening Post* did—yet even consideration for a Pulitzer was a notable achievement.

But the Gandhi scoop was to prove the final highlight of Farson's career as a newspaperman. The next five years were to offer fewer trips and shorter sojourns in foreign countries. Still, a few newspapering adventures lay ahead: following his months in India, for instance, Farson next traveled to Germany, where on September 25, 1930, he covered the Leipzig trial of three German army officers accused of fomenting Nazi ideas in the ranks. The star witness—the reason his editors dispatched Farson to Leipzig—was Adolf Hitler. Farson was the only American correspondent to cover the trial, in which Hitler testified that the Nazis had no intention of overthrowing the government because they planned to keep winning at the ballot box. In fact, eleven days earlier, in the 1930 federal elections, the Nazis had dramatically increased their seats in the Reichstag from 12 to 107, and Germans increasingly recognized that Hitler could find a way to power. Farson's dispatch began:

Leipzig, Germany, Sept. 25—The fiery fascist, Adolf Hitler, gave the groggy German government another brutal slamming today when, his voice rising to a roar, like a train in a tunnel, he declared:

"We are not crazy enough to stage a putsch! We have not the implement. We intend to conquer by legal means. How can any one expect a putsch, when our movement has already grown to 107 seats? At the next elections we will probably have 150 or even 200—probably even a majority ourselves."

The scene was the Supreme court at Leipzig, in Saxony. In the soft and richly carved oakroom Herr Hitler's voice roared like a loudspeaker to the entire German nation. Such, in fact, is actually the case, for Herr Hitler is obviously using this opportunity to testify in the defense of three Reichswehr officers under trial to put it indelibly on record that the national socialists are a legal party and intend to secure their victory by such means.

Maybe he means it and maybe he does not, but he appeared to be making every effort to establish confidence that any such thing as a putsch is absolutely out of the question.[2]

Afterward, Farson brought Eve and three-year-old Daniel with him to Berlin, where he covered debates in the Reichstag.

Farson then traveled to Poland to investigate reports that the government was persecuting its ethnic Ukrainian minority. Upon his arrival, according to the story he wrote for the November 15, 1930, edition of the *Daily News,* authorities hustled him to a police station, "where I underwent five hours of grilling by a dreaded political ordeal—which, while conducted with extreme politeness, ended in my being followed by spies every minute from then on—one an ugly girl in rubber boots who stalked me about the streets of Lwow and sat outside restaurant doors while I ate, destroying my appetite."[3] After Farson uncovered proof that Polish authorities had beaten two citizens to death, he was arrested, thrown into a cart, driven across the country, and expelled.

The following year, 1931, Farson was given the job of London correspondent for the newspaper. Though considered a plum assignment, the promotion meant that Farson would no longer be the newspaper's roving reporter. He would no longer be able to sate his thirst for travel and new experiences. The previous London correspondent, Carroll Binder, was reassigned to the Ottawa office. So began a more settled period in Farson's life. From 1931, when Colonel Frank Knox took copossession of the *Daily News*, through 1934, he ensconced himself in London and wrote stories on British politics, reviewed books, and covered the economy, labor strikes, the royal family, visits from American dignitaries, an interminable string of international conferences focused either on the European nations' debts (a hangover from the last war), or on rearmament (a harbinger of the next). His fellow correspondents also elected him president of the Association of American Correspondents in London; during his two-year tenure, meetings became drunken gatherings in which British leaders— Ramsay MacDonald, Stanley Baldwin, and Neville Chamberlain—delivered their sober assessments of world conditions, assessments Farson wearily dismissed as so much empty blather. But Farson showed that he had developed some wiles as a foreign correspondent in 1933, when, under his guidance, a group of journalists formed to swap rumors, tips, and tidbits gleaned from a host of informants, bankers, diplomats, and bureaucrats. Farson was apparently the only American correspondent in the group, giving him a leg up on his competitors from the New York papers. Twice or three times a week in gatherings in Farson's office in Bush House, or often over the telephone, he traded information with journalists from the powerhouse journal *The Week,* the Polish News Agency, the *Berliner Tageblatt,* and various French publications. As one participant recalled, it was "a group of what were then the best informed and most lively-minded correspondents in London."[4]

Farson returned to the United States for several months in 1934 to cover the labor strife across the country. One of the highlights of the trip occurred at the beginning, on May 15, 1934, when the ship he was traveling on, the RMS *Olympic,* sister ship to the *Titantic,* struck another ship in a heavy fog while approaching New York. Seven men died in the wreck, and Farson gave lengthy interviews to newsreel journalists while still aboard ship. The second highlight occurred when gangster John Dillinger was gunned down in Chicago on July 22, 1934: Farson was given a private viewing of Dillinger's corpse. As for the trip across country to interview labor leaders and businessmen, Farson was appalled to find that his prose had been altered by editors to fit Knox's anti-union prejudices.

He considered the trip a waste of his time and talent and was relieved to return to London.

Overall, these were heady days for American foreign correspondents like Farson in Europe. The *Daily News* offered its readers possibly the most exciting page 2 in all of American newspaperdom, stuffing it with reports from capitals around the world filed by some of the best correspondents on the beat. John Gunther, who would go on to fame as the writer of travel books and the memoir on the death of his son, *Death Be Not Proud*, filed dispatches at a furious pace from Vienna. Junius B. Wood, called "the greatest correspondent who ever lived," hopscotched from China and Japan to South America.[5] William H. Stoneman covered Rome, then Moscow. Paul Scott Mowrer, who would go on to marry Hemingway's ex-wife Hadley Richardson and serve as New Hampshire's poet laureate, held down the Paris beat and won the first Pulitzer for foreign correspondence in 1929. Meanwhile, his brother, Edgar Ansel Mowrer, covered Berlin. Edgar Mowrer would become slightly famous when, pressured by the Nazi government to leave Germany in 1933 and asked by a Nazi official when he planned to return, he replied, "when I can come back with about two million of my countrymen."[6] He won the Pulitzer in 1933 for his reporting on Hitler and various German political crises. Gunther later recalled those years as bubbling, blazing days of American foreign correspondence in Europe: "Most of us traveled steadily, met constantly, exchanged information, caroused, took in each other's washing, and, even when most fiercely competitive, were devoted friends."[7] Impressed by the newspaper's coverage, Sir Arthur Conan Doyle facetiously quipped in a 1928 piece of fiction that the *Daily News* monitored the globe with a giant telescope.[8] The newspaper's foreign service was "as distinguished a corps of correspondents as has ever been assembled by an American daily," judged press critic Oswald Harrison Villard.[9] Farson, then, was a jewel among jewels. Women adored him for his dash, men took to him for his dare. Beneath the tilted brim of his fedora, he squinted at life through a lazy whirl of cigarette smoke, using his job as a globe-roving reporter to carry out his boyhood wish to travel the world and write. He still bridled at the clock of an ordinary life.

When 1935 arrived, Farson had been a foreign correspondent for nearly a decade, and he still loved the work. Yet it had driven him to alcoholism. Yes, Farson was indisputably an alcoholic. He readily admitted that after filing his dispatches, he rushed to the nearest pub to gulp down double-whiskies—four of them. Waking up in the morning, he lamented the necessity of having to wait for the pubs to reopen. Several times London's bobbies arrested him for drunk driving. Farson put part of the blame on the demands of the job. American correspondents in London had early deadlines to fret over and competitors to worry about. Losing a scoop by half an hour was—and still is, in the world of journalism—abject defeat. The task of trying to beat his colleagues, all of whom were as competent and competitive as he was, drove Farson to near despair. He had also become disillusioned with the people who ran the world, diplomats and statesmen who held conferences, made speeches, and never seemed to keep their word or change anything for the better. Speaking of the job of foreign correspondents, Farson said he knew of "no profession more calculated to kill one's enthusiasm for the human race."[10] And on top of it all, Farson was a father of a young boy; and he was carrying on at least two affairs that left him with heavy guilt. His wife knew of the affairs, which made matters worse and sent Farson in search of the bottom of the bottle at every turn. (Before the decade was over, Eve would suffer public humiliation over the affairs.)

The most devastating affair was with a woman named Sybil Vincent. Daniel Farson would later recount the turmoil she brought to his parents' marriage:

> Eve had stuck by him all those years, traveling the world with him in greater or lesser discomfort and somehow coping with his relentless alcoholism. What she could not cope with, and what broke her, was his infidelity, especially with Sybil Vincent. This *femme fatale* loomed through my childhood and adolescence, with the added complication that the parents of my best friend at prep school, Anthony West, were Sybil Vincent's closest friends as well. There could be embarrassing confrontations if my father arrived for Parents' Day with my mother, for he knew the Wests far too well.[11]

Farson was hooked on the thrill of writing "with the gun against your head," with no time to rewrite.[12] The job had allowed him to travel the world—he held the dubious distinction of having lived in Stalin's Russia and Mussolini's Italy and in Germany during Hitler's rise—to talk to workingmen and peasant women. It had also paid him well: He and Eve were able to buy two adjacent worker's cottages on Walton Street in Chelsea and knock down a wall to create a single home. They dined out frequently, and occasionally traveled to Paris (where, Farson later recalled, "we sat listening to the bogus profundities of the Lost Generation as the saucers piled up, and how they dragged into the conversation, as their own opinions, the findings of every philosopher they had read or even heard of—having a wonderful time cashing in on their mornings of alcoholic melancholia").[13] And there was always plenty of money for Farson's liquor and his beloved Gold Flake cigarettes. Life was good. So when a letter arrived in January 1935 from one of his editors, Hal O'Flaherty, warning that the newspaper's owner, Knox, was on a warpath, Farson must have received a shock.

The letter read:

> Comment upon your recent dispatches leads me to write you immediately a word of warning. Colonel Knox has expressed the opinion and I regret that I am forced to concur, that your point of view is not that of an American looking at world affairs from our point of view.
>
> In other words, it is felt that you have lived so long abroad, and particularly in an Anglicized atmosphere that it would be far better for you to return than remain much longer.
>
> Consequently I would prepare, if I were you, for a move back to the United States within the next two months. I am certain that some order along that line is being considered and I want you to be warned well in advance.[14]

Farson seethed. For ten years he had labored for the newspaper and held down at various times the head office of the *Chicago Daily News* in Rome, Paris, Moscow, Berlin, and London. He had helped establish the foreign correspondent's life in the American imagination as one of unending romance and adventure. And for a score of years he had lived outside the United States. The States held nothing for him; he had no intention of returning. On January 16, 1935, Farson wrote to Colonel Knox to offer his resignation. He also suggested that Knox's claim that he had lost his American viewpoint was disingenuous:

From other quarters I hear that you were annoyed by the amount of drinking I did in Chicago. I must say I don't blame you. I gave you plenty of reason. I'm sorry.

On the other hand, I hope you will understand my position. My only capital is an experience of twenty years in Europe under the most varied conditions. It is my best asset. It would be folly for me to return to begin life all over again in the United States.

I hope therefore that you will understand my motive in herewith offering you my resignation. Of course I will stay here to suit your convenience and be of any assistance to my successor.[15]

Knox, vacationing over the winter at the Triangle T Ranch in Arizona, responded on February 8:

My dear Farson:

Your letter of Jan 16th was forwarded to me here where I am recuperating from the strenuous life of the fall and winter, riding a lot days and sleeping a lot nights.

If you actually feel that your own interests are best served by remaining in Europe to capitalize upon your long and varied experience there, of course, I acquiesce in your tender of your resignation, but before you make that final I do want you to know that Hal's letter was an exact expression of my judgement. I think you have so completely absorbed the English point of view that you no longer view the passing show as a detached American observer and commentator, which is the one quality I must insist upon. This is my sole reason for making a change. My decision was not affected by anything else. As a matter of fact the allusion you make was never a subject of conversation by me at any time or with anybody.

So please make up your mind as to your future course with only the actual facts in mind and let me have your decision. There is a place here on the local staff if you choose to avail yourself of it.

I plan to send a new man to the London office about April 1st.[16]

Farson didn't waiver in his determination to quit, and now he was out of work. The decision had been his, though the story that circulated for years was that he had been dismissed due to his alcoholism. The columnist Drew

Pearson speculated that Knox sacked Farson because Farson had trashed Herbert Hoover's latest book. Hoover was a political intimate of Knox's.[17]

For the third time in his life, Farson had given everything up to start anew. He had left St. Petersburg, Russia, as a hustling merchant to live a brief idyll in a floating cabin on Vancouver Island; he had given up a high-salary job as a truck salesman in Chicago to sail a boat across Europe; and now, at the age of forty-four, he had given up his newspaper work to remain in the United Kingdom.

In uniform in Egypt as a member
of Flying Corps, ca. 1917

Farson in
uniform, with
his leg bandaged,
ca. 1917

Wedding day, 1920

Negley, Eve, and Daniel
Farson in Yugoslavia,
ca. 1935

Farson hiking in the mountains of Yugoslavia

A successful day fishing for salmon
in British Columbia, 1921

Farson on the deck of his floating cabin in British Columbia, 1921

Fly-fishing, location unknown

Farson aboard *Flame*, sailing across Europe, ca. 1925

Eve Farson aboard *Flame* dressed against the cold

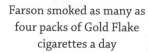

Farson smoked as many as four packs of Gold Flake cigarettes a day

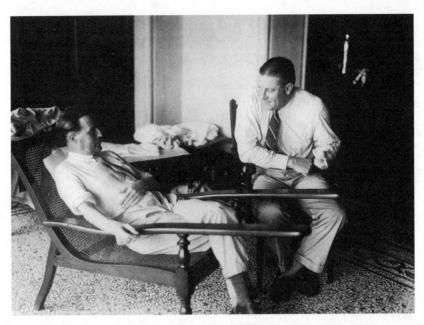

Farson with journalist Ellis Ashmead-Bartlett in India, ca. 1930

Farson's incurable leg injury

14

> • ←

Writing a Best Seller

WHAT NEW ADVENTURE AWAITED HIM? Even as he quit, he had an inkling. Back in 1931, Farson had confided in two friends that he felt he and Knox would not get along. Upon taking partial ownership in 1931, Knox had ordered a pay cut and dismissed part-time correspondents in Oslo, Madrid, Ireland, and Milan. Some suggested that Knox, who had charged up San Juan Hill with Teddy Roosevelt and the Rough Riders, had a knowledge of foreign affairs that was limited to the battlefield.[1] Farson therefore thought of Knox as the perfect Bolshevik caricature of a bloated American capitalist. (Years later, Farson would admit to a certain glee in the fact that Pearl Harbor was bombed while Knox was secretary of the navy.) One of the friends that Farson entrusted with his misgivings in 1931, Ivy Litvinov, the wife of Soviet diplomat Maxim Litvinov, told Farson that he should simply tell Knox to go to hell. Farson deemed the advice impractical. But another confidant, Maurice Hindus, a writer and correspondent for *Century Magazine,* told Farson to write a book—and not just any book, but the story of his life.

So, in the spring of 1935, with no money in the bank and their eight-year-old son in tow, Negley and Eve Farson set out to drive across Europe, to what was then Yugoslavia, where Farson would try to stay sober long enough to spin out the rich chapters of his life into a book. Farson was broke, and he chose to write from the Saint Janez Hotel on the shore of Lake Bohinj in Yugoslavia because it was cheap: "For what I should have paid for a double-whiskey in a smart London hotel, the Saint James gave us each bed and board: my wife, self and eight-year-old son."[2] The British publisher Viktor Gollancz told Farson that if he finished writing the book, Gollancz would publish it. The two signed a contract in which Gollancz paid an advance royalty of a mere twenty-five British pounds, plus a promise of 10 percent on sales up to two thousand copies, 15 percent on the next one thousand copies sold, then 20 percent on anything sold beyond that. The up-front money was meager, but Farson was ready to gamble that he could write his entire life story before the money ran out. Daniel Farson, though only eight at the time, vividly remembered the tiresome, weeks-long trip across Europe. The Farsons traveled in an old, battered Ford that broke down repeatedly with eruptions of radiator steam, forcing them to search for water in small villages. Daniel sat in the back seat with an oversized Mickey Mouse doll that the journalist H. R. Knickerbocker had given him. Knickerbocker had persuaded a friend in the U.S. embassy to issue Mickey a passport, and the French officials ceremoniously saluted the mouse and stamped his passport officiously, to Daniel's delight.

As they grew exasperated with filling out forms at the various hotels they stayed in, the Farsons took to registering under false names, such as Senor and Senora Alvarez from Mexico and Mr. and Mrs. Hirahoto Tagasi of Tokyo. The hotel clerks seemed oblivious until they arrived in Munich, where Eve angered her husband by signing them in as the Rosenbaums, despite the large sign in the foyer that read, "Jews are not wanted."[3] In Vienna, Farson disappeared for several days. Eve and Daniel stayed in the dark hotel room as Eve waited by the phone and tried to distract her son. Finally, Farson was carried into the hotel on a stretcher, blind drunk. As their journey continued, Daniel hunkered on the back floorboard beneath a blanket and pretended to sleep while his parents argued furiously, Farson demanding to stop so he could have a drink, his wife imploring him not to.

Daniel recalled life with a drunkard:

Even when he was sober the threat was a constant shadow. I doubt if my father was ever violent, but I do know that for many years I flinched and drew back if anyone raised a hand. Alcoholism isolates, and I had no brothers or sisters and few friends, for we seldom rested in one place long enough. Everyday details became dramas—but to us alone. Probably my mother tried too hard in her struggle. Her battle to keep him sober was like a military campaign—with ploys, feints, skirmishes and ambushes. I was spy, guerilla and decoy, running with the latest reports to my mother, stealing his trousers, searching the room for the hidden bottle while he slept. . . . For me, the worst part was the listening, while he lectured me, repeating everything over and over again like a Chinese drip torture, aiming a finger like a revolver.[4]

At last they made it to Lake Bohinj in northern Yugoslavia, where all their belongings, including Farson's trout rods and typewriter, were unpacked and carried into the Saint Janez Hotel. In the mornings the servant, Minka, brought them coffee, croissants with butter, and wild honey. Minka was the daughter of the royal huntsman, but King Alexander had been assassinated the year before, throwing all royal employees into a life of uncertainty. There, at a relatively unknown lakeside resort surrounded by beech forest and the Julian Alps, Farson began work on his book, typing away through the mornings and calling for refills of his coffee cup. He worked without pants, not putting on his trousers until he had met his daily quota of ten pages. Then followed a leisurely lunch during which he read his mail and any newspapers that had come up from the town of Bled. The waiter Joseph always looked at the newspaper pictures over Farson's shoulder. In the afternoons the whole family rowed across the lake and fished for trout, which Eve cooked in a frying pan she brought with her. Some days they lingered so long they had to row back in the dark. Every other week, they stuffed their rucksacks and went hiking. The setting and the seasons were perfect; Farson breathed the fresh mountain air and took pride in the quality of the work he was producing. Though he inevitably returned to the bottle in the evenings and embarrassed himself among the few other guests at the hotel, the routine was serene enough to give him the energy to keep working.

The fishing was also good for Farson's wounded spirit. Fishing with a black gnat-like fly in what he called the most "unfished" trout streams in all of Europe, he brought back six or seven trout a day. "Fishing those streams was my Nirvana," Farson recalled. "A short time after I was in the stream my mind was miles away from it, in another world. In this mood, letting my mind wander freely, I had moments when I was as close to some of the intuitive truths as any Hindu practicing yoga."[5] The experience, he said, "was the grace of life."[6] The fishing had a remarkable effect on his writing: as he stood in the streams, he was able to think back on the other places he had fished in his life, and the recollections brought his memories into relief.

Previous incidents came into focus. As he fished, he recalled catching catfish in the Chesapeake, fishing on old wharves in New Jersey, stalking smallmouth bass in the spring lakes of New York and fat salmon in British Columbia. The memories of fish led him to memories of places, which led him to memories of people and the moments he had shared with them. He realized that he had become fed up with the human race, but his anger and disillusion with world leaders and statesmen melted away when he held a rod in his hand, and scenes from his own life, his string of adventures, came into focus. Starting with his upbringing under the cash-strapped tutelage of General Negley and running through his days in Manchester, England, selling munitions to czarist Russia, flying his plane in Egypt, living on a houseboat in Canada, selling trucks in Chicago, sailing across Europe, wandering across the Shetlands, Spain, Russia—Farson threw it all into his book. At times, it was a painful ordeal. In his effort to be honest with himself—Farson knew he was an alcoholic, that his ongoing affairs had damaged his marriage—he found himself remembering things he had hoped to forget. But in the end, he concluded that sorrow was a necessary part of life: "A man should live with his mistakes."[7] Yet the book he wrote, which ran to about 300,000 words and contained more than one hundred references to whisky, wine, beer, assorted alcohol, and drinks, drinkers, and drinking, did not mention his own drunkenness, or his infidelities. Those private failings would only become public confessions decades later.

By the time Gollancz finished editing and polishing the manuscript, it had shrunk to just under 220,000 words.[8] From a bookseller's point of view, the words, though now fewer, were high-octane material capable of fueling huge sales. Farson titled the book "The Way of a Transgressor: Never Go Back." The first part of the title comes from the book of Proverbs: "Good understanding giveth favour, but the way of transgressors is hard." He never explained why he chose the biblical phrase as his title, but it had been rattling around in his brain for nearly two decades. One young woman who lived in Saint Petersburg in 1916 wrote in her diary on September 10 of that year: "A famous writer was here, Negley Farson who was in love with Vara, Mrs [sic] Sartisson's sister. She did not approve of him at all but he said he would write about the three governesses dressed in white in a book he was writing called 'The Way of the Transgressor.'"[9] Whether Farson was passing himself off as a famous writer or whether she misheard him say he wanted to be a famous writer is a mystery. But in either case, the title is nearly identical to the one he chose in 1935. As for the second half of the title, "Never Go Back," its origin is less shrouded: British diplomat and spy Robert Bruce Lockhart recalled in his memoirs that Farson once told him, "Wherever you have been happy, never go back."[10] Ultimately, Gollancz shortened the title to *The Way of a Transgressor*, excising the "Never Go Back" subtitle, and published the book in England in late 1935. The book landed on American store bookshelves the following year.

Critics loved it. So did readers. Somehow, despite the despair and the drinking, he had captured the lightning of his life in a bottle. Once again, he had emerged from the wreckage intact. He was now a publishing sensation.

In England, the *Daily Herald* called it "The Autobiography of the year—without a shadow of doubt."[11] The *Times* critic said, "Every page quivers with vitality."[12] And the *Sunday Times* joined the chorus of praise, calling the book "fascinating—a brilliant picture of a born adventurer's reckless and relentless experiment in living."[13] *John O'London's Weekly* said it was "full of wanderings and hair-breadth escapes, flying, fishing, yachting, wars and Bolsheviks," and its author was "a desperately brave and intensely curious man who had gone through an immense amount of living and sat down to write about it as an afterthought."[14] In Australia, the *Sydney Morning Herald* on January 18, 1936, had this to say: "Reckless, happy-go-lucky, adventurous, a born wanderer, this rolling-stone has gathered little financial moss but a wealth of experience."[15] And this: "Negley Farson knows how to tell his stories crisply, humorously, vigorously. He has an eye for the dramatic, a strong sense of Irony, the gift of the concrete telling phrase, and abundance of sheer gusto."[16]

American critics crushed on the book as well and penned reviews that drove sales to a furious pace. The *New York Times* on February 14, 1936, compared Farson to the great boxing champion John L. Sullivan, who refused to take a seat during his seventy-five-knockdown fight against the challenger Kilrain under the hot Mississippi sun: Like Sullivan, the newspaper explained, Farson seemed to never pause between his mishaps and adventures. "His life has been one of fast action, and has ranged all over the map," reviewer Robert Van Gelder wrote for the paper. "When very young he was a champion athlete. He worked for a while as an engineer, as an advertising man, as a salesman of munitions in wartime Russia, as a freelance writer, a newspaper correspondent, an aviator, a sales manager. Only when recovering from severe injuries at various times has he put much thought to the puzzle of what it is all about."[17] The book, Van Gelder concluded, was a "bombshell of vitality" and "the raciest reading of the year."[18] The day after the *New York Times* review appeared, the *Saturday Review of Literature* made Farson its cover story and featured a handsome photo of Farson (with a cigarette elegantly perched between his fingers) on its front page. The review on page 5 ran three full columns. "The thing about this book which is unique is the enormous zest for life and adventure which it discloses," wrote reviewer Frank H. Simonds.[19] Simonds compared it to Walter Duranty's recently published *I Write as I Please* in its ability to grip the reader, and he heaped praise on Farson's description of decadent czarist Russia, Egypt during the Great War, and the various adventures Farson had as a foreign correspondent. Like Van Gelder, he found a lack of geopolitical context in Farson's wanderlust and adventuring but did not hold that against him: "Farson's book is not history, just as the report of his travels is not geography. Journeying with him over Europe and through conferences and revolutions, the reader discovers no explanation of events and no elucidation of policies. But nowhere have I encountered a more vivid or more absorbing record of how people actually felt in moments which will one day be reduced to dry historical proportions and become at once unrecognizable to those who lived them and intelligible to those who stayed at home."[20] The reviewer for the Indiana *Evening Gazette* offered a similar assessment. While he complained that the book was "full of stirring incidents—and little else" and that Farson "seems to have come out about where he went in," the reviewer nonetheless gushed that "Farson is a man who has lived—and how! His life has been one long succession of exciting incidents, breath-taking events, and general turbulence. It has been Adventure with a capital A."[21] The *New York Times* published a second review of Farson's book, this one written by R. L. Duffus under the headline "A Stirring Life of Adventure." The review, which ran to four columns and included another dashing photo of Farson, was boundless in its praise: "It seems that almost nothing that can happen to a man in these days, except death, failed to happen to Mr. Farson. He attracted thrilling and high-colored experience as a light attracts moths. Some of his success in this, no doubt, was luck. Most of it was due to his passionate unwillingness to adapt himself to a conventional, steady-going existence. . . . A psychiatrist might say that he spent his life escaping."[22]

That same day, the *Washington Post* piled more praise on Farson and *The Way of a Transgressor* and compared him to the fabled "white-haired boy" whom fortune smiles upon.[23] Reviewer Theodore Hall wrote that "when a man can fill 602 pages of autobiography, narrating his jobs and tussles and escapades and loves and joys over the face of the earth, and not be forced to commit one solitary dull line to paper, then one is justified, I should think, in ascribing to him the lightness of hair traditionally associated with the blessings of good fortune."[24] On March 4, the *New Republic* weighed in: "Take out a map, pair off places with events—Russia and the Revolution, Ireland and the De Valera elections, Turkey and the Mosul oil affair, Gandhi and Civil Disobedience—add a whiff of life and a fiery personality and you have the main ingredients of Negley Farson's autobiography."[25] The review concluded: "It's a bird's-eye view with the bird perpetually flitting to the next tree. But nothing can rival the pungency and tempo and humor of these stories; which reveal, moreover, Mr. Farson's generous and engaging personality."[26]

Professional critics weren't the only ones to notice Farson. Old acquaintances with whom he had long ago lost contact wrote to congratulate him, including one colleague from Hans Renold Ltd. in Manchester, several friends at the Mack Company in Chicago, and one faculty member from Andover who asked for an autograph even as he confided that he had "assisted" in Farson's departure from the school. A Mrs. Harold T. Miller of Detroit likened Farson's book to "a piece of warm human flesh with a bit of soul attached," while an enthusiastic fan letter from a Mr. Harrison

Brown said the book "is as full of colour as a van Gogh and it reeks of living like the saga of a democratic and cosmopolitan Kipling!" Many of the correspondents confessed that they had written their letters as soon as they put down the book. The American Prison Association recommended Farson's freewheeling biography to inmates in its 1,000 *Books for Prison Libraries, 1936–1939.*

Farson had become famous. Readers snatched up his book by the thousands, then by the tens of thousands. It was a Literary Guild Selection of the Month. By July 1936, it had sold more than one hundred thousand copies. Harcourt Brace, the book's American publisher, announced plans to produce ten thousand copies of an illustrated version. By the end of the year, a year in which Margaret Mitchell's *Gone with the Wind* dominated the fiction best-seller list, *The Way of a Transgressor* was the number-three nonfiction best seller, and it would sell well for years.

The book was as honest as Farson dared to be. On one hand, it was an unvarnished look at the ups and downs of his childhood, his complicated relationship with his parents, his struggle to become a writer and his sense of insecurity, his mistakes and failings. Even when writing of his adventures, he remained modest, almost offstage, and the lack of embellishment brought clarity to his prose. On the other hand, the book drew a veil over his infidelity, the remorse he felt over betraying his wife, and his alcoholism, the great, guilty burdens of his life.

The book was behind him. Now what would he do? The world, after all, seemingly lay at his feet. Even before *Transgressor* rocketed to the top of the best-seller lists, he had asked himself how he would live his life "if that book hit the jackpot," if he suddenly had the financial means to live solely as he wished.[27] He couldn't figure it out. Or perhaps he did: "So thinking what sort of life I should go in for if that book gave me the choice, I answered myself with a negative: I knew there was one thing I was not going to do—and this was try for mere happiness. That also doesn't last. It can cloy. I wanted to go on *experiencing*."[28]

With his book selling well in England, Farson set off for the United States in the late fall of 1935, hoping to promote the book to an American audience. Perhaps more importantly, he wanted to reimmerse himself in the intense, messy life of New York City—but only temporarily. Farson had often daydreamed of returning to the city and living in a room on lower Third Avenue, where he could "soak" himself in the varied lives of thousands of strangers, the goal of which would be to increase his interest in his own life: "I want to feel that I'm living every day, instead of just being alive."[29] But he would never wish to remain in New York City; his home was forever England.

He boarded the *Berengaria,* which was also carrying writer Sinclair Lewis back to the United States. Farson and Lewis were acquaintances, having met at various parties in London. They had never become friends, though, because they had been too drunk to converse. (Aboard ship, their relationship deepened as they shared their amusement over a clueless English author who told them of his plans to lecture throughout America.) When he arrived in New York, Farson checked in to the Brevoort Hotel in Greenwich Village, where he had spent time recuperating in 1920 following his leg surgery. It was there where a newspaper publisher had rejected his full-page obituary of John Reed because, according to Farson, it had made the fiery writer too likeable. Farson spent his afternoons enjoying booze-soaked lunches, reading in bed, and scribbling notes for a new book he was contemplating to be titled *Created Equal.* The book would be about how Americans are born equal but fight their entire lives "to get over it!"[30] He also spent his days walking the streets of the city. To his dismay, everything had changed from the days when he hustled to sell oil to city merchants, from the days of Diamond Jim Brady, Delmonico's, the five-cent stein beer and the flophouses. The city seemed to Farson to be in the iron grip of a ruthless mafia.

Meanwhile, Farson had been offered a "big lecture tour," which he said he "unfortunately" accepted—unfortunately, because he was drinking too hard to work out the logistics that such a tour required.[31] He gave a single speech in New York City, which turned into a fiasco when he froze up fifteen minutes into the talk. He abandoned plans for his book. Freed from the workload and with his wife and son still back in London, his boozing reached epic proportions. He attended "some of the wildest parties you could imagine" and drank until he went blind and passed out.[32] The episodes went unnoticed, however: He was just another blind drunk among drunks in the city that never slept. Finally, he bought a black Ford V-8 and headed to the American South. He planned to write articles for the British newspapers and magazines.

One of Farson's first stops was Baltimore, where he hoped to talk to F. Scott Fitzgerald and hear what he had to say about the state of America. If there was one writer in the country who could sympathize with the wreck that Farson was making of his life, it was the author of *The Great Gatsby*. Fitzgerald was in the middle of writing "The Crack-Up," a series of articles on his own busted life that appeared in *Esquire* magazine in February, March, and April 1936. Like Farson's, Fitzgerald's life had been savaged by alcohol, hard living, financial pressure, and a troubled marriage. Unbeknownst to Farson, Fitzgerald envied his adventurous life. Later that year Fitzgerald wrote his editor, Maxwell Perkins, to bemoan the fact that, unlike Farson, he had an insufficient pile of real-life material to which to turn his writer's hand; while Farson mined his life for racy tales, Fitzgerald had to do the arduous work of inventing them.[33] Farson found him living on the top floor of a Baltimore apartment building. Fitzgerald was writing as he stood in front of an old-fashioned accountant's desk. Farson asked him why he wrote standing up. Because, Fitzgerald explained with a smile, if he sat down he'd start drinking. He pointed to a bottle of gin on the floor. Then he said, "Let's sit down."[34] They drank and talked till long past midnight. Farson admitted to not remembering much of that evening, only that he looked up from his drink to find Fitzgerald gone.

Farson next steered his Ford to Washington, where he interviewed a group of African Americans as part of his effort to collect material for the British press. He also attended a White House dinner, shook hands with Eleanor Roosevelt, and met President Franklin Delano Roosevelt. (Seemingly without trying, Farson had become one of the few people on the planet who had met Hitler, Gandhi, and Roosevelt, not to mention British prime minister Ramsay MacDonald.) Farson admired both Franklin and Teddy Roosevelt, imagining the former as a young man on his yacht, the latter on African safari: "These men, these lucky men, and their like, who knew how to get the most fun out of life in the United States, were far closer to the American working man, and the American working man knew it, than any of these great big bouncing know-it-all self-made Americans who are always so afraid of their own immediate past."[35] After meeting the next day with labor leader John L. Lewis and taking time to stand before the Lincoln Memorial—it was his favorite monument—Farson once more got behind the wheel of his big Ford and headed farther south.

As he drove through Virginia and North Carolina, the tension began to melt away from his muscles. Nature helped him find his center of being when he was at war with himself, and motoring slowly through the black-water swamps and admiring the wild cypress and the Spanish moss eased his anxiety. He accepted the unspoiled land as a blessing and tipped his hat to every swamp he passed. In North Carolina and Georgia, he stopped at prison camps to interview both wardens and black convicts. The casual brutality horrified him. Prisoners lay together, linked by steel wire like fish on a stringer. He took notes, plenty of notes, then fled. His drinking continued; he added moonshine to his list of sampled alcohol products. The combination of heat and booze wearied him, and as the endless black-top and booze ground him down he gave up any pretense of trying to write a book about America. If he had been cold sober, he concluded years later, he could have written the best book of his life. He would mourn the loss of the book until the end of his life. It was the fish that got away. Liquor, he realized, had betrayed him: "Drink has always taken all the guts out of me; I have never got a drop of inspiration, or courage, from a bottle."[36]

In a desperate attempt to win back his self-respect, he holed up in a hotel room in Atlanta with his Corona and banged out a story about a disbanding vaudeville troupe he had encountered in the lobby. He typed from morning to midnight, then sold the finished pages to the Manchester *Guardian*. But it was the only writing he did. When he reached the Florida state line, at last, he turned the Ford around and headed back to the Brevoort in New York. There, he packed his belongings, sold his car, and boarded a ship to England. He was done with America. During the voyage, he stayed deep in his cups and "was decanted from the ship" at Southampton.[37] In a hotel room there, he hallucinated, envisioning meteor flashes in the sky and torn faces laughing at him. He felt as if he were falling. In the morning, he lay abed and waited for the pubs to open. He was terrified that it was Sunday and they would not open till noon. Worse, maybe they would not open at all. He decided only one thing in the whole world could possibly save him: he needed to put a fishing rod in his hands and wade into a stream.

Desperate but at least with a plan to go fishing, he bolted to Norway. He had been to the country many times during his years with the newspaper. Now he sought solace in the simple values of the Norwegian people: unlike Americans, they did not strive to get rich or to become famous. To Farson, Scandinavian people were synonymous with hard work, strength of character, a passion for independence, and an appreciation for a strenuous life. These were the values that Farson cherished. As he noted, "Power, position, pomp—I wanted none of those."[38] For weeks he wandered over the mountains and brooded on the meaning of life—his life. He walked among the junipers and savored the crunch of the reindeer moss beneath his feet. He fished deep rivers until his strength waned and replenished himself the next morning by washing in the crisp air and breakfasting on fried trout, goat's cheese, and a whole jug of milk. Finally able to smoke his cigarettes without trembling, he returned to England, to his wife and son.

There, the Farsons bought an English Ford and set out once again to motor across Europe, back to the hotel in northern Yugoslavia where he had written his book the previous year. Was this Farson's attempt to reconnect with his family? He never said. But Daniel recalled that his parents' marriage was "dangerously near to a divorce,"[39] and the trip was a disaster. Tourist crowds had infested Lake Bohinj. A new hotel had risen in a single year. Soldiers pointed their rifles at Farson and forbade him from fishing in the royal waters—an article he had written for the *Sphere* in which he boasted of poaching trout in the king's lake had apparently angered authorities. Peace proved elusive. Norway and Yugoslavia were not enough, and he was tired of Europe anyway and needed to escape. He dreamed of trade winds. He asked himself, Where should I go? What should I do? He answered with the words of English explorer Sir Richard Francis Burton:

> Do what thy manhood bids thee do,
> From none but self expect applause;
> He noblest lives and noblest dies
> Who makes and keeps his self-made laws.

15

→•←

South American Bender

THROUGH THE HAZE OF heat, his polo shirt pasted to his back with sweat, Farson leaned out over the rail of the Dutch steamer and spied the snows of the High Sierras in the distance as his ship sailed into the Venezuelan harbor of La Guaira. As the East had beckoned to Marco Polo, so Farson's "manhood" had bid him come to South America. In front of him, three rusty destroyers bobbed at anchorage—the laughable entirety of the Venezuelan navy. They had rested there for years by the ancient and obsolete harbor fort and greeted incoming vessels with tinny bugle calls. A British oil-tanker captain, a fellow passenger of Farson's and an old hand in the tropics, told him the coastline was the most dangerous in the world: if you ventured into the jungle a mere sixty miles inland, the Indians wouldn't bother shooting you; they would shoot your guide and "leave it to you to find the way out."[1]

Farson had long set his sights on South America. As a young man with an engineering degree, he had dreamed of building bridges across the Andes. His motives for this trip were less noble. He was abandoning all pretense of respectability: He pocketed $1,000 in royalties from *The Way of a Transgressor*—a huge sum considering the average yearly wage was about $1,700—and turned over all future royalties to Eve, hoping to save her from financial ruin in case he didn't return, which was a distinct possibility. For he had determined to go on an epic, transcontinental bender. Farson paradoxically hoped to cure his drunkenness with an alcoholic debauchery, as if he could purge the desire for drink by surrendering to it completely for as long as he could endure it. He would drink to reach the bottom. "I have never been on such a round of drinking in all my life," he later wrote. "I went to South America with the deliberate intention of going the limit. I had abandoned all hopes of propriety."[2]

Farson began to drink heavily nearly five thousand miles from the South American coast, as his ship left Dover on its eighteen-day voyage across the Atlantic. He drank Singapore slings, concocted of gin and cherry mixed with soda water and a touch of lemon juice. He pulled corks so frequently that one fellow traveler, an older woman with a childlike but late-life enthusiasm for adventure, politely inquired after his health. Gallantly, he drank less, but only in her company. The length of the journey gave Farson time to study the idiosyncrasies of the other passengers over the rim of his glass. There was the young Englishwoman, possibly a teenager, whom he dubbed the Parrot. She was "a study in green and scarlet. Red hair (she wore no hat); sullen, scarlet lips; scarlet, and very dirty, fingernails; and the most daring collection of fake jewelry I have ever seen on any girl."[3] She carried chrysanthemums "plucked from the vase of some cheap Soho restaurant."[4] She was furious at having to leave her lover behind in England, but his farewell telegram had merely said, "Au Revoir. Carlo."[5] He had not even used the nine words allowed, she pouted. Farson admitted to making out with her below deck but lamented that she wore a chastity belt.

Farson bunked with a traveler he referred to only as the Bishop, an elderly man who had lived in torrid British Guiana for twenty-one years. To Farson's amusement, the Bishop awoke at 6:00 a.m. every day to take a bath, then returned to bed to drink two cups of tea and eat exactly one biscuit. He hung his pajamas on two separate hangers. "Here was a man the tropics couldn't break," Farson observed. "And his safeguard had been his unshakable daily routine."[6] Also on board were an archetypically pretentious aspiring artist and his girlfriend, who tossed his paintings into the ocean after calling them derivative. Finally, there was the young Syrian trader from Manchester whom Farson disliked. The Syrian exercised each morning by walking on his hands across the deck, a bit showoffy but a muscular feat that led Farson to conclude he was too much of a man to punch in the face. Farson remained in Venezuela for ten days and never ventured outside La Guaira, merely scribbling a few notes on the country's bloody history.

From there, he sailed to Puerto Colombia in Colombia, and from there to Barranquilla, where he hopscotched from barstool to barstool while waiting for a boat to take him through the Panama Canal. His goal was to reach Bogotá, and he discovered that the canal was a faster route than trying to travel inland.

While waiting for the boat, he accompanied a group of British tourists through the jungle outside Cartagena to a little village to witness a bullfight. The fight took place in the heat of the afternoon, in a bull ring fenced by bamboo that measured 200 by 100 feet. Peasants and cowboys sporting white cotton shirts and straw sombreros sat beneath the hot sun to watch, while the silk-clad Cartagena society watched from the shade. Young men sipped rum straight from the bottle, and the cowboys wore spurs on their bare feet. Two matadors fought that day, the first an older fighter no longer fit for the bull rings of Spain and consequently now consigned to ply his trade in the backwater villages of the New World. As Farson watched and the crowd looked on in horror, the bull's horn pierced the matador's lung: "The matador squirmed like a freshly caught fish on the hot sand."[7] The second matador, a young man named Ivarito, rushed to his aid. After a few spectators dragged the wounded man away, Ivarito entered the ring to fight the bull. He disdained to wear the padded gold jacket and elected to fight in only a white shirt. Farson was sober enough to appreciate the young man's bravery:

> He was unexpectedly handsome, with a pale, clean-cut face and fine forehead. He frowned thoughtfully as he stepped out from behind the barrier, and before he left it, I saw him drink about a third of a glass of dark rum. Unlike the vast rings of Seville and San Sebastian, where the bullfighter is usually so far away that he looks no bigger than a doll, we would watch every expression on Ivarito's face. It made the fight very intimate. And it was obvious that Ivarito, taking the matador's revenge, intended to humiliate the bull by driving it into a frenzy of frustration and fear. He exploited every risk for all there was in it. Time and again it was hard to distinguish man, cape, and bull. It seemed folly to take the chances he was taking in such a shabby ring for a mere country crowd. He was due to fight a few weeks later in Bogota, where he would get a hundred times the purse he would get for

this village exhibition. But if he had been fighting in Madrid itself he could not have given the crowd more for its money.

At last Ivarito was ready to kill the bull. He waited for the perfect moment to drive his sword down into its heart. As Farson watched, Ivarito placed his heels together, rose up on his toes, drew the bull toward him with a wave of his cape and thrust his sword down into the charging bull. The bull swayed slowly back and forth, then sank into the dirt. A man ran into the ring and stabbed deep into the bull's skull with a dagger. The crowd crushed the rickety bamboo stands and rushed out to the carcass.

"They will eat it tonight," an onlooker told Farson.[8]

Cartagena lacked sidewalk cafés and cabarets thanks to the strict customs of the Catholic Church and of old Spain, and life was still fairly primitive. Laundresses either beat laundry on rocks by streams or tossed the clothes into a vat with other people's laundry—usually dyed bright colors of scarlets, blues, and oranges—so Farson eventually found all his formerly white suits left him "looking like a rainbow."[9] During the day he ate papayas and green oranges and a fruit soft as an alligator pear and blood red inside. At night he drank hard and hit saloons such as the Navy Bar, the Pullman, and the Dancing Bar with a couple of ex-sailors, Barnacle Bill and his buddy Jock. Jock refused to return to his home in England "because my wife's a Christian," he told Farson.[10] Farson got drunk with the two old tars, until one night one of them took Farson's lit cigarette, touched it to a bottle rocket and threw it on the dance floor, causing pandemonium. "It hit a fat Colombian beauty where she did not expect to get a rocket," Farson said of the incident.[11]

At last, Farson caught a boat to Panama and landed in the seaport of Colón in the Canal Zone, where he spent his first night in jail. He had been out dancing at the Moulin Rouge, then hailed a taxi back to the Hotel Washington. There, he told the Jamaican taxi driver he could wait if he wanted, since Farson was undecided if he was done drinking. The taxi driver chose to wait. Farson, drunk, went to sleep. About 1:00 a.m., a hotel employee woke him to tell him the taxi was still waiting, and the driver demanded money. The ensuing argument between Farson and the diligent taxi driver ended when police escorted Farson down a corridor "stinking of human offal, and *clunk*—horrid sound—the bolt of a cell shut behind me."[12] He found himself with a dozen other miscreants in a "cement box. It was like a cage at the zoo; and smelt like one."[13] Farson wore a spotless white suit—at least it was white when he entered the cell. A Frenchman who approached him wore the dirtiest underwear he had ever seen. A Panamanian sat in a corner and rocked back and forth with his hands around his knees. His nose was broken, and a bit of bone protruded. The man he had caught with his wife had reportedly suffered worse—a stab wound.

Hours later, after meeting the magistrate, Farson was released and fined. But the magistrate bristled at what he perceived to be Farson's Yankee impertinence and decided to throw him back into the cell for a few more hours. When he was finally set free for good, a group of sympathetic whores commiserated with him—after he bought them a round of drinks. Farson continued his binge at Bilgray's Bar, one of the most famous saloons in the Caribbean, known for never cutting its whisky. When the bars closed, or when he needed solitude, he drank Johnnie Walker scotch on the balcony of his hotel room. Farson may have been drunk his entire stay in Colón. At one point he awoke sober enough to notice an anchor tattooed on his arm.

It was also in Panama's Canal Zone that Farson encountered an emaciated French prisoner who had escaped from Devil's Island and had been hiding in the jungle. Farson described him as a "walking mummy,"[14] but the Frenchman, Rene Belbenoit, would soon make his way to the United States, where he wrote a best-selling book about his escape, *Dry Guillotine*, in 1938. Unknown to Farson, Belbenoit had the manuscript with him when they met. He later sent Farson a signed copy.[15]

Farson eventually sailed for Buenaventura on Colombia's Pacific coast. From there he set out for Bogotá, boarding a train that pulled out from the "rust" of the city and pushed through sixty miles of jungle so "dense, dark and sickening that human beings rot in it."[16] Farson scribbled in his notebook that the jungle inhabitants lived in hovels of bamboo and banana leaves, and were eaten by yaws, a bacterial infection like syphilis, and hookworm ulcers "which seep into their calf muscles and jerk their heels up permanently."[17] Everyone, he noticed, whether adult or child, carried a machete: "For without that cane knife there is no way of passing through this misanthropic undergrowth, which shuts off forever any possible glimpse of the hot sky."[18]

Farson switched from train to automobile to climb the ten-thousand-foot passes of the Andes, which run the length of western South America. His companion on the car ride was a Dutchman who had been sent to Colombia by his church to find a jungle home for fifty refugees from Hitler. Mist drenched the Andes as Farson's driver carelessly wheeled up the narrow road of hairpin turns.

Bogotá, perched almost four miles above sea level, struck him as dreamlike with its limousines and luxury shops—in contrast to the rot of jungle and wretched people elsewhere. Farson noted that in Bogotá, everyone wrote poetry, "mooning under the cedars."[19] He played billiards in the Jockey Club with the sons of landowners whose immense property stretched to the horizons. Their spoiled sons attended good English schools such as Oxford or Cambridge. None of these big hacienda owners were "heart-searching about their duty to the peasants that had so tortured the old Russian aristocracy," Farson observed.[20]

Urged to visit Guillermo Valencia, Columbia's "perfect" poet, in Popayan, Farson flew over the Andes in a German plane with two dachshunds and a pilot who smoked a cigar under a "No Smoking" sign tacked to the cockpit. Farson looked down to spot the grandiose churches that marked the location of so many Andean villages. Valencia, clothed in a camel's hair dressing gown, ushered him to his study, where Farson sat on a couch of black leopard skins. Valencia showed Farson his trophies—the last letter of Simón Bolívar, written from his deathbed, and a glass statuette of Gandhi. Valencia had always sought to meet the great men of the day, and he had even managed to meet Nietzsche by disguising himself as a servant. While Valencia still grew animated in discussing his long-ago visit to the German philosopher, Farson was less enthralled by own his trip to Valencia. The old poet grumbled incessantly about politics:

> The instant he began to talk about the Colombian government, this great literary figure became quite childish. He saw a communist behind every bush. I no longer heard the voice of a poet: it was the voice of an angry landowner, disfigured by hate. But there was not the least doubt he believed what he

said. He was the perfect type of the old pure-blooded Spaniard of the Andes, still living in a world that had ended with that last letter of Simon Bolivar's on his study wall.[21]

East of Bogotá, hostile natives inhabited a jungle where they still waged wars with spears and stones. Farson viewed photographs of two men shot by Motolone Indians, a tribe that had been fighting European trespassers since the 1500s. In one photo, a man clutched a six-foot-long arrow jutting from his gut. In a second photo, the broken shaft of an arrow protruded from another man's chest. Boats that plied the nearby rivers were still outfitted with screened fences to fend off arrows. Farson concluded that "to be bow-and-arrowed in this year of our Lord 1937 did not seem at all bizarre . . . it was much too likely to happen."[22] In Popayan, a local druggist offered Farson three shrunken human heads for twenty-five dollars each: "They were about the size of oranges, black, with long strings of hair dangling from them. Their lips had been sewn up with white fibers of some sort; and they were all frowning."[23] Jivaro Indians, who lived deep in the Ecuadorian Amazon, were known to shrink human heads. They engaged in head-hunting raids once a year against neighboring tribes.

Farson stuck to the old roads, except for the five hundred or so miles over the Andes, between Popayan in western Colombia and Quito in Ecuador. He called those miles an "amphibious and aerial journey" where he was slung over roaring rivers by steel cable and paddled thirty-foot native dugouts down rivers beneath smoking volcanos.[24] At Quito, Farson found some "grand" drinking buddies, including a British army officer, Captain Erskine Locke. "Cocktail conversation in Quito consisted chiefly of 'How do you get your breath?' At 9,500 feet no one knows a good answer," Farson noted.[25] Locke and Farson eagerly awaited the opening of the bar at 9:00 a.m., and then drank Haig & Haig scotch—doubles. They ate prawns brought by train on beds of ice from the Pacific, and strips of fresh, uncooked fish displayed on platters of red peppers and rings of onion. Locke would later explore the Amazon and die in Ecuador. Farson also met a handsome couple who claimed to have made the first movie ever taken underwater. Farson considered them kindred spirits: "They were all out of the same bin, these people. At the word *adventure* they would shy like a horse, yet that is what they were living. One could feel at home and at ease with them. They had made their choice, and put money and 'success' below getting the best out of life. Their talk was young."[26] They were, in short, people after his own heart.

Farson boarded a dirty steamer at Guayaquil, a port city memorable to Farson for its mud, rats, mosquitoes, and winged cockroaches, and he headed down the Guayas River in western Ecuador. There the "bends" hit him— apparently a reference to fevers—and he curled up "like a shrimp."[27] He stopped in Lima to interview General Oscar R. Benavides, the dictator of Peru, and in Chile, he met with Don Arturo Alessandri, the president. Farson considered such meetings and interviews as tedious as a board meeting or a tour of a factory floor. But before he had left England, he had contracted with the United Feature Syndicate to write articles on South America's political situation. United Feature promised its readers a trio of delights in 1937: Farson's dispatches from South America, a serializa- tion of Erich Maria Remarque's latest novel, Three Comrades, and exclusive reports from a salvage expedition that aimed to "raise the treasure" from the sunken Lusitania.[28] (Unfortunately for United Feature, the salvag- ing of the Lusitania would be a bust, and the serialization of Remarque's novel never materialized.) Readers were no doubt delighted with Farson's arrangement, but the necessity to interview officials and diplomats and file his dispatches proved irksome for him, forcing unwanted intrusions of sobriety on his intentions to cross the continent as a full-bore drunk. The occasional sobriety kept him, he suspected, from enjoying "the experience I felt I must have at that particular junction of my life in order to set things right with myself."[29]

At the end of his trip, Farson decided to remain sober long enough to do some hunting for ducks with the Chilean diplomatic corps. Farson, still a steady shot despite the binge drinking, bagged several ducks. A bit later, local ranchers offered him a chance for fishing "that will take the hair off."[30] They took a train from Santiago down to the Laja River, a steep river that flows from the Andes. Farson used his little Hardy rod to catch a six-pound rainbow as an active volcano erupted into the sky every ten minutes, adding an exotic touch to the joy of virgin fishing. "I don't know any fish that ever gave me so much thrill," Farson observed.[31] The frenzied trout took him down the river for a solid half hour and left him with a mere ten feet of backing at one point as he stumbled along boulders, desperate to win back some line. The healthy rainbows and the strong river wearied Farson. "Frankly, after a few days, I was glad to get away from that fishing. That sound of the reel screaming was beginning to get on my nerves. They always made the same first, swift rush—and I always began to tremble. It's a terrible strain on the nerves. As it is on the legs."[32] His fellow fisherman, a Scot, suggested that the fishing had become crowded: he had heard that someone had been on the river fishing ten miles below.

That was it for Farson. He headed toward Patagonia, then hopped a plane to Buenos Aires and left the West Coast once and for all. On the East Coast, he caught a steamer for home. It was an abrupt and ignoble end to a transcontinental adventure, but he had seen enough of South America. He had drunk enough of its spirits, and he had learned that he could not drink his way out of his drinking problem. If there were any salvation from the torment of alcoholism, it lay not in draining the bottle but in abstaining from the bottle.

16

→ • ←

Taking the Cure

FARSON RETURNED TO LONDON from South America a wreck, both physically and mentally. His bizarre and draconian plan to drown his alcoholism in alcohol—how had such a rational man even conceived such a wrongheaded scheme?—had been a miserable failure. He suffered from fevers that doctors could pin neither on the effects of the Andean altitudes nor on the endless bouts of alcohol. They didn't know where his alcoholism ended and his illnesses began. If alcoholism has a bottom, Farson had certainly found it. So, after a few months back in Europe, Farson decided to visit the specialists at the Institute of Tropical Medicine in Hamburg. He checked into the Hotel Vier Jahreszeiten, in a room overlooking Inner Alster Lake. There, reinvigorated by the breeze that blew through his window, he sat down to finish writing his book on South America. But the lure of the city, the vision of liquor bottles standing row upon row behind the bar, pulled him away. He lunched at a different place every day, drank his way through the afternoon, staggered to the beer halls, finished the nights in the cabarets, then stumbled his way back to the hotel with the dawn. Boozing it up along Grimmstrasse, he watched as gangs of Nazis beat up anyone who expressed opposition to Hitler's rule.

He had reached the point where he recoiled at seeing daylight shine into his room. Against nearly all previous experience, he began to sleep with the blinds down and never knew what time it was when he awoke. Furthermore, he later admitted, "I never wanted to wake up."[1] He continued:

I wanted to be out of this world: sleep was the only way I could escape. My bedclothes were like sheets thrown in the laundry basket; in the paroxysms of my nightmares I had twisted them all over the bed. My clothes lay wherever I had flung them before falling into bed—I even woke up fully dressed without even having had the decency to take my shoes off. My suit-cases were a revolting mess: books, clothes, suits, all piled in confusion. My typewriter, untouched, was a constant reproach to me.[2]

The hotel proprietor, with whom Farson had started on good terms and enjoyed many friendly chats, began to avoid Farson, who knew he was making a fool of himself.

Despite his barstool life, he continued to work on his book, sketching in his mind all he had seen during his staggerings—the whimsical airs of oddball characters, the sweep of a cornice or a cupula on an old Spanish-style home, or a strongman boasting of his own clever corruption. The work allowed him, at least, to avoid the Nazi bombast that he found so tedious. He had only come to a fascist country because he felt the Institute of Tropical Medicine in Hamburg would provide the best treatment available for his alcoholism. He continued to drink heavily in the evenings and sat in beer halls eating shrimp mayonnaise or attended a cabaret where a sailor played accordion music that reminded him of Old Europe. At a party given by the U.S. consul-general he met an acquaintance, a German doctor who had in fact warned him against seeing the Hamburg specialists. The doctor told him of the penchant of German women to tattoo Hitler's face on one breast, and sometimes Hermann Goering's on the other. Occasionally, when a woman would change her mind about the aesthetics of such patriotism, he would remove the tattoos. The doctor offered to remove Farson's tattoo, the anchor of unknown Panamanian origins. Farson agreed, and the doctor simply chopped out a piece of Farson's hide as thick as a banana peel and as big as a magnolia leaf.

Farson came to loathe the dawning of day in his room, and yet, between bottles, he managed to write the concluding chapter of his South American book, *Transgressor in the Tropics*. Perhaps more amazing, given the drunken stupor he was in while collecting his material, the book proved successful and briefly landed on the *New York Times'* best-seller list for nonfiction.[3] Somehow, Farson's alcoholic haze did not impede his ability to observe and connect with common folk; even drunk, he could apparently charm stories from the everyday people he always sought out. Critics praised his vigorous writing and his skill at absorbing information and crafting it into compelling vignettes. The *Daily Mail* called it a "fascinating book" and noted that Farson possessed "a genius for adventure."[4] The *Bystander,* a British weekly tabloid, gushed that "Negley Farson is a born writer and raconteur: he is also a very vital person, and it is impossible as one reads not to be carried along with him in his adventures, not to experience something of his zest, his insatiable thirst for knowledge—and his loneliness."[5] The *Times Literary Supplement* averred that "any one of its thirty-nine chapters . . . is an inducement to read another."[6] The American journalist Ernie Pyle, writing as the Scripps-Howard roving reporter, liked Farson's book, noting that they shared the same impression of South America's West Coast. But Pyle took umbrage with Farson for not going to Rio de Janeiro. It's "like going to New York and not seeing the skyline," Pyle wrote in his column. "Farson did himself a great disservice by leaving too soon. He says in the book he will probably never see South America again. But he's got to go to South America again. He's got to see Rio. D'ya hear that Farson? You've gotta see Rio!"[7]

Though critics greeted the book warmly, Farson treated it like an unwanted child, chastising himself for playing up the comic-opera side of the land, an easy task in a place rife with pompous bureaucrats, boorish tourists, spoiled aristocrats, and keystone cops with both palms out. He never returned to South America, which he dubbed the "Sad Continent."[8] He remarked with disparagement that it "left a mark on me for the rest of my life. It is like a tattoo."[9]

Farson recalled his final days in Hamburg as "disgusting," yet he could not remember how or when or why he left the city. He simply awoke from a daze one day to find himself on a train headed for the Harz Mountains. He hurriedly disembarked at the next station, in a little town called Quedlinburg. There, he found he was too tired to go on. Farson spoke little German but had come to know the word for the sanatorium's nerve doctor—*Nervenarzt*. He dropped into a taxi and told the driver to take him to the sanatorium. On the way, he began to shiver uncontrollably. He would later find out he had a violent infection as a result of the surgery to remove the tattoo. A doctor operated on him at once, cutting a four-inch gash down his right arm below the elbow. Farson spent two months recuperating in the Quedlinburg hospital.

Eventually he moved into a local hotel, returning to the hospital every other day to have his bandages changed. But after one of the doctors, a Nazi named Fritz, invited him home for dinner, he again began to hit the bottle. Hard. He and Fritz became drinking buddies—Farson had no Nazi sympathies, ridiculed "the Brown Shirts with their fat behinds,"[10] and scorned Nazi ideology, but he was sympathetic to anybody who would share a bottle with him. When not out drinking with Fritz, he stayed in his hotel room and drank. He even drank in the mornings. Eve wanted him back in London, but he made the excuse that he needed to stay in Germany to give his arm time to heal. The hotel had become too comfortable to leave: He ordered the waiter to bring him wine and he drank it as he lay in bed. Because he kept bandages with him to constantly repair his leg, he stopped going to the hospital altogether and used his leg bandages to bind his recuperating arm. He used the chair to steady himself as he wobbled from his bed to the toilet. He kept a bottle of Martel cognac by his bed, to steady his nerves when he awoke from his nightmares at four in the morning.

At last, even Farson realized he had had enough; he could sink no lower. He decided he must go to Munich, to a neuropsychiatric institute run by the famous neurologist and professor of psychiatry Oswald Bumke. How or when he reached Munich, Farson couldn't say. He only remembered Fritz driving him to the train station. Then he woke up in a hotel in Munich, lying fully dressed in a bed. His bags were stacked beside a nearby table. After a bath and a half glass of cognac, he went down to the front desk and asked the manager to call Professor Bumke. But Bumke was out of town. So for the next few days Farson roamed the streets of Munich and desperately tried to slow his drinking. He walked the streets and forced himself to "be interested in the passing crowd."[11] Whenever he passed a hotel, he would enter the lobby and sit in a chair as if waiting for a friend. In the afternoons he strolled through the museums. Meanwhile, his money was running out. When the advance on his book on South America arrived, he cashed most of it and handed it over to the hotel—unsure if his drinking bill had already exceeded the amount of the advance. One day in April 1938, as Farson was beginning to doubt that his legs would hold up if he walked outside the hotel, the manager told him Bumke had returned.

Farson wasted no time and set out for the institute. Bumke, now a gray old man, had once been called to Russia to attend to the dying Lenin. More recently back in Germany, he had, according to Farson, opposed Hitler's program in which doctors euthanized the insane, the physically handi-capped, and the mentally ill. But Bumke had escaped without punishment. Now, he asked Farson a string of questions. The going was slow, for Bumke spoke little English and Farson spoke just enough German to order beer at a Hofbrau Haus. They used their subpar French to communicate, and finally Bumke called a young woman into the room to give Farson his assessment. "The Herr Professor," she told Farson, "says he will try and help you. He asks me to say that, so far as he can tell—that is, up to the present—there is nothing that cannot be put right."[12] A relieved Farson registered to undergo treatment in the institute.

For the following months, he lived in a small room along a corridor with eight doors. One of the doors was his, but he saw only three of the seven other patients: One was a weatherbeaten man of about fifty, a German ex-officer suffering from shellshock who marched up and down the length of the corridor all day; the second was a little man with a twisted face who was eventually carried out on a stretcher, dead; the third was a young man who was "not there" mentally and who always made an effort to straighten up and look sane whenever Bumke entered the corridor. As for Farson, he underwent a regimen of daily shots from a syringe whose barrel was one inch in diameter. Farson never knew what was in the syringe—he noted only that it looked like wine and he wished it were.

The treatment seemed to work, easing Farson's mind and leaving him in a state of euphoria. One day, however, a friend wrote from Vienna to invite him down. The lure of "all the fun we could have" was too delicious to resist, so Farson packed and dressed, and when Bumke's chief assistant came to give him his morning injection, Farson asked him to return his passport so he could go into Munich and withdraw some money from the bank.[13] The assistant implored Farson to stay, which only enraged him. He began yelling. Finally, Bumke unlocked the door and tried to reason with him. "Mr. Farson," he said, "your mind is in grave peril. You must believe me."[14] He continued in the same vein and finished with a plea for Farson to stay. As Farson looked out of his barred window to where the schizophrenics were sitting or walking about in the courtyard, he pulled off his tie. He would stay.

As it turned out, he had made the right decision.

Bumke began his treatment of Farson by simply spending time in conversation with him. Their talks ignored the past and focused on the present. Farson had to talk about himself without relying on excuses from the past, such as a troubled childhood. He had to explain himself to Bumke, to bare his failings and insecurities; at first he recoiled. He loathed himself, had come to find all of civilization disgusting, and wanted to escape from humanity. At night he lay in his bunk and dreamed of the little cabin by the isolated lake in British Columbia.

But gradually, he came to enjoy the experience of talking about his present life. He awoke each morning with a sense of expectation, with hope. Bumke also sent in his chief assistant to chat with Farson. At first Farson chafed at being asked to talk about the places he had been and the things he had done, especially with a doctor with Nazi leanings, but eventually this too became cathartic for him. He began to take an interest in the assistant's stories as well. Eventually Bumke told him: "You have had an unusually wide experience of life. Why don't you give yourself the benefit of it? Be kinder to yourself."[15] He concluded that, though Farson had lived a colorful and adventurous life, he had not allowed its lessons to "become cumulative"—a criticism that had been leveled against Farson's memoir.[16] He had piled up experiences but had not added them up to a greater sum. The assessment struck home. Farson realized that he had always been a great worrier, and one of the ways he had tried to break himself of the condition was to live every day as if time didn't exist at either end of the twenty-four hours—there was no past, there was no future, there was only this exact moment, to be lived as fully as possible. His writing and his journalism created the impression that he had succeeded in believing his myth: each place he visited seemingly sprang up from nowhere just before he arrived; each journey he took yielded people and customs over which he gushed in amazement. But in reality, beyond the written word, he had never been able to bring himself completely to that state of nirvana.

From now on, he would deal with the difficult, everyday realities head-on, with no pretense that this was his only day of existence. He would attempt to live with more mindfulness. He walked out of the sanatorium a sober man with no desire to drink. "My friends and family, to explain the miracle, think Bumke must have hypnotised me," he later recalled.[17] In the end, Farson said he found giving up drink as easy as falling off a log.

When he said goodbye to Bumke, he was ready to start life anew. He was refreshed as if from a swim.

17
➔•←
His Life in a Novel

I F FARSON THOUGHT THAT Bumke had cured him, he nevertheless did
not feel ready to return to Eve in South Kensington and instead went
straight to the Sailing Club in Chichester Harbor, not far from Ports-
mouth. He explained to Eve that they could not be together yet, that he
needed time to burn up some of the creative energy he had stored up at
the sanatorium. Holed up at the Sailing Club—an odd choice of residence
for a man trying to stay off the bottle, given the club's well-stocked bar—
he wrote his third novel, *The Story of a Lake*. In terms of his personal life,
it may have opened more wounds than it closed.

Though nominally a novel, it was in fact almost pure memoir, a confession in fictional masquerade, perhaps the result of Bumke's push to force
Farson to be honest with himself. Farson did almost nothing to disguise
the biographical nature of the book, even though it exposed the pain of his
private life and cast his wife in a terrible light. She probably took no comfort in knowing that Farson treated his mistresses equally harshly under
the cover of fiction. Their son Daniel said the book humiliated his mother.

That the book was a fictionalized version of reality is not in doubt. In
fact, one former resident of British Columbia, where the Farsons once
lived and where much of the novel is set, said Farson's portrayal of the real
people who lived there explained why "Farson headed the list of people
to be gut-shot should he return to the vicinity."[1] The novel's protagonist,
Tony Lynd, is a London-based foreign correspondent for an American
newspaper who once served in the Royal Flying Corps. He walks with a
limp, once traversed the Pyrenees by mule, and once interviewed Gandhi.

Lynd recalls good times with his wife on the Danube and smokes Gold Flake cigarettes. He loves to hunt and fish, drinks at least three double-whiskies after dispatching his stories, and covered Hitler's testimony at a trial in Leipzig. The character sketch fits Farson perfectly. Also like Farson, Lynd is arrested for drunk driving. Lynd's wife is a former nurse (as was Eve) named Christina. Tony Lynd's two mistresses are named Luba and Felicity, nicknamed Flick. Farson's true-life mistresses were Shura and Sybil. Daniel Farson said changing Shura's name to Luba and Sybil's name to Flick represented Farson's bare-minimum effort to hide their identities, and the two women likely were as mortified as his mother to read the book. In his memoir, Farson portrayed Shura as sweetness and innocence, a teenage runaway who had sung heartbreaking Cossack songs to him as they sat on the docks of Archangel and even taught him to sing one. Years later he claimed he could still sing the song and it never failed to make him sad. He also maintained that he had not forgotten the sight of Shura as she poked her head out of the train window, waving until he disappeared from view. Somewhere years later the two had met again—her family had apparently moved to England—and he had rekindled his romance with her, only partly behind Eve's back. In the novel, Shura surfaces as aloof and slightly mercenary. Felicity, or Flick, meanwhile, though described as the woman of the protagonist's dreams, comes across as nothing more than a tiresome nag with all the charm of a grenade. The book, said Daniel, had the "painful candour of a diary."[2]

The novel, although full of political scenes and diatribes, provided rich insight into Farson's domestic life. Farson glossed over the inner workings of his marriage in his nonfiction books, and Eve would later burn much of their acrimonious correspondence. In the novel, or fictionalized autobiography, the plot centers around Lynd's disintegration—brought about by his frustration with his wife's near absolute distaste for sex, a fact Lynd discovers within a month of his wedding day. Farson painted a devastating picture of Lynd and Christina's life in the bedroom, as Lynd at one point reflects that, "If she had known how often he had got up and walked to the window and simply bitten at his fingers at nights, then she would have suffered unbearably because she would have known that she had not satisfied him, and even the companionship they did have would have been spoiled." Daniel Farson would later note that his parents' indiscreet and awkward comments to him about sex—and the lack thereof—confirmed that his father was an intensely frustrated man. In the book, Farson's frustrated stand-in, Lynd, turns to heavy drinking, then to an affair with Luba, a girl he once knew in Russia and runs into while returning from an extended reporting assignment in India. He then meets Felicity Correl, a red-haired, green-eyed, hard-drinking correspondent for an Australian newspaper. They begin a stormy affair.

Daniel Farson identified Felicity as the real-life, red-haired, green-eyed Sybil Vincent, noting that she and his father carried on an affair for years, even after Eve discovered it. Eve's mother, Enid "Smee" Stoker, once told Daniel that Sybil had driven three men to suicide.[3] If the novel is any indication, her affair with Farson was torrid: Lynd (Farson) and Felicity (Sybil) argue vehemently—in one scene she calls him a "cheap edition of Ernest Hemingway!"—match each other whisky for whisky, then copulate with wild abandon. Lynd tries to give her up but can't shake the thought of her—not until remorse over his wife's death drives him to return to heavy drinking. As for the novel's other mistress, Luba, she appears only occasionally, but long enough to knock on Christina's door and beg her to stop Lynd's affair with Felicity. Daniel Farson said the incident really happened: Shura turned up at their home in South Kensington to ask Eve to intervene in Farson's affair with Sybil.[4]

The novel seemed to be Farson's effort to blame his wife for his unfaithfulness. Daniel, writing years later, partly agreed: "What drove my father away? The easy explanation was sex, or the lack of it."[5] The affair with Sybil Vincent, meanwhile, emotionally broke his mother, Daniel said, and tormented his father: "Unable to choose between the two women, my father divided his life disastrously. When he was with my mother he suffered the agony of frustration; when he was with Sybil, he was tormented by remorse. If he had been more cynical he might have enjoyed himself more, but he was too 'decent', to use one of his favorites words, for his own peace of mind."[6]

In addition to airing out his affairs and his wretched addiction to alcohol, Farson used the novel to unburden himself of his frustration with journalism. After admitting to his love for daily journalism in

Transgressor, he now, a few years later, had little good to say about the line of work. It was a most interesting profession, he conceded, but one that left its increasingly cynical practitioners no time to lead their own lives. Eventually, journalists who should have felt shock at events felt only numbness. At the same time, Farson considered the work easy: politicians and world leaders argued and called each other fools; correspondents had merely to transcribe their words and fire off a cable to the home office. Correspondents could also express their own opinions without fear of being called wrong: politics was too imprecise; no one could prove, exactly, that a correspondent's argument or point of view was incorrect. There was a certain joy in trying to steer the global conversation on a particular topic, Farson admitted, but he concluded that it would be more joyous still to receive a cable telling him that he was out of a job, because then he could rest from the fear that always lurked in the correspondent's heart, fear that a rival correspondent would get the story first. It was enough to drive a man to drink.

The book, with its political rants, scathing portrayal of his wife, the unsympathetic descriptions of his mistresses, not to mention the details of his binge drinking and his acquired disdain for the life of a foreign correspondent, left critics unsatisfied. *Kirkus Reviews* opined that Farson's reputation as a journalist and the success of his memoir were sure to lead to big sales but added that, despite the fast-paced story, "the characters are superficial, externally motivated, and the story goes fast nowhere in particular."[7] The *New York Times,* in a review titled "The End of the Lost Generation," was slightly more ambiguous. Though the book is "sincere and honest" and "very easy to like," according to the newspaper's critic, *The Story of a Lake* "is the work of an untamed amateur in fiction. Irritating at times, and again ridiculous, there is vehemence and energy in it, an unusual vigor."[8] In a final swipe, the critic noted that the book's characters could not have been invented: first because some of them appeared in *Way of a Transgressor,* and second because "any man who could invent these characters would have written a better novel. Evelyn Waugh, or Aldous Huxley or Hemingway might have created them."[9] *Time* magazine dismissed it as an "awkwardly constructed, Lost Generation novel."[10] Joseph Henry Jackson, reviewer for the *San Francisco Chronicle,* likewise interpreted it as a Lost Generation novel, unfortunately written after the glory days of the Lost Generation had long passed:

> No one can deny that it is fast paced, full of action, even pretty well pep-
> pered with spice. And it's written, I feel, with an honest desire to explain
> what can go on inside a certain type of man—even maybe to present that
> type of man sympathetically, so that his sins may be forgiven him, or if not
> forgiven, at least understood. Yet, well—even if it is a sort of latter day "Sun
> Also Rises," Mr. Farson isn't Hemingway, and anyhow, the time for that kind
> of rising sun is past. Indeed, come to think of it, that's really what ails this
> novel. It has a dated flavor. If you listen very closely as you read, in spite of
> the current topical touch, I believe you will be able to hear the faint familiar
> echoes of other places and people, maybe even Mr. Fitzgerald's beautiful and
> damned, tinkling hollowly somewhere this side of paradise.[11]

Yet the reviews weren't all bad; some friendly critics gave the book a passing grade. First Lady Eleanor Roosevelt said she found it "an interest-ing psychological study."[12]

With his book written and sent off to the publishers, the royalty advance in his pocket, Farson was ready to abandon the Sailing Club's premises. But still he refused to go home—he was not ready to see Eve, and if she knew about the contents of the upcoming novel, no doubt she would hardly want to see him. Their marriage was on the verge of collapse, and only time would tell if it could survive.

But wanderlust was upon Farson again. He recalled his brief stay in Quedlinburg, Germany, where he and Fritz the Nazi had once stopped outside a bookstore on a snowy evening to feel the warmth from within. Farson had noted with amusement all the books in the storefront win-dow were about Africa—or more precisely, Germans in Africa. There were books on German big-game hunters on safari, German explorers on the Great Lakes, Germans in West Africa, Germans in East Africa. Fritz asked him if he would like to go to Africa. Farson replied, "I think that's where I shall go."[13]

And he did.

18

> • ←

Mired in African Mud and Acrimony

ARSON BOARDED A GERMAN ship in December 1938 for the seventeen-day journey from Southampton to remote Walvis Bay in what is now Namibia. In Farson's time, it was still known as South West Africa and constituted a sizable piece of the African territory that Germany had managed to grab during Europe's rapacious scramble for empire. By the time Farson arrived at Walvis Bay, the Germans had lost the territory to the British as a result of the Great War, and South West Africa was ruled by British administrators under a League of Nations mandate. Twenty German youths, seeds of the Nazis' future on the continent, boarded the ship with Farson, bent on returning to their South West African homes carrying Christmas trees from the fatherland.

Farson had often drunk himself insensible during his previous voyages, but he strode the deck of this ship as both a world-renowned writer and a sober man. The bottle was behind him. He saw the African journey as a way to deal himself "a fresh hand of cards," to restore his sense of himself as a writer and adventurer capable of journeying through life without firm plans or smooth roads.[1] But it was a herculean task he had set himself—to travel across the continent without succumbing to drink.

For almost any lifelong drunk, giving up alcohol is difficult under any circumstances; adding the challenges of travel—bad roads, foreign tongues, lost luggage, the hostile hotel concierge, the broken telephone connections, the thousand other things that typically go wrong—would both create stumbling blocks and raise the stakes. The amply stocked hotel bars, always a favorite haunt of Farson's, would be a constant temptation when he was not out traversing the plains or the jungles. Added to the task of staying sober was Farson's determination to do it without the help of Eve, whom he had left alone in their London home to wonder what the sanatorium had done to her husband.

Farson had seen revolution and riot aplenty, but he greeted his first sight of Africa with fear. Two barge loads of ragged, miserable natives, towed by a tug, plowed through the water toward the ship to help unload the baggage and the passengers. The natives included Zulus, Damaras, Hereros, Ovambas, Khoikhoi, and "Portuguese boys," all fighting the cold and damp by wearing castoff European rags—old school blazers, scarlet berets, and Buster Browns. The Portuguese had their teeth sharpened to a point—a custom usually ascribed to spiritual motivations, though Farson thought it a remnant of the days of cannibalism. Overall, Farson concluded he had never seen such a collection of broken men outside a prison. He was appalled. But what he witnessed was merely the consequence of nearly three hundred years of Europe's brutal exploitation of southern Africa.

In 1652, the Dutch had established a permanent settlement at Table Bay on the southern tip of the vast continent. The settlement's purpose was to serve as a resupply point for Dutch ships. At the time, the Dutch were the world's preeminent maritime power, with a fleet of six thousand ships, and many of them made frequent voyages to the Pacific around the Cape of Good Hope. From a few dozen settlers at Table Bay who negotiated with the Khoisan tribe to provide cattle for the fleet, the settlement grew to several hundred, then several thousand. Soon the settlers were using slaves to help keep up with the demand for labor to provision the ships.

Then the settlers turned their back on the sea and rolled their wagons inland from the shore, expelling the native tribes from the best land, the land with green grass and plenty of game. To survive, the landless natives were forced to take jobs as laborers for the white colonists. Decades passed; the Dutch, now known as Boers, killed thousands of Khoisan and forced others into labor. But in 1795 British forces took the Cape Colony from the Dutch, and their ownership became ratified in a peace agreement reached in 1814. By the 1830s, the Boers were chafing under the yoke of British rule. The British had outlawed slavery in 1833—so the Boers began to migrate farther into the wilderness.

The Germans, latecomers to the European race for African land, arrived in southern Africa in the 1880s, establishing South West Africa and beating and abusing the natives there as brutally as had the other European powers. Now, with Hitler in power in the fatherland, the German settlers who greeted Farson were openly confident that Germany would soon regain control of the territory from the British. The sight of the misery of the African natives sickened Farson; the smug arrogance of the Germans depressed and infuriated him.

Farson spent several weeks at Walvis Bay but found little to like there beyond the Herero women, whom he likened to birds of paradise in their fine clothes and regarded as the most beautiful women in all of Africa. His small hotel room had a single window, which looked out on a sandy compound where empty beer bottles had been piled into small pyramids. He claimed that not a single blade of green grass grew in the town, and as for the lagoon, once a week the sea bed would rumble and belch up a noxious gas that killed the fish, which then floated up on shore. Behind the town lay the Namibian desert, bleak and inhospitable.

Seeking to escape his grim surroundings, Farson traveled twenty miles north to explore Swakopmund, the colony's summer capital. There, he lounged on the shore and swam in the ocean, but the sight of the insufferable Germans he met irritated him. The night he arrived, the local Nazis were boycotting the hotel's evening entertainment because the five-piece band featured more than one non-Aryan. Farson declared the seaside town "120 percent Nazi."[2] The Nazis in turn scorned Farson, ostracizing him after they discovered that he intended to interview a Jew.

"You *shouldn't* talk to men like that!" the owner of the hotel told him.[3]

Farson's African adventure began in earnest when a group of Boers from Angola invited him to join them on their trek to discover new farmlands. The group hoped to find uninhabited land—uninhabited by whites, anyway—north of Outjo, more than 250 miles northeast of Walvis Bay. Farson jumped at the offer and declared that he would take part in the latest iteration of the Boers' fabled Great Trek, a white migration into the heart of Africa as legendary and cruel as that experienced by America's westward pioneers. In a series of migrations begun in 1834 and known as the Great Trek, the Boer wagons rolled north and northeast, and the Boers claimed vast landholdings—six thousand acres per family head—and started life anew. By the end of the decade, roughly six thousand Boers had left the Cape Colony, or one in ten of every white inhabitant. The Boers packed all their belongings into wagons and forded the Orange River to create the Orange Free State and the Transvaal. While some settled, others splintered off to wander toward the edge of the Kalahari Desert, pushed on by any threat of government control or whiff of civilization. The treks continued in the following decades as the Boers continued to search for the promised land—or a few thousand acres of it—in the African interior.

Farson found himself in the company of discontented Boers who, like their ancestors a century before, were convinced that paradise was just over the next white anthill or down in some broad valley where giraffes and elephants thundered over green grass. "They felt suffocated if they saw the smoke of another man's fire on the horizon,"[4] Farson noted, expressing a sentiment that likely described the feelings in the deepest hollows of his own heart. He accompanied a clan of thirty Boer families. The men carried .303 Mausers and wore black veld sun hats that flapped in the wind as the expedition headed out into the Outjo frontier to find farmland. To be successful in the abusive climate and on such barren soil, the farms would have to be twelve thousand acres each, a size approved by the British government.

The expedition's trucks followed game trails (since there were no roads) and broke out into the open arid land by crushing whole thickets beneath their axles as they headed north on their way toward Outjo. At camp under African skies, sober, his belly full of Vienna sausage and his Mannlicher rifle by his side, Farson marveled at the sight of millions of stars flickering in the black sky. "For the first time in years I felt completely at peace with the world," he reflected.[5] The Boer men sported long beards or goatees, their blue eyes sunk into faces tanned to leather by the sun. They fashioned their shoes from kudu skins, their luggage from rhino hides. Farson saw in all their primitive equipment a high level of "contentment and security; the ability of the men, in almost any circumstances, to fend for themselves."[6] They were close to the earth as they slept with their rifles by their sides.

The days rolled by and the trucks ground forward, but the Boers found the valleys too small or the land too parched for the big farms they planned. Farson chain-smoked cigarettes and enjoyed the scenery as his hosts scoured the wrinkled terrain for the promised land.

Then one day the truck ahead of Farson's abruptly stopped. The Boers jumped out. Still holding their rifles, they pointed to something far in the distance below. Farson was certain their hands were trembling with excitement. After weeks of bulling through the bush, they had found a broad green valley that stretched to the sunset. Farson looked out into the valley and saw grass so dark and green that he remarked that he wanted to eat it. The Boers had reached the end of their trek—paradise found—at least for now. But a cynical Englishman traveling with Farson said they would never settle down, their stay in the valley would be temporary. Farson knew the Englishman was right when he confided: "As soon as they've killed every living thing in this valley, they'll get restless, pack up and move on. These Boers will go on, and on, and on—just as long as there is any new land left in Africa."[7] Farson knew he had witnessed civilization encroaching on a wild land, and it galled him.

He left the Boers in their newfound paradise and trekked alone through South West Africa, traveling in a country that had only five miles of paved roads. He sought out the Germans who made up the majority of white settlers in the country. Farson held mixed views of the Germans: he admired their vitality and ingenuity, especially in raising cattle, but disdained the Nazi ideology that inflamed them. The twenty young Germans who had disembarked with him at Walvis Bay had all just completed two years of military service, which in Farson's mind made them fully trained Nazis. Hermann Goering's father had once ruled as governor over South West Africa; Nazi sentiment had only intensified since his day. A Nazi movement dubbed the Greyshirts had emerged in the 1930s in South Africa, and the group hated Jews with a passion that would have made Hitler smile. "To be 'Heil Hitlered!' and given the Nazi salute in the African bush was almost too much to bear," Farson noted.[8]

He drove to Windhoek, the colony's capital city, where the fastidious Germans had blanketed the ground with scarlet geraniums and purple bougainvillea; to a nearby farm where the owner showed him a rusty wire noose on a tree where unruly natives were hanged; then to nearby Ovamboland to witness a tribal dance where virgins were covered with red ocher and drummers pounded out a fierce beat. In the pulsating frenzy of movement and noise, the Ovambo chief bestowed a native name on Farson, an honor reserved for important white men. He earned the title of "The Man with the Big, Strong, White Stomach." Farson was not pleased.

In one small, upcountry town, Farson spoke with its *fuehrer,* a garage owner who told him there would be no war because Hitler "doesn't want a war. The *fuehrer* wants peace with all mankind."

"Well," Farson replied, "you're going about it in a queer way."[9]

All along the way, Farson remained sober. He attended the usual "sundowner" cocktail parties, comfortable affairs where the settlers unwound at the end of the long, hot days, but he studiously rejected every drink thrust in his direction. Although at Swakopmund he had enjoyed a "heavenly" beer served to him by a beautiful German girl with bare, sunburned legs, Farson apparently imbibed because he did not consider beer a real alcoholic drink. In his mind, he was still riding high on the wagon.

Tired of seeing how the whites had brought "civilization" to the natives, he commandeered an interpreter and drove out to meet the Bushmen of the Kalahari, the indigenous hunter-gatherers of southern Africa who, modern genetic studies conclude, are the oldest population on earth. He admired them for living as they had for thousands of years, without the curse of progress or the discomforts of civilized life. Some white settlers considered them subhuman. Just a few decades before, a magistrate had turned down a request by white farmers in the area to classify the Bushmen as vermin—to be shot all year-round. The magistrate asserted that the Bushmen were in fact human. The ruling did little practical good. A man who shot a Bushman dead was never tried for murder. So, Farson noted wryly, Bushmen were shot. The farmers were only following the example of the Boers, who had spread "civilization" north from the Cape. The Boers "shot the Bushmen as if they were baboons," according to Farson.[10]

Near the Okavango River, Farson contacted some King Bushmen who were, understandably, fearful of white men. Farson earned their trust, however, by setting up a bow-and-arrow shooting match in which they took aim at his hat. One arrow poked a hole in it, and Farson ruefully stuck his finger through it, eliciting a burst of laughter from the entire tribe. He described the Bushmen as tiny in stature, eager to joke. One night, around a campfire, Farson watched four witch doctors dance an "initiate" of the tribe into a hypnotic state. The boy's body became icy cold, his arms limp in Farson's hands: "The dance, under a cloudy moon, had the definite element of magic about it. The men alone danced. . . . The women provided the rhythm by claps of their hands and a high, thrilling chant. . . . The flames gilded the branches of the tambut trees. Sworls of red sparks flew up towards the few stars." Farson called the Bushmen the "last wild thing in human form."[11]

Farson kept on the move and penned sketches of the Bushmen and other natives for armchair adventurers back home, most of whom were familiar with Africa only through the lens of Johnny Weissmuller's Tarzan movies. Though he had regretted signing a contract with a news wire before embarking on his South American trip—he felt it had crimped his style and curbed his freedom of movement—he had nevertheless agreed to send the London *Daily Mail* occasional dispatches from Africa. The articles helped pay for his journey. Playing to an audience of *Daily Mail* readers, he used personal anecdotes to soften ugly tales of brutality and illuminate the different mind-sets of Europeans and native Africans. In one sketch, for example, Farson wrote that he killed twenty-five ducks and geese one morning as they flew overhead. After the shoot, he gave a native chief, Nehemiah, eight shotgun cartridges with which to hunt. A week later, Farson returned and asked Nehemiah how he had done with the cartridges. Nehemiah claimed he shot five ducks with each cartridge.

"Nehemiah, you incredible liar!" Farson replied.

"I no lie," the chief responded. "But I don't shoot the way master does; I shoot 'em on the water. I crawl up—bang! Bang! One time I kill ten! Master, he go bang! bang! in the air. When duck drop, that is luck!"[12]

Farson continued by train through the western part of the Union of South Africa and lingered briefly at Cape Town before turning northeast to Johannesburg and the coastal city of Durban, from which he planned to catch a boat to sail up the eastern coast of the continent to Dar es Salaam. But while still in South Africa he managed to score an interview with Jan Christian Smuts, the South African leader who had been prime minister from 1919 to 1924 and was again from 1939 to 1948. When Farson encountered him, the former Boer War commando, known as General Smuts, wore his trademark gray goatee, which Farson thought helped to give him an air of philosophic detachment. Smuts told Farson that the South Africans would fight the Germans to keep South West Africa out of Nazi hands.

Farson's African journalism didn't stop with interviews of high-placed officials—a type of journalism he abhorred: repeating his technique of gathering stories from common folk and society's downtrodden, as he had during his trip by boat across Europe and during his postings to Russia and India, Farson also shared his eyewitness accounts of how natives were systematically abused in South Africa. First, he noted that the government forced the natives to pay taxes with money—something they didn't have unless they went to work in the gold or diamond mines or ports or farms of the whites. Hundreds of natives lined up outside recruiting offices for the chance to work in the mines, a scene that Farson said resembled a slave market. Those natives who worked for any length of time in the mines returned to their villages with their health completely wrecked. Outside Johannesburg, hundreds of thousands lived in mining compounds, where a 9:00 p.m. curfew was imposed and vans of police officers drove around arresting any natives found outside their area past curfew. But perhaps the biggest scandal was the overcrowding. In the Transvaal, for instance, 70 percent of the population lived on less than 4 percent of the land. It was worse in the Free State, where 67 percent lived on 0.2 percent of the land. Farson accused the white man of doing nothing less than setting up "black zoos" in Africa.

He departed South Africa from the coastal city of Durban and steamed up the Indian Ocean by boat to Dar es Salaam, a small fishing village in Tanganyika (now part of Tanzania) that the Arabs called the "Haven of Peace." The ship, crewed by rival groups of Hindu and Muslim Indians, carried fifty goats and 9,876 bags of cashews. The trip took six days, during which Farson scored another important interview, this one with the head of the South African Indian Congress, who happened to be aboard ship, sailing back to India where he planned to agitate against the discrimination that Indians were suffering in South Africa. In 1939, more than 220,000 Indians lived in the country, imported in droves since 1860 to help meet the tremendous labor demands of the settlers and plantation owners. But the white settlers had grown alarmed at the large number of Indians and were now working to limit where the Indians could live. Farson detailed the entire argument for readers back in England, delighted to give the *Daily Mail* the "real news" it was paying him to deliver.

Farson enjoyed a brief respite from his travels in Dar es Salaam, whose blue waters and palm-fringed lagoon, crowded with Arab dhows, he considered one of the most welcoming ports in the tropics. He watched as hundreds of Hindu women in rose-colored saris strolled past, along with bearded Sikhs, "gold-turbaned Mohamadans" and hundreds of black natives in red fezzes and white gowns that looked to Farson like nightshirts.[13] As for the English who controlled the colony—and Farson lamented repeatedly that Britain had stopped sending settlers and farmers to Africa and was now sending only bureaucrats—Farson found their dominant characteristic to be a never-ending complaint that the British policy of treating natives equally was being taken too seriously. Still, Farson considered the British officials honorable and enjoyed exchanging pleasantries and opinions with them in their sun-kissed villas.

Then Eve showed up. At Farson's request, she had left England before Farson departed from Durban, and she sailed into the harbor of Dar es Salaam on a French ship, wearing a wide-brimmed felt hat against the tropical sun. Their son, Daniel, remained in England, where he attended Abinger Hill, a progressive preparatory school in Surrey. Why Farson asked Eve to join him is a genuine puzzle. Did he feel he needed help staying sober? Or was he so confident of staying off the bottle that he felt he could once again tolerate her company? Or were things going so well that he now judged the two could be together without the old acrimony? Perhaps he was simply lonely for his wife's companionship or felt the time was right to salvage their marriage. Whatever her wandering husband's motives, Eve jumped at the chance to be with him again.

As the two settled into their stone bungalow at Dar es Salaam, things went exceptionally well. They rose at 6:00 a.m. to swim in the warm ocean before a modest breakfast of toast and tea. Barefoot Indians served them lunch before they dressed in whites for tennis, followed by drinks each night before dinner. As quickly as that, with Eve's arrival Farson had begun drinking again. But it was casual and carefree, not the full-bore drinking of a foreign correspondent stressed about deadlines. Farson lay back and enjoyed the world created by the British. "It was all very easy, and English," he wrote. "And, as I look back on it now, very worthy. For the British empire was not the result of an accident. There may have been, in the eyes of some critics, too many 'gentlemen' at Dar es Salaam. But there were some splendid men among them. And the tone of the service was friendship, even love, for the natives under them. Do not minimize that."[14]

The sentiment is, at best, paradoxical, given what Farson had witnessed of the British Empire in India. His admiration for the British had clouded his judgment when it came to Africa.

At last, with the arrival of spring, it was time to leave, to continue the journey. Farson bought a powerful eight-cylinder Ford. His plan was simple: he would motor across Africa from east to west with Eve as chief navigator and campmate (shades of their boat trip together down the Rhine and Danube). He dismissed warnings that the trip in the rainy season, on muddy roads, would end in disaster. It would prove a major error in judgment—but perhaps Farson felt the need to escape the louche life of Dar es Salaam with its leisurely tennis matches and its evening round of drinks. The route the couple chose would take them from the rain forests of Tanganyika to Kenya, from there through Uganda, Rwanda, Burundi, the Congo, the Central African Republic, and, finally, on to Cameroon. Along the way, they would stop at Mount Kilimanjaro, the Serengeti Plain, the African Great Lakes, Nairobi, Ituri (home of the Pygmies), and Stanleyville, now Kisangani, on the Congo River. There Farson hoped they could float the car by barge west down the river until they reached Aketi in the northern part of the Congo, then drive north to Bangassou. The final leg of the journey would take their Ford west to the Atlantic Ocean. From the port of Duala, Eve would sail for home while Farson would continue by plane to Accra in Ghana, then known as the Gold Coast.

Even today, in the era of GPS, cell phones, and modern roads, the route would be ambitious. The distances between African capitals are vast. In Farson's day, such a trip was considered foolhardy. Ahead of the two adventurers lay swollen rivers, muddy trails that passed for roads, insect-borne illnesses, and deep jungles that were home to wild predators and deadly snakes. And where would they find gas along the way, not to mention engine repairs and medicine?

Farson ordered two white linen suits, custom tailored by the Indians at Dar es Salaam. They made him two pairs of shoes too—one of suede, the other sturdy Norwegian-style brogues. He packed shorts and polo shirts and two safari shirts that could be stuffed with gear. Eve took a gabardine jacket and skirt—made in London—and asked the Indians to make her several khaki trousers. They brought water bags, an aluminum cooking pot, coffee and tea pots, frying pans, pounds of groceries—much of it apparently tinned Vienna sausages and pears. Most white explorers traveled with servants in 1939, but for lack of room in the car, the Farsons did without the usual "boy," a decision that caused consternation among the natives, with whom they lost standing. Instead of a servant, they filled the car with shovels, an ax, forty yards of heavy rope, and extra jacks in preparation for the boggy roads they would face in the wet season. In fact, at the very beginning, the rains at Dar es Salaam forced the Farsons to ship the car by freight truck to Dodoma, one hundred miles away.

Farson felt a deep thrill, as he had on every other launch of an adventure, when he rolled the Ford off the truck and he and Eve headed out from Dodoma with the "breadth of Africa . . . before us."[15] But the red clay roads immediately turned to slick butter. They drove five hundred to six hundred miles across Tanganyika and found themselves repeatedly mired in mud. With the help of natives, the voyagers managed to dig themselves out of the mire. Miles later, deep in another muddy rut somewhere in the middle of nowhere, they were forced to repeat the process; several miles later, they would become stuck once again. Then the roads turned to "black cotton soil," an African phenomenon that, despite the exertions of the natives, left the Farsons moving at a snail's pace.[16] One day the muddy roads swallowed the car so many times that they made only three miles. Their car, even with chains on the tires, would simply sink, leaving the rear end deep in mud, the wheels spinning futilely. Farson was repeatedly forced to haul himself out of the car and into mud as "jellified as a bed of an estuary at low tide."[17]

Farson developed a system. He would work his way to the back of his car, slipping and sliding, to retrieve an ax, a shovel, and four burlap sacks. He would then chop down a nearby thorn tree, lop off its branches, and place them in front of the submerged rear tires, cover them with the burlap and drive over his handmade road until the car mired again. Even for a young man, the work would be exhausting. Farson was closing in on fifty, maneuvering with a permanently damaged leg. Between his backbreaking labors, however, he was able to marvel at the surrounding beauty: wild acacia forests, the occasional twenty-foot-thick baobab tree, and the weird euphorbia, a plant shaped like a gigantic green candelabra. Forest life abounded in the thorn groves, fully abloom with morning glories with violet heads, wild gladioli, and cactus sporting primrose blossoms. Doves whirred off the road as he drove, and tiny kingfishers hunted streams he forded. Hawks, talons out, scooped up snakes that writhed in the air. Monkeys scurried about the treetops, some with babies clinging to their bellies. Baboons barked as the Ford trundled along. The sight of wild nature, Farson observed, "made up, a little, for the brutal drive."[18]

The Farsons had first traveled south: Farson wanted to talk with the fuehrer of Tanganyika's German population, a baron who lived on a tea plantation in a rain forest at Mufindi. The trip ended in disaster, though, when Farson discovered that the German was a Hitler fanatic. The baron, meanwhile, was equally horrified to discover that Farson had refused to allow *Way of a Transgressor* to be translated into German because he would not sign the papers avowing he had no Jewish blood. The Farsons motored down the slopes from the baron's plantation without a backward glance.

The couple turned north toward Mount Kilimanjaro when, just outside Dodoma, high in the heart of Tanganyika, Farson had another of his near-death experiences. The Farsons were descending into a valley where they saw a nameless, swollen river flowing from end to end. There was no bridge. They pulled up near a village of beehive huts built on the river's banks, and the natives crowded out to greet them. The villagers, some of whom spoke English, told the Farsons that a cement causeway ran to the far bank of the river, though it was now submerged. Farson couldn't see the causeway, but decided to gamble: He slowly drove into the roiling water where the natives said the bridge might be. Farson felt the solid cement under his tires as the river lapped at the bottom of the engine. Unfortunately, when they were almost across, they found their way blocked by a huge thorn tree lying in the raging water.

With the sound of the river roaring in his ears, Farson stepped into the water to push the thorn tree aside. Immediately he was swept under the car. The current scraped him across the car's undercarriage and the rough cement causeway, shredded his clothes, and ripped flesh from his body. Flailing desperately underwater, he grasped the rear passenger tire and established his footing on the concrete just as he would have been swept downstream. After righting himself and marveling at his survival, he discovered that he had driven on the extreme edge of the causeway. "It was just a gift from God that I hadn't driven the car overboard," he later wrote, adding:

> A naked native rushed from the near bank, and we shifted the thorn tree. I was shocked to watch the speed with which it was swept away. Then, getting the car to dry land, I stripped, regardless of the proprieties, while Eve painted my scratched nakedness with iodine, from head to foot. We spread out the pound notes, the letters of credit, the precious traveler's checks, in the murky sun. My signature on all of them was a bit watery, but still legible enough to permit cashing. Another pair of dry shorts and a safari shirt were exhumed from the back of the car with some golf stockings. We went on.[19]

Eve told him afterward that she had never seen such a look of amazement on his face as when he disappeared into the water. She thought he had drowned.

At Arusha, the two snow-capped peaks of Mt. Kilimanjaro loomed to the east. The Bantu-speaking Chaga lived on the slopes of the mountain, growing coffee and making spears for Maasai warriors. A single spear was a work of art and required a master's skill to fashion—it cost one ox. Farson drove up Kilimanjaro on the roads the Chaga built, past rows of green coffee bushes, banana plantations, and a forest of trees festooned with gray moss. Along the way, Farson did voluminous work in collecting population statistics on the various Europeans and tribes, along with other information important to the journalist's trade: immigration numbers, wage rates, labor and agricultural statistics, coffee and tea prices, bureaucratic policies, herd sizes, and local opinions on how geopolitical forces interacted with the tribal reality on the ground. He talked to nearly everyone he encountered. But most of all he loved mingling with the tribes, and of all of them, Farson idolized the Maasai warriors, semi-nomads who measured their wealth in cattle and children and regarded the white man with contempt. He called them "blood drinkers" for their custom of drinking the blood from living animals without harming them.[20] Farson described the warriors as "the most beautifully built men in Africa, perhaps in all the world. I have never seen such men elsewhere!"[21] The Maasai warriors brandished eight-foot steel spears and wore their hair in long pigtails colored red with ocher and hanging down their back. They covered their nakedness with a soft, red skin draped over one shoulder, the tips of their painted buffalo shields touching the ground. Though warriors, they didn't hunt game for food. The warriors stalked wild beasts, especially the African lion, to prove their courage.

The Farsons pushed on to the Serengeti Plain, to the most famous of all hunting grounds in Africa—the Ngorongoro Crater in the Crater Highlands of Tanganyika. The crater, formed when a volcano erupted and collapsed on itself, teemed with lions and also boasted rhinos, hippos, zebra, waterbucks, and wildebeest. "I have stood on the running board of my car and looked across a single herd of wildebeest, and their backs glinted in the sun as far as I could see," Farson wrote. "And here, among the acacias and thickets of thorn, prowls the greatest lion population in all Africa."[22] They drove toward Lion Hill in Kenya. The Farsons watched in awe as a leopard leapt from a tree in front of them, "and it dropped in what seemed nothing less than a stream of spots."[23] Angry hyenas grudgingly moved out of the path of their Ford. The Farsons had planned to drive across the roadless plains to reach Musoma on the shores of Lake Victoria, then ship the car across the lake to Entebbe in Uganda. But the heavy rains stopped them, and Farson, staying at a hotel in Arusha (decorated with the heads of eight buffalo), determined to drive up to Kenya, then west to Uganda. The little English colonel who ran the hotel delighted in showing them his plantation and the herd of giraffes he refused to hunt. When Farson wondered out loud how the Boers could kill such an animal, the colonel responded, "I'd much rather shoot a man."[24]

The Farsons had now driven for weeks, mostly over muddy paths that were roads in name only. The Ford's springs were nearly worn out by the miles of rough road. Driving and camping had taken on a routine. They settled in quickly wherever they stopped. Farson set up the camp beds and mosquito netting while Eve lit the alcohol stove to warm a tin of mulligatawny soup or Vienna sausages or the delicate meat of jungle birds Farson had shot. Coffee always simmered while they ate. After dinner, if the swarms of flies and gnats were not too troublesome, the Farsons would read or write.

Remarkably, or perhaps because they had encountered no liquor stores as they drove from village to village, no alcohol had passed Farson's parched lips. But all was not idyllic. Back in Dar es Salaam, Farson had injured his lame leg in one of their tennis matches. The leg had become infected during their journey; the pain grew increasingly intense. Farson dressed the wound twice a day, but the bone was becoming exposed as the infection ate away at his flesh. As they drove through jungles and across plains, Farson constantly sought out doctors and in the process became somewhat of an expert on the lack of adequate health care in Africa. Whether he could complete the journey became an open question.

On the slopes of one crater, the Farsons stopped to talk to German planters, who warned about the thick herds of elephants that ambled about. They drove up to the crater's lip at eight thousand feet on a road that wound upward for nearly ten miles, then spent the night on the crater, able to see the views from both sides. Behind them lay the green jungle, in front a vastness—the smooth floor of the crater some two thousand feet below and as green as a lawn. In the far distance rose the mountains of Kenya. On the trip down the crater, the rains fell hard, and Farson failed to keep the car on the road. The rains had turned the volcanic dust into a slippery stew. The constant skidding off road and into ditches and fields eventually broke the car springs.

The next morning, they bought new ones from a German planter at Oldeani (a miracle, according to Farson, to find the right springs for his Ford in the middle of nowhere), then took the road north past Kilimanjaro to Nairobi. There, the Farsons rested for four days, stopping at the stately Norfolk Hotel, where Theodore Roosevelt and Hemingway had previously holed up.[25] Farson called Nairobi the Paris of the East African coast, packed with gay cafés. The couple enjoyed a series of lunch, tea, and dinner parties in the city during which they met various colorful characters. At one lunch, a young, gin-soaked Englishman implored him to go diamond hunting by a nearby lake. The Englishman had no idea if any diamonds were there but tried to entice Farson along by noting that the fishing was fantastic. Farson didn't bite. At a dinner, a seventeen-year-old girl informed him that two distinguished Nairobi bachelors had killed themselves over her within the past year. "I never, in all my life, got myself into so many tight spots as I have right here in Nairobi!" she told Farson.

"It never occurred to any of these young men to shoot you, did it?"

"No. But it's so embarrassing, to have people going around shooting themselves!"

"Must be," Farson replied laconically. Such was life for the English expats living in the outposts of the British Empire.[26]

Earlier in his journey, Farson resolved not to leave the continent until he had killed one lion and one buffalo, so he teamed with Sidney Downey, a white hunter, to kill his first lion. The two drove across the plains to reach a suitable hunting ground. There, in a single day, Farson saw buffalo, leopard, zebra, wildebeest, gazelles, various species of buck, hyenas, jackals, monkeys, giraffe, and a host of other animals.

They awoke at dawn in their tent—Farson slept with his double-barreled rifle and .400 cartridges by his side—to hear the unmistakable grunt of a lion. Downey exclaimed that the lion was circling them. "We've got to cut him off," he told Farson.[27] Farson slipped on a dry shirt and a damp jacket and his boots and followed Downey outside, into a torrential rain. The two zigzagged behind trees, stalking the lion in broad daylight. "It was the rain which killed him," Farson recalled:[28] the lion, its belly swinging from a recent gorge, couldn't hear the men over the sound of the downpour. Big and black-maned, the lion had headed to a nearby river to lie up; it didn't see Farson and Downey until they were 120 yards away. Farson looked into its face as he shot.

He missed with both barrels. Hurriedly, he slipped another cartridge into the right barrel, carefully aimed at the lion's shoulder and shot again. The lion disappeared. Farson suddenly remembered that the Nairobi graveyard held the bones of many men who had only wounded a lion. He cautiously approached the beast, saw it struggle to rise on its front legs, and shot it again. "He was dead. And suddenly all the reaction of it hit me. I won't say that I felt ashamed, because I was tremendously satisfied. But I knew then, when I looked at the noble face, that I would never want to kill another lion."[29] Later in life, reflecting on his lion kill, he elaborated on the moment. He had told Downey, "'I'm sorry. I wish to Christ I hadn't done it.' I expected triumph; all I felt was dismay . . . there is something damned silly about this business of killing animals."[30] The instant remorse was not a new emotion for Farson: while still in South West Africa he had shot a springbok and immediately vowed he would never shoot another.

The Farsons pushed on to Uganda and the Congo, with both Farson and the car seemingly on their last leg. The lion hunting in the rain had aggravated Farson's old injury. The leg had swollen, and more bone was showing; Farson was bandaging it twice a day. Still, he refused to let the danger of infection stop him. He relied on his grit to get him through. At the Ugandan capital of Kampala, twenty-five miles north of the equator, they stopped at the Hotel Imperial. There, Farson, his crippled leg be damned, set up his headquarters for his next big-game hunt, this time for buffalo. It would be a far tougher ordeal. A white hunter named Kennedy, wiry and bug-bitten, accompanied him on the hunt, and the two camped in an enclosed pen called a boma that sported a huge gate of sharpened stakes. Opening the gate required the strength of six men. The safety precautions were due to the buffalo's reputation as the most dangerous game animal in Africa. Kennedy had been in the wilderness thirty years killing buffalo.

May had arrived, and still the skies poured rain. Farson carried a Rigby Magnum, a high-powered, bolt-action rifle that could hold three .416 cartridges. The natives beat through the tangle of a swamp just ahead of Farson and Kennedy in an effort to scare the buffalo out. The ancient technique proved sound. Five of the huge beasts—they could weigh up to 1,300 pounds—rushed out and charged the two men. Farson shot one in the shoulder. The buffalos took off, then came charging back.

At twenty-five feet, Farson shot the wounded bull again and watched it shudder as the bullet struck. The buffalos, including the wounded one, again thundered off. For the next five hours the hunters pursued them through tall grass—Farson as usual ignored the pain of his leg—knowing that the wounded animal might backtrack and stalk them. At last, the bloodied bull galloped out of a river bottom, and Farson shot him in the neck. He watched as the beast suddenly slid on bent knees into the reeds. "It was the supreme thrill I have had of all my shooting," Farson later wrote. As usual, he also felt regret: "The wet, blue muzzle would never again smell the night mist under a Uganda moon."[31] Later in the evening, Kennedy estimated they had walked seventeen miles in pursuit of the buffalo. Farson had limped the whole way.

The Farsons drove into the forests of the Belgian Congo, tired but determined to slog on. The trip had now stretched on for months, and Farson had spent countless hours digging the car out of mud, and the car itself was a mobile disaster: Farson had changed flat tires, busted several sets of springs, and driven the car off the road and into fields too many times to count. The radiator constantly threatened to explode. The oppressive heat of the jungle enveloped them as they descended, driving through mahogany forests and gangs of baboons swinging through the trees. Watusi, the African giants, watched them from the side of the road as they drove by. Even a six-foot, six-inch Watusi was not considered tall and could jump over a bar set six feet from the ground, Farson noted. They drove briefly through Rwanda and Burundi, where they encountered missionaries bent on converting the natives to followers of Jesus. "Changing Gods was a tricky business," one missionary told Farson.[32]

Farson, who desired to see everything interesting in the world, wanted to glimpse a gorilla. He pressed the Belgian administrator in the Congo to allow the natives to guide him into the rain forest. The administrator was reluctant: gorillas enjoyed legal protections, and he wisely feared disturbing the animals would lead one to attack. The last gorilla that had been killed, as a specimen for an American museum, had a nine-foot arm span, the administrator told Farson in hopes of dissuading him. But the Farsons persisted, and soon found themselves inching through the jungle. Some eight hundred gorillas lived in the region. Farson called it a "gorilla wonderland" blanketed with mist, tall ferns, impenetrable clusters of bamboo and huge, flowering lobelias some twenty feet high.[33] Hiking with a native hunter, the Farsons came upon three steaming balls of dung—a gorilla was nearby. Farson carried a thin metal spear, seven feet long, as his only defense. The administrator had forbidden them to carry guns.

Then they heard a band of gorillas begin to beat their chests, mouths open, "a horrible sound, meant to strike terror into everything in the forest, and it certainly worked with me, all right," recalled Farson.[34] Moments later, a bush collapsed and Farson saw his first wild gorilla. It stood a mere fifteen feet away. "The sight of him was worse than his shrieks!" he wrote.[35] The gorilla, in turn, frightened by the sight of Farson, bolted. But Farson had checked another item off his Africa to-do list: he had shot a lion and killed a buffalo, now he had seen a gorilla in the wild.

The Farsons continued their westward trek as Farson's health visibly deteriorated, but the two were delighted to discover that the roads here were better due to the presence nearby of tin, copper, and gold mines: trucks needed good roads to carry the ore out. For once Farson could speed up to 40 miles per hour for hundreds of miles, so they "raced" to Stanleyville (now Kisangani), in the heart of the Congo. On the way, near the Ituri Forest, Farson met Pygmies carrying bows and arrows and flitting from tree to bush. He found twenty, some with crowns of feathers, standing in a clearing. The unsmiling Pygmies, potbellied, with thin arms and standing about three feet six inches tall, carried a small dead deer in a net. The Farsons were at a loss to communicate with them. "Ages of evolution lay between, and we could not cross," Farson sighed.[36] But he found their attitude impish. They examined Eve with puzzlement.

By the time they reached Stanleyville, Farson had lost thirty pounds. Before they left, Farson and Eve shot down the cataracts of the Stanley Falls (now the Boyoma Falls) in a native dugout with forty paddlers. He called it exhilarating.

At last, after a two-week respite, they drove their trusty car onto a paddleboat and spent four days floating down the Congo and gazing at the unbroken wall of green jungle that lined the banks. The river itself seemed to have no life. When they stopped for coal or to unload goods, Farson saw natives emaciated from lack of food, some of them lepers, some with elephantiasis. Others had carved scars onto their bodies from head to toe. They landed finally in Bumba, where they planned to take a new road past Aketi to Bangassou in French Equatorial Africa (now the Central African Republic). By now, the romance of the adventure for both Farson and Eve had evaporated in the jungle heat. Farson suffered from malaria. There remained only steely resolve. And a desperate need for medical attention.

At Aketi, Farson found a surgeon who ripped the oozing bandages from his leg. The entire shinbone lay exposed. The doctor, an exiled White Russian, concluded that Farson's previous doctors had been trying to murder him. The Russian carved out the infection and sent Farson on his way, and the Farsons drove on through the heat and savannahs. When they stopped at a hotel in one remote village, they witnessed almost an entire colony of French inhabitants drunk by 10:00 a.m., "a symposium of everything that can happen to the white man under the equator's sun . . . they drank white wine with their breakfast—or, more often, instead of it."[37] The French officials despised their post, and "for ten, twenty, even thirty years all these men had lived with the thought of just one day; the day when they would receive their pensions and sail back to retire in cool France."[38]

At Bangui, Farson's malaria deepened, and he suffered gloominess and impatience. They headed for Douala in the Cameroons, where Eve planned to catch a German steamer home. The many miles had prompted so much marital bickering and bitterness that Farson could bear her company no more. The positive effects of Bumke's treatment had apparently worn off after more than fifteen months of near sobriety.

Weakened by malaria—and possibly by overdoses of the sulfa drugs he took to treat his gangrenous leg—Farson had begun drinking again, and hard. Somewhere in the Cameroons he had successfully sought a liquor store, where he bought a bottle of French cognac, pulled the cork, and downed half the bottle. In his own mind, he was officially off the wagon. Farson himself blamed his renewed drinking on the fever "grilling" his bones; the suffering even prevented him from taking notes. He remembered this stretch of the trip as "just drive—drive—drive; unload—load; unload—load."[39] The drinking unleashed "a torrent of accumulated bitterness" against Eve, Daniel Farson later claimed. "Things were said and things happened that were too vile to be more than hinted at afterwards."[40]

The drinking had brought out the worst in Farson, as usual. He treated his wife cruelly. Though Farson dedicated the book he eventually wrote about the trip to Eve, there was no hiding the acrimony that bedeviled their marriage. To Daniel's mind, the book dedication was merely his father's attempt to assuage his guilt over his treatment of Eve. The dedication read: "To MY WIFE—My sole companion on the drive from coast-to-coast across Africa; she was better than any man."[41] In the book itself, he added that "to a great extent, she made the trip. It was her love of beauty and adventure . . . that gave it its tang. In her eagerness to 'get places' she nearly killed me."[42] But the reality was different, or at least more tense, than the kind words pretended.

Putting her aboard a ship, he said, "Well, that one is over."

"We might have gone up to Timbuktu," she lamented.

"Haven't you ever got enough?" he asked angrily.

"No!" she said. Then she was gone.[43]

Daniel vividly recalled his mother's arrival in England, alone. He found her hopeless and devastated: "I have seen few people so destroyed, her face puffy and her eyes red from weeping. . . . His cruelty must have been refined to cause such utter desolation; an excess of decency can be as dangerous as the lack of it."[44]

Farson, meanwhile, flew to Ghana, sick with malaria. So ill was he, in fact, that he checked into the local hospital at Accra. There he lay in bed, eating his dinner, on June 22, 1939, when his last African adventure occurred. To his puzzlement, his bed began to shake, the electricity failed, a piece of plaster fell from the ceiling onto his head. A mutton chop, meanwhile, slid off his plate and onto his chest. He was in the middle of an earthquake. By the time it was over, Africans five hundred miles away had felt the ground shake; in Accra itself, more than 1,500 homes lay in ruins, more than one hundred people were injured, at least seventeen were killed. Farson, now a seasoned journalist, grabbed his pen and jotted down notes on the activity around him. Village bells rang constantly; residents walked the streets banging drums and chanting. Dust from all the collapsed structures turned the moon to green that night. The ostentatious British government buildings crumbled. The natives' mud-and-wattle huts survived. Immediately after the quake stopped, Christian natives as well as the unconverted rushed to churches to hear ministers wailing to God for help. Then the natives, Christians and pagans alike, ran into the streets, firing shotguns and muzzle-loaders to ward off evil spirits. "They were playing it both ways across the board," a bemused Farson noted.[45] Taught that gin was the most precious gift to God, natives bought it by the caseload, only to pour it out on the streets as a sacrifice to the deity.

Through it all, Farson, unhurt, read poetry and drank "far too many whiskies than were good for me."[46] He had made the trek from coast to coast, and he knew he wanted to leave Africa. The malaria had left him melancholic. He had grown to hate the broiling African heat and yearned for the cold: "I vowed that when next I traveled it would be to a land of perpetual ice."[47] A short time later, he boarded an Italian tramp steamer for home. He had arrived in Africa the previous year to find Nazi enthusiasts among the German settlers. He sailed home two months before the German invasion of Poland in September 1939.

So what had Farson gained for all his trouble, besides more marital turmoil and a renewed dependency on booze? At the very least, a better understanding of Africa. And that understanding would pay good dividends: he would call upon his knowledge of the continent for years to come as news organizations sought experts to write articles and give radio interviews. He also wrote prefaces for the books written by subsequent British travelers to Africa, and African scholars cited his observations in their own books. Farson, in short, had established himself as a bit of an expert on the continent. Though personally fascinated with the African landscape of jungles, savannahs, and mountains, Farson had focused much of his attention on colonial policies toward the natives and the relationship between white settlers and the African natives. More specifically, he had witnessed the so-called noble intentions of white European colonizers in action, along with the attendant racism. He believed that white Europeans, afraid of the power of millions of Africans inherent in their sheer numbers, were disgracing themselves with their brutal treatment of the natives. It was a viewpoint he would share in news articles and radio broadcasts for years to come, arguing that the native's "capacity for suffering, his vitality, his faith that one day things must come all right for him, are indestructible. They shame you. What are you going to do with him? In Africa, the black man, by his very presence, has made the white man do mean things. Demean himself. And the white man hates him for it."[48] Farson believed the Africans would never forget the duplicity of Christians. An old Zulu saying that he heard cut to the dark heart of the matter: "You had the Bible—and we had the land; now we have the Bible—and you have the land!"[49]

19

→ • ←

A Bomber's Moon

HEADING INTO LATE 1939, the Farsons were back in their small South Kensington home in London and leading what seemed an idyllic life once more. The unexpected success of *The Way of a Transgressor* had allowed the family to plump their bank account, and the relative success of the novel *The Story of a Lake* had dropped a little extra drinking money into Farson's pocket. Now he was hard at work pulling together his notes to write his book on their African journey. Gollancz had paid him a five-hundred-pound advance and promised the same royalty rate as for *Transgressor*. But the uneasy truce that the Munich Pact of September 1938 had brought about collapsed completely on September 1, 1939, when Germany invaded Poland. France and the United Kingdom responded by declaring war on Germany, and nations throughout Europe and the world prepared for a greater global conflict.

Londoners, the Farsons included, braced for invasion, convinced that their city was an ideal target for the German war machine. London was, at the time, one of the greatest cities in the world, with more than eight million inhabitants. Its port handled more cargo than any other port on the planet, the wealth of the world churned through its financial institutions, its banks, stock exchange, and insurance companies. London was also the British seat of power, as well as the fulcrum of the British Empire. Furthermore, the city had become a destination for the tens of thousands of refugees who had fled Europe as German aggression roiled the continent. The city seemed too valuable for Hitler *not* to invade.

The British government and the city were slow to respond to the threat of war, but the shift to a war footing must have seemed rapid and unsettling to the Farsons, changing as it did the face of London. As early as October 1938, days after the Munich Pact, city workers had dug a million feet of trenches in the Greater London area. Volunteers had stacked sandbags around some of the public buildings deemed vulnerable to bombing. Vans with loudspeakers began rolling up and down the streets, telling residents to report to collection points to pick up their gas masks; within days, nine out of ten residents had received one. Everywhere the Farsons looked the city was changing: the first barrage balloons, or blimps, appeared in the skies shortly after Munich, and at times they would number as many as a thousand; neighborhoods held drills in which wardens and firefighters responded to mock bombings; the BBC reduced its radio programs to a single channel; newspapers began to offer advice on how to store food and build bomb shelters; hospitals began to release patients to make room for war casualties. And on September 3, 1939, Prime Minister Neville Chamberlain announced to the nation that it was at war with Germany. Soon afterward there sounded the first air-raid alarm—a citywide blaring of sirens that Farson almost always referred to as "the Banshees."[1]

"The first air-raid warning was the worst," he recalled. "Before this war began the experts were predicting that when the Nazis made mass air attacks on London the casualties would be from 30,000 to 35,000 a day. We believed them. So, when the Banshees began their howling on that sunny Sunday morning of September 1939, my knees shook. So did a lot of other people's."[2]

It was a false alarm, and so began what the English came to call the Phoney War, the period between the declaration of war in September 1939 and the spring of 1940, when the Battle for France and Britain began in earnest and the German Luftwaffe began its bombing of the United Kingdom's shipping and ports. For months the city's residents were tortured with sirens and false reports of imminent invasion. As the months dragged on, thousands of wives, mothers, and children who had been evacuated began to return to London. Cinemas that had closed reopened. Pubs were doing a booming business. Where once an air-raid alarm had sent patrons scrambling to the cellars after leaving their pints and whiskies behind, soon they were staying long enough to finish their drinks, and eventually they were not bothering to put down their drinks at all. Shops continued to do business, though now blackout curtains graced their windows, and whenever Farson made his way to the Tube he had to step around piles of drab sandbags (though one restaurant, Prunier's, had painted its sandbags blue to match the woodwork out front). People had grown accustomed to the blimps overhead, the anti-aircraft guns, gas rationing, the trenches through the parks, the vegetable gardens on the courts of Wimbledon.

But the Phoney War could not last forever, and in April 1940, German troops invaded Norway. A month later they dashed into Belgium, the Netherlands, and France. By the end of June, all three countries had capitulated. Winston Churchill took over as prime minister in May; by the end of the month, British forces were scrambling to avoid wholesale capture at Dunkirk. They completed their evacuation of France on June 4, and four days later the first real German bombs fell on the London area, tearing up the countryside of Addington. Bombs landed on Colney two weeks later. The Farsons vowed to remain come what may, German bayonets or bombs, but they decided the time had come to evacuate their son. Daniel was still a student at Abinger Hill and had achieved distinction by becoming head boy. In the last week of June, Daniel and about forty classmates and twenty-five of their sisters sailed from Liverpool to Canada. The young boys all assumed that the Germans would overrun England in their absence, Daniel recalled in his memoir, *Never a Normal Man:* "One pretext for the school's evacuation was expedient: that we should return from Canada when we had grown into young men and join the British resistance in helping to free our country."[3] Daniel and his classmates attended Ashbury College in Ottawa and lasted out the war there with no need to return and fight.

In August 1940, the heavy bombing began in earnest as the Germans targeted the airfields around London. By the end of the month, central London was ablaze as the docks of the East End fell prey to German bombers. In September, waves of bombers appeared in the skies above London day and night, officially marking what history books now call the Blitz. Farson was among the many foreign journalists who witnessed the bombing and was one of those who established the legend of British courage, dignity, and even humor under fire and against insurmountable odds as they faced the seemingly invincible German forces.

In September 1939 he and a friend, the illustrator Tom Purvis, had agreed to publish a book on the bombing, should they both survive. Purvis would provide the illustrations, Farson the prose. When the bombing became intense, in September 1940, Farson and Purvis prowled the streets at night and climbed their way through the debris and toppled storefronts by the light of the burning buildings and anti-aircraft gunfire. Soon they were also making early-morning jaunts to witness the destruction and talk to the newly homeless. The book they produced for Gollancz in 1941 came out under the title *Bomber's Moon*. Though it rapidly got lost in the massive pile of books later published on the war, it won immediate praise for its down-to-earth portrayals of Londoners struggling to survive as their neighbors died and their world burned and collapsed around them. For readers who relished action and adventure, Farson did not stint in his descriptions of the bombardment.

"Around the corner from where I live is a row of little shops. . . . Well, the other night a bomb hit the block of modern flats across from these shops," he wrote in *Bomber's Moon*. "When I saw them a few minutes later most of them looked blown in. I saw one or two of their inmates being helped down the street, and one stretcher case. Others were emerging from where most of them had been sleeping during the raids: in their cellars. And they were covered with that peculiar cement-like dust that seems the accompaniment of all bomb-debris. They looked knocked-out, finished."[4]

On another night, he and Purvis took cover with a crowd in the crypt of St. Martin-in-the-Fields—where thousands of coffins had been removed to make room for those seeking shelter—as waves of German bombers passed overhead:

While we were talking there was a frightful screech, and we knew that a whistling bomb was on its way. Deep down in the catacombs we knew it; and we waited for the crash. When it came it seemed almost to lift the church; the lights dimmed and almost went out. Then they rose again to full power. There was a small burst of excited talking from the huddled mass of people in the main crypt. It reminded me oddly of the cries I had heard on the Gold Coast after the shock of a recent earthquake. Then the life of St. Martin's settled down again.[5]

In another sketch, he recalled making his way to his club, the Athenaeum, with Purvis as enemy bombers hammered away at the city docks. The bombing was so intense, Farson noticed that even the hardiest taxi drivers had abandoned their cabs and dashed for the shelters. "Strange night," Farson wrote. "We moved out into a windswept, rainy street illuminated at fearsome intervals by the flash of gunfire, bombs, and the fingers of moving searchlights. 'O-o-o-o-o-oh!' could have been our signature tune of that night as we walked hurriedly along, trusting to the slight protection of [small metal helmets called] 'battle bowlers.' And mine did not fit. It sat like a button on the top of my head."[6]

But Farson didn't have to search far for sights and sounds to record: the war was, fearsomely, all around him. September 7 awoke Londoners to the reality of war. That day, hundreds of German bombers flying in impressive order filled the skies above the great city. Londoners stopped to watch them and admire the precision of their formations. Seconds later the bombs hit the East End and all but obliterated entire sections of the city. The docks burned deep into the night—there had been more than a million tons of lumber piled on them—and the working-class homes around them lay in broken piles. More German bombers returned that night and kept up the bombing into the next morning. More than 430 Londoners died. The following night's raid killed another 400. The night after, 370. London was ablaze, as warehouses and their contents burned for hours. Making a circuit of his immediate neighborhood in South Kensington, Farson was able to witness the resilience of Londoners.

Additionally, his reporter's gaze fixed on the inefficiencies of a government that, in Farson's view, often failed its citizenry. The Tube tunnels had been converted into shelters, but all that really meant was that people were welcome to spend nights in them. There were neither beds nor provisions, no separation of men from women, and only a bucket or two to serve as latrines for the thousands trying to survive the bombs. Farson watched elderly men sleep bolt upright, while children dozed fitfully on urine-soaked platforms. The smell was almost unbearable. Adding insult to their injury, residents endured night after night of filth, then read in the morning papers about the marvelous job the government was doing to provide bunks for several million residents. In reality, thousands and thousands who couldn't fit into the Tube simply spent their nights jammed in adjacent warehouses. Still, Farson admired the way the British carried on. At dawn he watched as they hurried from the shelters to get a few hours of sleep in their own beds before they headed off to work. Others he admired for limiting their breakfast to a single cigarette. Londoners cheered when their own guns fired back at the German bombers, and Farson silently cheered the Londoners.

In September, the government calculated, British gunners had fired thirty thousand shells for every enemy plane destroyed. Gradually, Farson noticed the great city's inhabitants begin to develop a technique to endure the raids. In pubs in the morning, they joked to relieve the tension from the previous night's horror. At dinner in the clubs, people began to say, "Well, see you in the same place tomorrow—if it's there!"[7] It was a dark gag. People began to make as few dates in the West End as possible and invited fewer friends over for dinner—keeping the crowd small in case everyone had to sleep over during a bombing raid. Everyone lived with the gut feeling that invasion was imminent.

Farson and Purvis took trips down the River Thames in ferryboats, hailed cabs to carry them through the rubble to get closer to the burning buildings, and rode buses through decimated neighborhoods. But getting about in wartime required patience and luck: the Auxiliary Fire Service had commandeered a third of all of London's taxis, and eight hundred buses had been removed from service. Severe gas rationing meant people kept their cars in their garages during the week and saved their precious fuel allotment for weekend jaunts out of the city. Driving through the city on broken and bombed-out streets was burdensome in any event: between September 7 and November 13, about 27,500 bombs and incendiaries had fallen on the city, the result of an average of 160 bombers arriving daily.

At the beginning of the Blitz, in September 1940, Gollancz published the British edition of *Behind God's Back*, for which Farson received a five-hundred-pound advance. The book, on which Farson had been working steadily since his return to England, immediately established his reputation as an expert on Africa and won unstinting praise from reviewers. His grit and determination to complete the cross-continental trek— despite his leg, his malaria, and the unspeakably rugged conditions—had their reward. Critics celebrated his account of the ordeal as a true achievement. The London *Observer* called it "one of the best travel-books of our time."[8] The *New Statesman & Nation* hailed it as a "brilliant, chaotic, contradictory, vivid, immensely readable book."[9] *The Scotsman* summed it up as "excellent,"[10] and the *Daily Telegraph* called it "remarkable."[11] The Glasgow *Herald* was more fulsome and described *Behind God's Back* as "an absorbing book—the racy, vivid travel tale of a cultured, knowledgeable, and shrewdly observant man."[12] Reviews from the United States also glowed brightly. "No other book written in this generation contains so much sound information and so interestingly presented about Africa," the *Washington Post* reviewer wrote, calling attention to Farson's "vivid descriptions of the many tribes he encountered" and "scenes of great natural beauty."[13] The *New York Times* praised him for "writing even better and more to the point than he did in his interesting biography." The review concluded with the observation that "Mr. Farson came out of Africa with malaria and an ulcer on his leg. He came out with a story that is not only well told but which is of a piece with today's news."[14] The book found a steady perch on the newspaper's best-seller list, alongside Hemingway's *For Whom the Bell Tolls*.[15] As bombs rained down on London, bookstores began to feature Farson's book in their display windows. One day as Farson and Purvis surveyed the damage from the latest raid, they came across a bookshop whose storefront had been blown out by a bomb. Farson was amused to see a copy of *Behind God's Back* lying in the street.

Gollancz published *Bomber's Moon* the following January and gave Farson a 250-pound advance for the slender volume. The book included forty-eight illustrations by Purvis. While Gollancz published it in England, Harcourt, Brace released it in the United States. Americans could read for themselves about the war that would soon arrive on their doorsteps. Again, Farson scored a success. British newspapers praised the American for accurately capturing their plight. The *Times Literary Supplement* said the book was "enthralling to read now" and would be "invaluable in the future."[16] The *Illustrated London News* called it "a little masterpiece of sympathetic collaboration."[17] Novelist Graham Greene, writing for the *Spectator,* said Farson had not quite got the English accent right, but nevertheless "we cannot help liking the things he says about us."[18] In the United States, reviewers also hailed the book as a gem of homefront reportage. "Sustained air attack took England unaware, in the sense that until the thing happened there was no way of knowing how to prepare for it," the *New York Times* wrote. "The people adapted themselves quickly; the workers on the spot gave not only patriotic devotion but swift intelligent activity to the 'small immediate practical thing' which was needed to make life tolerable as well as safe. But Whitehall was psychologically far away from the air-raid shelters and the bombed-out families. Government processes were enmeshed in red tape."[19] According to the reviewer, Farson's depictions of an inactive or inept British government offered the United States government a valuable lesson, one it should heed as Americans watched war clouds gathering.

Farson was now entering his fifties, but the years and the miles had slowed him only slightly. The way he wrote and the way he lived remained chock-full of vitality. He had bulled his way across Africa and borne the bombing of London, and he had two successful books, worthy follow-ups to *The Way of a Transgressor,* to show for the effort. The times were tumultuous, but he seemed to thrive in them. And his best work still lay ahead.

20

→•←

Writing a Masterpiece

A S THE GERMAN BOMBING of London eased up, Farson penned *Going Fishing*. He was fifty years old and at the height of his storytelling power. If his previous books brought him fame, this one brought him a measure of immortality, drawing hallelujahs and bows from fishermen and critics alike, both then and now. It is his masterpiece. "It remains the supreme lyric on the impenetrable romance and anguish of fishing," opined journalist Christopher Wordsworth of the *Observer* decades later.[1] That's tall talk for a sport steeped in a literary tradition launched by Izaak Walton in 1653, when he wrote *The Compleat Angler*— the first written celebration of the art of fishing. Though Walton had decreed that no man is born a fisherman, Farson might have been the exception: he apparently sprang from the womb knowing how to roll cast to a rising trout. He fished his entire life with determination and passion, from the wild seas of the Hebrides to the placid chalk streams of England and the roaring rivers that sliced through the mountains of Chile.

Farson introduced his one and only fishing book as "just a story of some rods, and the places they take you to."[2] The phrase marked the height of Farson's achievement in understatement: he stuffed the book with riveting tales of fighting fish—rainbows, goldens and browns, salmon and channel bass, perch and blues, smallmouth bass and largemouth bass, sturgeon and even whales. The book was also chock-full of fish counts, fish weights, and fish lengths, for size mattered to Farson when it came to fish: "Every man has a fish in his life that haunts him; that particular big one which got away. Sometimes even I lie awake and groan at nights over an 8-lb. sea trout I had on for 2 hrs. and 40 mins. on a 3x leader up at Laxo in the Shetlands. It gets a pound bigger every time I tell about it."[3]

If any of Farson's books can be said to contain incandescent prose, *Going Fishing* is the one, with its sundry reflections on the beauty of rushing trout rivers and of a magical moment when a trout jumped "between me and the sun" and "the drops he shook off were golden."[4] The 147-page book was a paean to fishermen as fish-crazed as Farson. In it, he unveiled himself as the kid whose pulse still raced at the first tug of a fish on the line. He admitted it: he was at heart a trout bum, more interested in the fly and the ring of the rise than worldly success. As he explained in the book, fishing filled some metaphysical need in him: "with a boat, a shotgun and a couple of rods, you could have a far fuller life than I was finding in the cities of Europe."[5]

Writing the book, published in 1942 by Country Life Ltd., allowed Farson to reflect quietly on the calmest moments of his life, to explore his feelings for a sport that had rarely failed to bring him solace. He had endured the yearlong Blitz by the Luftwaffe and spent months scrambling through bombed-out buildings with Purvis. With the book, he washed himself in the memories of his epic fishing life:

> At sunset Joe and I (he was killed at Chateau Thierry) got out our shotguns and took the dinghy ashore to go after some snipe we saw feeding along the waterline. We got three, and they were the treat of that night's dinner. After dinner, with the water lapping gently against our sides, and with a full moon rising, we lazily fished for catfish. Although we were hard up for any kind of food then, we did not care whether we caught any or not; the night was so beautiful. We were hushed by it. I was not writing in those days, except to amuse myself, but I wanted so much to put the enchantment of that night into words that it hurt. And then as we were sitting there, not talking, a hound bayed far up on the hill . . . a hound baying at the moon. I shall always remember that.[6]

Farson's obsession with fishing began as a child, surf-casting for channel bass and bluefish on the New Jersey shore, where the book begins. In New Jersey, where he was born, the state remained a wilderness, especially on the ocean's shores and in its marshes. As a boy, his enthusiasm was so great that he played gillie to other fishermen, including one old German neighbor who fished at night in the surf for channel bass as he watched by the green glow of a driftwood fire. Sometimes they ate the bait—fat clams roasted over the fire. One night the old German waded into the surf and cast his line far out, walking back to rest his rod on a forked stick. A big fish struck, bending the stout rod, and the German sputtered as he grabbed it. His reel jammed. The drags were frozen. He ran into the surf as the fish burrowed deep and then up and down the shore as the bass struggled. Finally, the German pulled the fish in far enough that Farson could tug the line to bring it farther in to shore. The line broke, and the boy, in terror of losing it, fell on the fish and shoved his hand and arm up its gills. "It won no prize," Farson said of the 25½–pound channel bass. "But it won an imperishable place in my memory, for it was the first *big* game fish that I had ever seen killed."[7]

The following chapters detailed his fishing mania throughout his travels around the world. Wherever he went, by foot, horseback, or car—Russia, British Columbia, the Shetlands, Ireland, the Caucasus, Germany, Chile, France, Norway, and Yugoslavia—he packed a rod and reel. He cast in public rivers, paid to fish in private streams, and, when necessary, poached in forbidden waters. He picked the highlights of his fishing life for his fishing book and intertwined those tales with glimpses into his thoughts about life. He believed fishing made a man philosophical or that a philosophical man chose to fish. Fishing, Farson asserted, made you think. He added that "what you get out of fishing is infinitely more than fish."[8]

Beginning in 1921, when he and Eve lived in the British Columbia wilderness, he had to fish so much to survive that he rarely took his rods apart for two years. Broke and eager to live off the land, he fished for food, for salmon and bass and big trout. "For many months of the year trout were our staple diet, and I do not remember ever getting tired of either catching or eating them."[9]

Or cooking them:

With so much trout to be had we were prodigal with our cooking. Our favorite way, with ones around two pounds, was to fillet them. These fillets we fried in breadcrumbs. My wife, who makes a nice, stiff mayonnaise sauce, contended that I always ate the fish for the mayonnaise. So I did. So I do, even here in London; salmon trout with *sauce verte*, or salmon with *sauce tartare*. We might have been both broke and primitive in our log cabin in British Columbia; but fillets of Rainbow trout with *sauce mayonnaise* we had at least once a week in the days when trout were on. . . . Mere frying of them we reserved for quick meals, like a breakfast, and there were long periods, at the beginning of the season, when I loved to eat my fill of those that we had boiled the previous night cold for breakfast. In some ways, I think that simple style was the best one of them all. The only seasoning was salt!

You could never tire of this firm, pink flesh.[10]

In the Shetlands, which he described as a "geologic debauch where the rocks seem to have gone mad," he caught sea trout in salt estuaries and brown trout in windy lochs.[11] Hooked to a Shetland brown trout, he captured the fears of all veteran fishermen:

I had been casting automatically and a trout had hooked himself. I fought him. I could not see him, of course, in the coffee-black water. I could just see my thin gut leader cutting the water and then zip under as he made a run. I let him have the line gingerly, feeling him. My rod was bending beautifully, absorbing his tugs; and I could feel each movement of his in my wrist, telegraphed along the taut line and slender split cane. I began to tremble a little—what if I lost him? Was I fighting him too hard? Was this leader any good? Had I soaked it enough? Had he taken the tail fly or a dropper? If he had taken the dropper then I was out of luck, because there were some weeds at the bottom. Ah—what a rush! He must be two or three pounds anyway.[12]

Farson admitted the trout weighed "rather under a pound. But a Shetland brown trout with his dappled sides and red spots is not to be considered on his ounces—you must consider his beauty."[13]

At Uxbridge, a short drive from London, an exclusive fishing club invited Farson to fish a mayfly hatch—the ultimate in fly-fishing—where he caught the "most beautifully shaped fish I have ever seen" from under overhanging blackberry bushes.[14] The fish was a club record and entered in the club's "book" as such. Club officials mounted the trout and presented it to Farson, who hung it on the wall behind his desk.

In Ireland, Farson bet and lost heavily on horse races, and in remorse poached every stream he could on the country's west coast. In the Caucasus, with Wicksteed by his side, he fished among the natives. On a river near the Turco-Tartar village he hooked thirty-five trout, the most he had ever caught in one day. These were the trout a Cossack girl cooked to ruin in rancid sunflower seed oil.

In 1937, Farson fished in the wild, big rivers of Norway, yet England still held his fishing heart: "I think the best thing to call it is a certain quiet decency. This almost unchanging English scene, with its red and green rolling hills, holds a romance that wild rocks, and wild rivers, or snow-capped volcanoes could never give you. It has a gentleness, a rich rustic worth, and an unostentatiousness that is like the English character. An imperturbable scene which fills you with contentment."[15] Fishing in the West Country streams, he enjoyed "the luxury of my own solitude, my own idle reflections—the inner solitude. There are times when I don't want trouble, I don't want thrills; I have come here for just a lazy contentment.[16]

Fishing satisfied Farson's compulsion to thumb his nose at the conventions of his era that dictated a contempt for leisure. Farson believed such an outlook was wrongheaded, driven purely by the money urge. For some odd reason, Farson noted wryly, society did not consider golf a waste of time, but it frowned on fishing as a symptom of an absence of proper ambition. For Farson, each cast of his line onto the water, each second he spent hip deep in a stream, was a middle finger at convention. Fishing offered an opposing philosophy to the quest for material goods, wealth, and success.

Farson's attachment to his fishing gear helped establish his reputation as a fish-mad man, and *Going Fishing* made it clear that tackle was as important to him as his typewriter. Dispatched to various foreign capitals, he armed himself with both, confident that, between diplomatic conferences and political trials, he could steal enough time to fish. He boasted of having dozens of reliable flies and of his fondness for rods, one of which, his little Abbey & Imbrie Duplex, he carried everywhere. He loved the look and feel of his fishing rods, built by skilled craftsmen of split cane, greenheart, and snakewood. "I love rods, I suppose, with the same passion that a carpenter, a violinist or a Monaco pigeon shot love their implements," he wrote in the book's introduction. "I love using them. But, if I can't, I can get a lot of fun by just taking them out of their cases and looking at them."[17]

The rods, adorned with an expensive Vom Hofe reel or a workman-like Pflueger with ratchets and drag, took him, he said, to the loveliest corners of the earth. Farson was equally fanatic about flies, though he lamented that too many anglers preferred "to accumulate tackle and terminology" rather than to actually go fishing.[18] Fishermen, he said, could foolishly argue for hours about the four best flies in the world. But having harshly critiqued the argumentative nature of his fellow anglers, he weighed in with his own top-four list of well-known flies, some of which anglers had been casting for decades: The Butcher, March Brown, Blue Upright, and Red Spinner. Then he couldn't resist adding a fifth—the Silver Doctor.

The book's publication prompted critics to swoon. Maurice Richardson, writing in the *Observer* in December 1941, praised the "romantic-tough, leathery high spirits of Mr. Farson." He added that the book brought Hemingway to mind: "In one of Hemingway's stories a man who can't get to sleep goes over in his mind all the rivers he had ever fished. This is very much what Mr. Farson does in 'Going Fishing.'"[19] Fowler Hill, writing in the *New York Times,* deemed the book "a wise and amiable volume; it is an explanation of an outstanding literary personality. . . . Here you will meet no stuffed shirts. Farson's people are the Cattyrackers of Delaware Bay, the tenders of lobster pots on the Coast of Maine, Canadian lumberjacks, the fishermen of Haute Savoie."[20] H. E. Bates, writing in *Cosmopolitans,* said you don't "need to be a fisherman to enjoy this book any more than you need to be an expert to enjoy fishing. The title is a piece of skillful bait. It is designed to lure you into the reminiscences of an excellent foreign correspondent who spends his off-days, quite properly, in a more intelligent occupation than politics."[21] *Kirkus Reviews* called it a "perfect book," a "book of quiet delight."[22] The U.S. Army purchased eighty thousand copies to give to GIs during World War II. (All of Farson's books were popular among soldiers during the war.) In one of the book's many later editions, World War II pilot and renowned angler Hugh Falkus wrote the introduction, which consisted of a few paragraphs: "I first read *Going Fishing* in 1943 when, as a prisoner-of-war, I was serving a term of solitary confinement following an escape attempt and a friendly guard smuggled the book into my cell. For a couple of months it was my only literature, so I can claim to have read it pretty thoroughly! But Negley Farson proved more than a solace; he was a revelation. Of all the fishing books I had read, his was the best. It still is."[23]

Indeed, the book has held up through the decades and remains his most reprinted book. In the last four decades, it has been republished at least ten times by various publishers, most recently in 2016. The 2013 *Sportsman's Library* listed it as one of the "100 essential, engaging, off-beat, and occasionally odd fishing and hunting books for the adventurous reader." Reviews glow each time it hits the bookstands, whether today or in past decades. *Angler* magazine said it "does not contain a single boring line," while Conrad Voss Bark of the *Times* dubbed it "one of the finest fishing-travel books of all time."

His publishers must have known it would become a classic. They recruited C. F. Tunnicliffe, a renowned artist, to illustrate the book. Sixteen years later, Tunnicliffe illustrated another famous fishing book, Hemingway's *The Old Man and the Sea*. Which brings to mind the words of Charles Lillard, the Canadian historian who wrote that "as a man Farson outdrank 'Papa,' as a journalist he out-adventured him, and when it came to trout fishing Farson outwrote Hemingway."[24] Lillard was right. Farson had outshone Hemingway in some important ways. He was the better fisherman and sailor, for one, and he had proven himself to be a more lightfooted adventurer—not merely traveling to Pamplona as a tourist or enjoying a guided safari in Kenya, for instance, but hiking and riding a mule across the Pyrenees, climbing the Caucasus, and pushing through the heat and mud of Africa to understand its politics and people. And as for writing, Farson had written more and under more trying circumstances—under tight deadline, amid confusion, and to the sound of gunfire. He had mastered the art of writing by campfire and starlight, on trains and on boats, in jungles and on riverbanks. Farson was by far the better journalist and, consequently, had seen more of the world and seen it in a more honest way.

Writing *Going Fishing* was, in a way, Farson's gift to himself, a stolen moment of quiet and solitude in the middle of a war and after years of roaming the globe. And in reminiscing about his fishing exploits, he had given readers a great book. It had also further illuminated his character—here was a man who relished the outdoors and hardships over the ease of a comfortable life in commerce. But the war continued; it was passing Farson by. Now he was ready, once more, for action.

21

⇥ · ⇤

Back to Russia

I
N LATE 1942, WITH the German army a dozen miles or so from Moscow, Farson decided to return to the Soviet Union. London's *Daily Mail* accredited him as its correspondent in Moscow, and he set sail in December. The trip to Murmansk was perilous: the ice of the White Sea temporarily trapped all sixteen ships in Farson's convoy, and the crews and passengers waited nervously to see who would show up first, German submarines or a Russian icebreaker.

Eventually, the Russian ship arrived, throwing its pale-blue searchlight across the wide expanse of the jagged ice field and turning it into a blazing sapphire that Farson always remembered as the most startingly beautiful thing he had ever witnessed. During the voyage a rough storm sent a cabin boy skidding across the dining saloon on his bottom and knocked a large trunk off a shelf and squarely onto Farson's raw left shin bone, reopening the old wound. For the next four months in snowy and icy Russia, Farson had to wear shoes instead of boots due to the thick bandages now wrapped around his leg.

When he arrived in the newly built port of Molotovsk on Christmas Eve 1942, he felt as if he were on another planet, or in a concentration camp. The Soviets demanded papers, asked brusque questions, barked loud orders, and treated their allies, the American and British merchant mariners who had risked life and limb to bring them supplies, as enemies. Farson discovered that he was the only foreign correspondent to arrive on that particular convoy, and the Russians who greeted him railed against the perfidious intentions of the West. Farson in turn harped on the

Molotov-Ribbentrop Pact, which did nothing to improve their relationship. He was off to a bad start. After a brief party with members of the British diplomatic mission in Moscow, he took off for Kuybyshev (now Samara) to join the other foreign correspondents. He was finally able to crack the angry exterior of the Russians by sharing some of the two thousand Gold Flake cigarettes he had brought with him.

The trip to Samara took five days; all along the way Farson's train had to pull over onto sidings as other trains carrying entire factories hurried south. Farson marveled at the immensity of the war effort, which he considered totalitarianism at its best and worst. Everywhere, manpower substituted for machinery. Every log station along the rail route was guarded by civilians, usually women with rifles slung over their backs. Soviet soldiers patrolled the countryside on skis. Unlike the British, the Soviets didn't form committees when crisis came. They instead set to work. So Farson looked on admiringly as he watched a group of peasants felling pine trees along the railway to rebuild a bridge that German bombers had just obliterated.

But the reporting assignment was a nightmare, thanks to Soviet censorship and control on the one hand, and on the other, Farson's own ferocious attitude toward being censored and controlled. Officials wouldn't let the foreign correspondents anywhere near the front lines. The only gunfire they ever heard was German artillery as they pulled back from Borodino. At interminable press conferences, Soviet officials refused to say anything the reporters could use. Farson and the other correspondents were forced to listen to BBC broadcasts to get news about the war in the Soviet Union. (Presumably the BBC had gleaned its information from Allied officials.) Officials herded them from place to place—from Moscow to Samara and back, with a few other destinations in between—"like a troupe of trained apes."[1] Farson filed a few dispatches on the Russian homefront, but mostly he began to drink heavily once more. "One or two of us were so full of vodka most of the time (I know I was) that we scarcely saw Moscow," he recalled years later.[2] Journalist Walter Graebner, *Time* magazine's bureau chief in London before the war, confirmed Farson's account: foreign correspondents in Moscow, he recalled, were forced to search for scoops in the four Soviet newspapers available to them, *Red Star, Pravda, Izvestiya,* and *Komsomol Pravda;* every morning their "interpreter-secretaries" read the columns out loud to them. When the correspondents ate lunch together, which was every day at 2:00 p.m. in a private dining room at the Metropole, they spent much of the meal trying to discover what stories the others were working on. They weren't above planting false stories in the ears of their adversaries. Gloom hung over the correspondents in the hotel, according to Graebner:

> When anyone has a date with a girl, it's almost an item of news worthy of a cable. Except for three correspondents, there are no American or English girls in Moscow and most of the Russian girls are either at the front, in factories, or unavailable. Many evenings are therefore spent playing poker or chess. There's almost nothing to read: books, magazines and newspapers make a complete round of the correspondents' rooms.[3]

Though they all lived virtually identical, miserable lives, Graebner admired Farson's secretary—a "buxom, middle-aged woman known only as Sophiana"—as the most gifted interpreter of them all, calling her the Mother Superior and noting that she also had worked for novelist Erskine Caldwell when he came to the Soviet Union to work as a journalist, as well as for world-famous photographer Margaret Bourke-White.[4]

James McCargar, a young diplomat serving in Moscow after graduating from Stanford University, recalled that diplomats were unable to mix much with the local citizenry, so they socialized with the correspondents. McCargar got to know most of the American and British correspondents but remembered Farson only as "a sad case." He recalled: "When I was at Stanford I had read a book by Farson called Way of A Transgressor, which greatly impressed me. . . . Obviously, I was eager to meet him, but his colleagues in the news corps advised against it. Apparently he was in great pain from an incurable leg injury, did not want to see anyone, and drank heavily."[5] While the other correspondents gathered on a balcony of the Metropole Hotel outside the room of Harold King of Reuters, Farson lay in his room, drinking alone.

Farson's one trip to reach the front ended in disaster. In January 1942, a group of journalists left Moscow for Mozhaisk, sixty miles west of the capital, under escort by three officials from the press department and three Red Army officers. An official known to the reporters as the Goon commanded the convoy. When Farson and the other correspondents reached Mozhaisk, the Wehrmacht was a mere dozen miles to the west. Along the road to Mozhaisk, the correspondents had seen the wreckage of tanks and numerous crosses over freshly dug graves, signs that clashing armies had passed. The correspondents were herded into a schoolhouse for the night and assigned rooms, but they slept little, instead spending the hours drinking vodka and listening to the rumble of cannons in the distance. When they awoke the next morning, hungover, they drank vodka with their breakfast. Several correspondents declined to go any farther, saying they were now too tired, but Farson and several others agreed to press on toward the front. It was–20°F outside.

Farson bundled into an old automobile, without a heater, with fellow correspondents Eddy Gilmore of the Associated Press and Frederic McLoughlin of the *Sydney Morning Herald*. Soon after their departure, Gilmore noticed that Farson was "in bad shape." His face was blue, and when Gilmore asked him if he was alright, he couldn't respond. Gilmore had the driver stop the car, which in turn halted the entire convoy. After a press department official examined Farson and remarked that his nose had turned white, they decided to rush him back to the schoolhouse. Farson wisely did not object. Two men hauled him up and helped him toward a car that would take him back to Mozhaisk. But before they reached the car, Farson collapsed on the road. Gilmore, who later won a Pulitzer Prize for his 1946 interview of Stalin, recalled the incident in his memoir:

> We knew we had to act quickly to prevent him from freezing, and a press department censor named Skvartsov put action to thought. He dove under Negley's large and prone body to protect him from the ice and instructed us to lift.
>
> Farson weighed well over two hundred pounds. He was hard and muscular, and with all his clothes he was some bundle. But we got him into the car after a struggle, and muffled in blankets, he went off in the direction of Mozhaisk, a driver beside him.

From Mozhaisk, a car took the ailing Farson back to Moscow.

Despite the story's ignoble ending, Gilmore admired Farson's grit, noting that Farson was the oldest correspondent in the group and his injured leg was causing him obvious suffering. He was, Gilmore said, "a very brave fellow to have come along at all on such a cold day."[6]

Finally, Farson and the Soviet Union had had enough of each other. Unable to reach the front, he felt himself a fraud. When officials came to say all the foreign correspondents staying at the Metropole Hotel must go to Samara, he refused. He composed a cable to the *Daily Mail* telling them he was returning to London. He instructed the young woman who had been assigned to him as secretary to take the cable to the censor's office for approval, confident that she would also tell the NKVD, the precursor to the KGB. Immediately Farson sensed the Russians around him begin to treat him differently, as if he were defying Stalin personally. His food allotment was cut off. His secretary disappeared. When he went to the Intourist office to buy a train ticket to Murmansk, they backed away "as if I had just told them I had smallpox."[7] None of them wanted to get involved with a man heading for trouble.

Before he left Moscow (he did manage to get his ticket), a colleague agreed to leave the Soviet Union with him—McLoughlin of the *Sydney Morning Herald*. McLoughlin's trajectory was the same as Farson's: he had arrived in the Soviet Union in December 1941, encountered a bureaucracy that would not let him get close to the war, and steadily drank himself into a stupor. The two left together on the train to Murmansk. Halfway there, though, at an unnamed station, they were pulled off the train and held for what Farson called "the three worst days of my life."[8] The station sat at a junction of rail lines, and Farson sat and watched NKVD troops come and go on the various trains. Meanwhile, he overheard the NKVD official in charge of the station talking about him on the phone. He was convinced that somewhere, somebody was deciding his fate, and that fate could involve a quiet execution. He felt terror.

At last, though, the official gave them permission to continue, and they jumped aboard a train heading to Murmansk. There, they proceeded to drink one bottle and two decanters of vodka. Knowing that Soviet paperwork would hold them up, possibly for weeks, the next morning they secretly slipped aboard a small craft that carried them out to a convoy preparing to sail back to England. They boarded the *Temple Arch* and were underway. It was only in leaving Russia that Farson at last got his taste of war in the east. The Soviet air force gave the convoy no cover going out, and soon German bombers were attacking the merchant ships, diving at them relentlessly. A quarter of the ships were sunk. One of them, loaded with turpentine, went down in flames behind the *Temple Arch*. Ahead of it, the guns of the destroyer *Sabre* blazed away as bombs fell into the sea around her. Farson watched as a submarine torpedoed the ship opposite the *Temple Arch*. It sank in less than three minutes. Three bombs struck Farson's ship, though two failed to explode. Farson survived once more to tell the tale.

Unbelievably, the trip to Russia and back nearly cured Farson of his wanderlust. He was tired—the pigheaded Soviet bureaucrats had worn him down. The pain in his left leg was a constant irritant, as it had been most of his life, so he decided to let sunshine and salty air help him heal it. He sent the *Daily Mail* a bill for his expenses, which totaled 528 British pounds and included seventy nights in a hotel room in Moscow, then he and Eve traveled to north Devon to relax. Also, Farson needed quiet time for another project: he had agreed to write a film script for the actor Clive Brook, who had survived the silent film era to become one of Britain's most popular actors of the 1930s, playing Sherlock Holmes three times. Farson completed the script, titled "Blitz Hotel," but the project died. So too did the producer, who shot himself.

But the Farsons enjoyed their time in Devon. They rented a house off the beach at Woolacombe, and the two strolled some of the most beautiful shoreline they had ever seen. Walking along the sands of Putsborough, they repeatedly passed a little gray house built of local stone that they wished they could buy. A rickety set of wooden stairs connected the property to the beach, which ran from the rocks of Baggy Point on the southern end to the rocks of Morte Point to the north. Across the water, visible from the house's front window, lay Lundy Island, once the home of pirates. The Farsons longed for the home, and as luck would have it, a year later it went on the market. Its owner had died in Kenya, and his son wanted to sell the house to raise the money to pay the death taxes.

Farson bought the house from the proceeds of *Going Fishing*. When he and Eve moved in, he was outraged to find no evidence that the seller had ever owned or read a book. The walls were a dreadful chocolate brown. So, while Eve spent her time laying on coat after coat of fresh paint to hide the insult to color, Farson set up a work bench in the garage and built bookshelves out of Oregon pine planks that had washed ashore. The time spent in the garage he would later call some of the happiest days of his life. Living a life of quiet self-sufficiency on their two and a half acres, they both began to enjoy the solitude. It was if they had returned to Vancouver Island. From the narrow country lane that ran past the six houses along the beach, only the roof of the Grey House (their name for their home) was visible. The Farsons were the only inhabitants who lived in their house year-round, except for another writer, Henry Wilkinson, author of the children's classic *Tarka the Otter,* and his wife. But both couples holed up in their homes and sometimes didn't see or speak with each other for a month. After Wilkinson kicked Farson's dog, he would never again be invited in to visit. From the end of September until the end of May, Farson noticed that not a single footprint appeared on the little stretch of beach in front of his house, except those left by a lone coastguardsman on his dawn patrol. Sitting in his bed at dawn or on sleepless moonlit nights, Farson could stare straight out on the gray Atlantic. He confessed that it made him brood.

It wasn't all rest and relaxation and a slow sinking into retirement, however. Farson was a world-renowned foreign correspondent, and he had no desire to move to a remote coastal village simply to become a sun-dial in the shade. He signed a freelance contract with the *Daily Mail,* and he continued to write stories for it during the war. From the comfort of his writing office, he penned dispatches on how things were going in the Scandinavian countries, on South Africa's aid to the Commonwealth's war cause, and on other British outposts in Africa and India. He acquired grist for his articles by listening nearly nonstop to the radio, spinning the dials all day when the Russians crossed the Dnieper. Additionally, he wrote political commentary for the Central Press, which distributed his work to Britain's smaller, regional newspapers, and contributed to the *Sunday Empire News.* He also continued writing for magazines, as he had since leaving newspapers a decade earlier. His contributions often appeared in journals such as *Britannia & Eve* magazine, the *Sphere,* the *Sketch,* and *Men Only.* The latter, in fact, published an anthology of Farson's shorter stories under the title *Men of the World.* In the pages of the various publications he repeatedly rehashed his life's adventures. All in all, with the closest pub three miles away in the village of Georgeham, Farson felt he worked harder than he would have if he had been given a desk in Fleet

Street. Still, he worked only in the mornings, then spent the afternoons planting fruit trees, pine, and birch, and creating a dense copse so that he and Eve could watch the birds nesting in the branches. The coast guard in nearby Croyde, meanwhile, held annual boating competitions for the Negley Farson Cup (named in his honor by Farson's sailing neighbors), and officials asked Farson to present it to the winning crew.

Finally, the war ended. Quietly, for the Farsons in their little home on the far western coast of England. There was no big celebration. Daniel returned from Canada, arriving on a Sunday at his grandmother's house in Pelham Place. "I scarcely recognized my mother, a fat woman with her fingernails bitten down to raw stumps," Daniel recalled. He heard his grandmother whisper to his mother, "Too bad on Danny's first night home." "I knew this referred to my father who was out drinking," Daniel wrote, "but that was what I expected and I loved him drunk or sober."[9]

In the years following the war, Farson tramped off to the downs behind his house with a gun to shoot rabbits and partridge. He rented shooting rights from a couple of farms along the Taw River to expand his hunting territory, and often went looking for ducks with a Welshman. Thus, he learned that his hearing had gotten so bad that he could no longer hear the beating of the duck wings, a skill that had, in his youth, enabled him to successfully shoot at the sound of the birds in the darkened sky. A doctor opined that the hearing loss was due to his overdosing on the sulfa drugs he had taken to fight malaria in Africa. Farson watched the curlews fly over his house every morning from the sands and was saddened that he could no longer hear their mournful cry. After a morning of listening to the radio and writing articles and an afternoon spent fishing or hunting or working in his ever-expanding garden, Farson used his evenings to reread the books he loved the most: the Russians. Tolstoy, Dostoyevsky, Pushkin, Chekhov, Turgenev, Gogol, and Gorky—Farson found himself drawn to them after listening to war news from Russia. Throughout his days as a journalist, they had been his companions. He carried their books with him in train compartments, foreign hotels, customs houses, and censors' offices. When he was sober and not fishing, he reread them.

The tranquility had done nothing to abate his thirst for liquor, however. The life of solitude also meant great stretches of boredom; boredom meant a turn to the bottle. Trips to the more exciting life of London ended in disaster. On the train ride to the capital, Farson sat in the dining car, watched the clouds roll over the green hills of the West Country, and drank one gin after another. By the time he reached Waterloo station he was too drunk to enjoy the theater or the company of friends whom he had longed for.

The potential for ample fishing—Farson's go-to antidote to drink—was one of the reasons he moved to the shore. At last, he thought, he would live somewhere where he could grab his fishing rod and tumble straight out his front door to the ocean. But for once, the fish defeated Farson: for two straight years he fished the ocean in front of his home, night and day and with every turn of the tide, but he caught nothing. Bells of dismay tolled within his spirit. His drinking, which was already setting a furious pace, increased. He became convinced that had he only had a little success surf-casting, he would not have turned so hard to the bottle. Twice he traveled to Norway in the hope of wading in its pure streams and fishing for trout. But that too became a sad joke and offered no respite from alcohol. He went on drinking binges that left him unable to stand in the rushing Scandinavian waters.

At last, in 1947, he decided to seek help once more: He traveled to Switzerland and checked into an asylum outside Bern. The institution, the biggest of its kind in the country, housed nine hundred patients, mostly schizophrenics. When Farson saw the tenderness and kindness with which they were treated by the staff, he forgot that he was a patient himself. When anyone reminded him, he became ashamed and admitted that he had caused his own problems, whereas those suffering around him were the victims of psychological forces beyond their control. The asylum was surrounded by a large farm, and the patients tended the flowers and sent baskets of them to Bern. Farson loved to stroll to the dairy at sunset and stand behind the large Swiss cattle and soak up the smell of the animals and fresh hay. He was ready to begin work on his final novel, *The Sons of Noah,* in the asylum. But the doctors had little success with his alcoholism. At last, one of them told Farson: "Keep your conflicts. The best thing for you is not to be normal. A normal man is a mediocre man."[10] Farson returned to England. But not for long.

22
→•←
Back to Africa

WHEN FARSON LEFT THE earthquake-devastated town of Accra on the British Gold Coast (now Ghana) in 1939, shivering from malaria, angry at his wife, bowed by the heat, he had vowed to never leave another footprint in Africa. By 1947, however, he had changed his mind. He and Eve flew to Kenya at the request of British governor Sir Philip Mitchell, who had been dismayed at the scant attention paid to the country in *Behind God's Back*. Farson agreed to investigate the complex problems facing the British colony, beset by racial animosity, violent religious cults, overgrazing, erosion, the tsetse fly, drought, and famine. The governor told him: "Go where you like, see what you like, say what you like. I imagine you will want to be rude about many things."[1] Farson responded gleefully in the resultant book, *Last Chance in Africa*, published in October 1949: "I have taken him at his word."[2]

He spent four months in Kenya, interviewed white colonizers, native leaders, and colonial administrators, and he detailed the rapacity of some settlers and the heroics of others. Though he didn't hunt in the country, he fished for trout under the gaze of the Mau Maus, who had revolted against the white man's effort to "civilize" them. He lunched with Danish author Baroness Karen von Blixen-Finecke, whose 1937 memoir of her seventeen years in Kenya, *Out of Africa,* he admired. He met with the great and the small, with Jomo Kenyatta, who would found Kenya as a nation years later, and with poor Kikuyu women bent almost double under impossible loads of bananas, wood, or manioc, and their babies perched on top. Farson's travels, mostly by car, took him to all corners of the country—to its volcanic mountains and torrid deserts, plains, and jungles—where he camped under African skies and talked, smoked, drank, and wrote. The campfire talks he took part in, and enjoyed, were liturgies that summoned men to put themselves right with nature and their fellow men, he concluded: "I have heard talk around fires such as ours . . . that the same men just would not dare to go in for in any convention-ridden city. They would have felt ashamed of themselves. Yet you will always look back on these talks, because they came so miraculously near the truth of life."[3]

Kenya's governor had also asked the writer Elspeth Huxley's mother, Nellie Grant, to house the Farsons on her farm for Christmas, and while she agreed, she had mixed feelings: her daughter was working on her own book about Kenya, *The Sorcerer's Apprentice*. Both mother and daughter felt that the governor had wronged Huxley with his invitation to Farson. Grant was polite to the Farsons but over several days insisted that Farson read Huxley's *Red Strangers* and *White Man's Country*, her goal being to slow Farson's writing down while her daughter worked on her own book, and to "dishearten" Farson by exposing him to Huxley's superior talent. Grant reported to her daughter that her scheme seemed to be succeeding: Farson read Huxley's books out loud at breakfast and lunch and appeared to become depressed.[4]

Still, the Farsons left Grant's home on good terms, and Farson later described her in warm tones. Eve may have inadvertently exacted a revenge of sorts: in the New Year, Farson began boozing hard, supposedly drinking the Nairobi Club dry, and Eve imposed upon Grant to shelter them once more while he fought against writer's block.

Farson had returned to Kenya to write a book for money. The mercenary nature of his task showed in the completed book, which read in some parts like a dissertation, like a farm bureau report in others. He became repetitive and at times surprisingly tin-eared. He copied dry governmental reports, including one titled *Report of the Taxation Committee, Kenya, 1947*, and another on soil fertility that ran on for four tedious pages.

Farson held conflicting views on the morality of colonizing Africa—a political and economic strategy still popular in the 1940s. Since the 1500s, Europeans and especially those in England viewed the European example of hard work, education, and Christian ethics as the savior of savage

Africa. Farson wasn't particularly impressed by the European example, and he characterized colonialism as a mere "money-making business . . . shot through with unctuousness and hypocrisy."[5] The white man's burden of saving Black Africans usually ended up on the Black man's back, he concluded. Colonialism had turned Africa into a great factory to supply Europe with its dainty needs—tea, soap, cotton, bananas—and the continent be damned. He noted, bitterly, that the Abyssinians trapped leopards to near extinction for their lovely spotted coats, sold to drape the shoulders of fashionable women in New York City. "And in this new age we should see that the black man has every right to live a full life irrespective of the pigment of his skin—and not be made to feel an outsider even in his own country, as he unquestionably is to-day," Farson wrote in a missive that was bold for its day, though now perhaps paternalistic.[6]

Farson loved Kenya, which he called the loveliest country on earth. Yet his eyes widened in dismay when he landed at Victoria Nyanza and saw a group of Sudanese dressed as Englishmen in shorts, khaki stockings, and pith helmets. He preferred Africans to be authentic and "primitive." His excursion in Kenya began with tea and coffee with the sultan of Zanzibar, followed by a safari through the game plains and into Tanganyika, then a trip through the lava beds of the Somali desert to the frontier of Abyssinia (Ethiopia), where Eve came down with malaria. Her fever reached 105 degrees and lasted two days.

The most stirring moments for Farson were those when he sat around campfires or on a veld in the shade of acacia trees, and the best parts of Last Chance in Africa surface far from officialdom and meetings over tea or gin. The highlight, at least for Farson, involved fishing. Early in his visit he broke from his ponderous dissection of colonial politics to fly-fish for trout. Kenya offered the best trout fishing in Africa. He summed up his experience: "To fish in forests of bamboo or wild fig and olive, under the darkness of giant podo trees, to see that startling beautiful sight of hundreds of little golden weaver birds shoot into their hanging nests over a pool you are fishing, or a white-breasted fishing eagle shining in the sun—yes, even to feel shortness of breath, as you wade, say, at 7,500 feet, up towards the bronze-blue rocks of a mountain towering above you—these are all part of the delight of handling a rod on any Kenya stream."[7] Eve fished with him.

They fished the Thika, a rainbow trout river high in the mountains that supplied Nairobi with water. Hippos and crocodiles swam in its deeper waters, leopards prowled its banks. Farson caught seven browns and one rainbow fishing upstream, dragging a wet fly slow and deep. Fishing the fast-flowing, gin-clear waters of the Southern Mathioya, he crawled on his hands and knees to the tail of a pool, casting a weighted fly to sink slowly to the bottom, where the feeding rainbows faced upstream. He hooked a heavy brown. The trout flashed down the stream and rubbed against the bank in a fury to loosen the fly. Farson reeled him in—his scarlet and silver spots iridescent in the sun.

Farson lost another brown—a huge one, he claimed—that he had fought for fifteen minutes under a crescent moon. Yes, Farson was now night fishing, a sure sign of a fanatical, big-fish fisherman. The biggest trout, the smartest fish, the cannibals feed only at night, and only the most impassioned fishermen go out looking for fish by moonlight. A gillie stabbing at the trout that lay gasping in the water on its side clumsily scraped the fly from the brown's lip, setting it free as Farson looked on helplessly. But, like any veteran of the stream, he knew how to handle the agony of the lost trophy trout, the one that flips its huge tail fin and rockets away into the depths. "It is always well to leave some regrets—a fish that will haunt you and make you ache to go back to that river again," Farson mused. "If you caught every fish you hooked, why, there would not be any fun in fishing at all."[8]

Farson, the hunter, the outdoorsman, also realized a startling change in himself—his desire to kill things had almost vanished. He still liked to pot a duck or goose for the table, but he carried no rifle in Kenya this time around. Kenya abounded in a stunning array of beasts, some dangerous and all beautiful to Farson's eyes. Yet Farson continued to sympathize with the hunter's atavistic impulse, despite losing the urge himself. He argued that there was something "aesthetic" about the hunt.

His machismo—seldom evident in his writing—bubbled to the surface in his musing over hunting African game. He believed that wounding a lion or buffalo tested a man—that a real man would track the dangerous beasts through tall grass or thick bush no matter the peril; a coward would abandon the animal and return to camp. And that danger, the chance that a pain-enraged lion waited in the brush to hunt the hunter, added spice to the adventure. "There is the ultimate thrill of making yourself experience danger," he said, "for no man tastes life unless he puts it in the balance."[9]

The forest and jungles, the plains and deserts, mountains and rivers always proved an anchor, or perhaps a lighthouse, for Farson the incurable wanderer. His eyes opened wide in wild places, allowing him to distill the experience in straightforward prose. Farson traveled without Eve to join the Somali nomads in the brutal desert where even the camels barely survived, emaciated and dejected, from lack of food and water. Farson noticed roosters were kept, not to be eaten, but to crow at dawn so the men could pray to Allah. At one set of wells he saw more than ten thousand camels, their hoarse cries for water almost deafening him. He found the trip the toughest of his life because of the high altitudes and the heat of the inhospitable desert. He continued to drink heavily throughout the journey. In Kenya's northern frontier, a land of volcanic desert, he reproached himself after repeatedly waking up drunk from a night of "grisly dreams" every quarter hour.[10] He had reached, he realized, "the age where I loathe myself for taking too much drink."[11]

On a foot safari from a camp outside Wajir in northeast Kenya, Farson noticed how the nomadic Somalis drew water from their ancient limestone wells—cut with astonishing precision by hand—by passing buckets made from giraffe hides from person to person. Giraffes made the best buckets because their hide was a half inch thick. Farson called such romantic sights the "real Africa":

If I have talked a great deal about the drama of Somali nomadic camel life, the chanting of the five-and twelve-man wells, the weird sensation of hearing singing far out beneath our feet at the eighteen-man dog-leg well at Buna, the sensation of seeing secretive Somalis passing you in the bush at night like grey ghosts under the stars, if I have talked of the dignity and the cruelty and the toughness of Somali life, and of that almost insane self-respect that seems to possess all desert-living Mohammedans, it is not that I have stressed these thing because of the mere picturesqueness of Somali life. It is because you get a sense of rhythm from them. Our own lives, those of the Europeans, have lost that sense of rhythm—that you are living in accord with some incorporeal *rightness* of things—even in the free lives which many white men still manage to make for themselves in changing Africa. But the Somalis still have it; and as you witness it, you feel that it is a life that should be perpetuated.[12]

The *New York Times* lavished praise on the four-hundred-page book Farson eventually wrote, titled *Last Chance in Africa*. In his review of May 5, 1950, Orville Prescott called it "an extraordinarily lively and well-written book about one of the most interesting spots on earth, Kenya Colony on the African east coast. The combination is a good one, a first-rate reporter with tireless energy and insatiable curiosity and a wildly dramatic country which has received little attention from journalists."[13] A second reviewer for the *New York Times* followed up the first review two days later, claiming that the "detailed, intelligent study of Kenya is by far the most valuable book Mr. Farson has yet written."[14]

Other critics panned *Last Chance in Africa*, dismissing it as a volume written at the request of the governor (and therefore suspect in its conclusions), too fat with dry facts and statistics, and too lean when it came to the lively impressions for which Farson had become famous. *Kirkus Reviews*, however, opined that Farson's "four months journeying through deserts, fertile plateaus, jungle and settlements" had resulted in a book that would probe the British conscience.[15] Farson had indeed used the book as a bully pulpit from which to sound off on colonialism and his strong opposition to the widely accepted notion that "primitive" people needed civilizing—especially by Englishmen.

But perhaps the writer Elspeth Huxley most trenchantly summed up Farson's quixotic view of Africa. Rather than focusing on his prescription for a happier Africa, she detected a whiff of upper-crust nostalgia in his prose: "The truth is that he is a romantic looking to a golden age in the past when virile naked warriors roamed the plains and bronzed, hard-bitten pioneers drove away the lions from the first crop of mealies. Even the Happy Valley set of socialite spivs is glamorized. One reads with a faint lift of the eyebrow of men who lay under a tree with a bottle of iced champagne in one hand and a copy of Horace in the other."[16]

The Kenyan government chartered a three-seater plane to fly the Farsons from Zanzibar to Mombasa to catch a plane back to England. They would never return to Africa.

Back at home in Devon, Farson got down to work, and he had plenty to keep him busy. When he wasn't typing up the manuscript for *Last Chance in Africa,* he was putting the finishing touches on his fourth and final novel, *Sons of Noah.* It was his best. Gollancz, who gave him an advance of one thousand British pounds, must have been relieved at the quality. For while there were critics who found reasons to not like the book, overall it was a mature work, with none of the political, polemical tirades that had slowed *The Story of a Lake*'s otherwise brisk pace and energetic story line. Farson's passion for his material shined brightly. Much of the action of the book takes place on boats, in waterways familiar to Farson: the Delaware Bay, the Chesapeake, and myriad streams and harbors. Dialogue, plot exposition, narration—so much of it occurs while the protagonists are hoisting sails, tying down cargo, standing at the wheel while the cold spray drenched their faces, or struggling to light a Primus stove before taking over the night watch. The book, set in the 1920s, reads as if Farson were daydreaming about the life he yearned for.

The narrator of the book, Richard Fenner, is a stand-in for Farson, a newspaperman who is weary of his work. He has been a foreign correspondent in Europe and has lived a glamorous, cosmopolitan life, even enjoying rambling conversations with Hemingway in Paris. But the constant churn of diplomats and statesmen has worn him down; he is now at work on writing a book about the United States titled *Created Equal* (the same title as Farson's aborted book on the American South). Fenner is also passionate about boats, especially the bugeyes that ply the oyster beds along the Maryland shore. Fenner's other passions, in addition to boats and oysters, are ducks, fens, marshes, creeks, and the assortment of colorful characters who inhabit the little ramshackle homes in various harbors. A second male character, Dr. Caspar Greer, is also a stand-in for Farson: He not only loves boats, he lives upon one. The circumstance that drove him to a life upon water, a doomed love affair, provides the thin but serviceable plotline that allows Greer and Fenner to be thrown together often. In the end, their tangled lives reach their inevitable destinations, but not before Farson has painted the Delaware and Chesapeake Bays with thousands of words, educated readers on the convoluted nomenclature of sailing, and excoriated the breakneck pace of modern life with its never-satisfied hunger for material wealth. The book received generally favorable reviews. The BBC called it a "gripping story" and a "masculine book,"[17] while the British publication *Punch* opined that the "boats in this book are as alive as the humans, and that is saying much."[18] The *New York Times*, however, was unforgiving and called the characters dead, the dialogue banal, and the narrative undistinguished.[19] Did Farson care? Probably not. He is not known to have ever said a single kind word about his own fiction. Additionally, he had already cashed the thousand-pound check from Gollancz.

23

→ • ←

Road's End

THE YEAR 1950 KICKED off Farson's final decade—a decade full of misery and a few surprising successes—and Farson greeted it by once more essaying a cure for his alcoholism, this one at an asylum in Denmark. There, he met a young nurse who became infatuated with him. When he returned to England, she pursued him with letters, and with Eve's unintended approval he called her to Devon, where she moved in with them in 1954.

She slept in a sleeping bag on the floor but often entered Farson's room in the dead of night and lay down at the foot of his bed. During the day she sat in the room for hours, never saying a word. While Farson tried to assure his wife that there was no hanky-panky afoot behind his closed bedroom door, Eve and Daniel wondered. They were baffled: Daniel considered the young woman "not at all smart" and not pretty,[1] while Eve confided in her diary that Farson had brought home a "bull-doggy little schoolgirl" who was possibly a mental case.[2]

Eve eventually concluded that Farson had foolishly fallen in love and was having another affair. The thought devastated her. "It is horribly cowardly & self-pitying to keep thinking of suicide—but when I look at the sea I can't help thinking how easy it would be to rush out into those clean icy waves and finish it all," she wrote in her diary on January 27, 1954. "This spring of love for Negley that . . . always makes me say and do the wrong thing is tearing me to pieces. Far better really just to leave him—but I can't face being without him while we both live."

The young woman eventually left. "Did he have an affair with Miss Svenson?" Daniel later asked, using his made-up name for the girl. "I should have thought so if I had not met her. Probably it was a yearning for one more new horizon."[3]

Earlier in the decade, Farson compiled the notes that he had penned along the Russian rivers and in the mountains during his long-ago horseback ride through the Caucasus with the eccentric old Englishman Alexander Wicksteed. The short articles he had written about the journey for the *Chicago Daily News* had already appeared in book form, comprising the back half of the book *Black Bread and Red Coffins*. The book appealed to a few critics, but readers had not embraced it as warmly. That was in 1930.

Now, two decades later, Farson's thoughts turned more frequently to Russia, to the Caucasus more specifically, as he read news accounts of Stalin's brutal deportation of whole tribes from their homes in the Caucasus to the wastelands of Siberia. The Chechens, the Ingush, the Balkars—all of them suffered from Stalin's policy of collectivization and forced removal. So, in his home in Devon, on the quiet shore of the Irish Sea, Farson gathered his notes and began typing out anew the tale of his journey. Against a backdrop of desolate beauty, he detailed the hardships of the trip, the comical behavior of his companion, and the dignity of the horsemen and tribes he had encountered all those years ago. The travelogue, titled *Caucasian Journey,* not even 175 pages, appeared in 1951; it has since become generally recognized as a classic of the genre. The *Guardian* called it one of the "supreme specimens of the adventure book, packed with thrills and spills and wonders."[4] Like *Going Fishing,* it has known multiple editions and multiple publishers, starting with Evans Brothers Publishing in 1951, Penguin Books in 1988, and Long Riders' Guild Press in 2001. The edition that Doubleday Books issued drew one of the best reviews Farson ever received—for any of his books. It appeared in the *New York Times* on April 13, 1958: "In this calm, nostalgic book, Farson has fulfilled the promise of 'The Way of a Transgressor.' It is the book of an adventurer written when the days of adventure are over, and the best he has ever written—the warmest, the most human, the one which sings with the clearest note of music."[5] What Evans Brothers Publishing paid Farson for the work is unknown, but whatever the sum, it was a testament that Farson could still cast his line out into the deep lake of his years as a newspaperman and reel in enough money to keep him in comfort, liquor, and cigarettes.

But the decade was not calm seas and smooth sailing. In early 1951, he took his last trip to an asylum in a feeble effort to cure his alcoholism. The asylum was in England, not too far from his Devon home, and he was never sure afterward how he had arrived there. He had gotten blindingly drunk in London and apparently humiliated himself in public. Soon after he woke up on a low-slung bed—the mattress was no more than a foot off the floor—surrounded by two doctors and a head nurse. In the corner of the room sat a man in a worn camel-hair dressing gown. The stranger rushed over to shake Farson's hand, and Farson was conscious enough to recognize that the stranger was an admirer. Farson's treatment involved a series of insulin shots (it was much worse for his new friend: he was the beneficiary of electroshock therapy). In the end, though, the treatment did little good. Just as the doctor in Switzerland had told Farson to keep his conflicts, the English psychologist now treating him opined, "The one thing that will ever make you stop drinking is your own common sense."[6]

One night in the asylum—which Farson called his "private looney-bin" in a letter to his publisher, Gollancz[7]—Farson awoke to find an Australian inmate hiding under his bed. The laugh it gave him, Farson recalled, was the first real laugh he'd had in years. Farson left the asylum in an upbeat mood and with good intentions, convinced that the psychologist's comment about common sense was a revelation, a profundity that, if he merely worked hard to keep it in mind, would help him stay sober.

But failing health and a complete and total surrender to booze dominated the end of his life. His unchecked alcoholism—for he could not and would not give it up—exacerbated his grim condition. He drank, then he and Eve fought, and he invariably aired what Eve called "the old grievances"[8]—mainly odd and unsorted complaints about her family. Eve noted the turmoil in the few diary entries that survive from the decade. Typical entries depict Farson sitting alone in cafés drinking sherry after sherry and her attempts to beg embarrassed friends to help her carry him to bed. She sought refuge in gardening, in entertaining neighbors, in driving into nearby Barnstable or Ilfracombe to see a movie. But Farson was often eager to catch a ride with her, to be dropped off at some pub (the Foxhunters Inn in Ilfracombe was a favorite), and that meant Eve had to collect him after the movie and bring him safely home. There, he emptied the cupboards in search of alcohol and occasionally drank up her cooking sherry. Once she came home and was surprised to find him drunk: he had happily found a forgotten bottle in an old suitcase.

But Farson, heroically, could still be productive. He published his second memoir, *Mirror for Narcissus*, in 1956. Gollancz gave him an advance of one thousand British pounds, along with the usual royalty rates. The book picked up where *The Way of a Transgressor* left off, beginning with Farson's departure from newspapering, then moving in quick succession to his trips to South America and Africa, the war years, and his return to Russia, ending with his move to rural Devon and his tranquil life by the sea with his wife and sundry cats. But more than a mere recitation, Farson dwelt on his alcoholism and offered readers an eyewitness account of the several treatment facilities he had enrolled in, his shameful and often public drunkenness, the guilt and remorse he carried within him through life. It was all a little fuzzy, with hints and suggestions of abominable behavior appearing between the lines, but it was a confession, nonetheless. Admittedly, the chapters of his life were decidedly lacking in epiphanies, but that's because he had found his truth early on, that life was not about earning money or holding onto a steady job—to really live meant doing things you hadn't done before, seeing new places, meeting new people; it was in experiencing as much as you could in whatever time you had, not as a mere bystander or bon viveur, but as a curious surveyor of difficult terrains and unfamiliar cultures. To experience life that way was always Farson's goal, and his book was a robust collection of such experiences.

As with almost all his books, critical reaction to *Mirror for Narcissus* was positive, even ecstatic in some quarters. The *Sunday Times* called it "irresistibly readable" and "splendidly told," and added that it "reveals a man packed full with rich and varied experiences, enough to fill a dozen lives."[9] The *Times Literary Supplement* was more conservative in estimating Farson's lives, calling him a "man who has packed five lives into one." But the review, which ran on June 22, 1956, was generous:

It is the restlessness of the frontiersman that is deep in Mr. Farson's blood: an American type of frontiersman, the type of Lewis and Clark. Plus, and it is a plus which greatly matters, an extraordinary sensitivity to natural beauty, and an extraordinary gift for direct communication. Plus also a capacity far beyond the ordinary for taking physical punishment, almost a pride in seeking physical punishment, coupled with a capacity for self analysis, a searching of the interior frontiers for the self which may run but cannot hid. Contrariwise, plus ever an outward-looking feeling for the oppressed, the underdogs. Plus—not to be forgotten in summing up Mr. Farson's work—the evidence of first-class ability.[10]

Kirkus Reviews was equally effusive: "Bouts—blackouts—hangovers— one gets a bit saturated and disgusted. Then suddenly the magic of a pen that always spins a yarn picks one up again. Negley Farson lost successive jobs; tried successive cures; always seemed to be at strategic spots to get yet another story. The eternal journalist operated through the bouts and the blackouts and the hangovers. Sometimes the stories suffered; sometimes he let his audiences down; usually he came through."[11] The modesty in the review's assessment of Farson's career, coupled with its unabashed admiration, might have amused him, for he admired the achievements of other journalists while laughing at the ludicrous nature of the profession itself.

But not all the reviews were good. Some critics found the close-up view of drunkenness too much to take. The *Washington Post,* for example, gave its reviewer a mere five paragraphs, five paragraphs in which he compared the book unfavorably to its predecessor—*Mirror* was less absorbing, the reviewer noted—while all the talk of booze and blackouts and failed vows to stay sober became a drag: "His bout with the bottle, treated lightly in the earlier book, becomes an agonizing clinical analysis here."[12] Perhaps the summary headline atop the review in the *Buffalo Courier-Express* summed it up best: "Author Deplores Ways of Self, All Human Race."[13]

Overall, the 1950s were the decade in which the bill for Farson's years of hard living came due. Though there were occasional trips to the continent— Italy, Portugal, Spain, France—and to the Scandinavian countries (where Farson's books were popular, and one restaurant had even named a dish for him), the letters and journal entries from his final decade make it clear that the price was indeed steep. By the end of his life, he estimated he had spent more than five and a half years of his time on earth in a hospital bed or otherwise recuperating, and he had undergone twenty-eight operations on his leg, each one of which, he grumbled, only made his condition worse. Whole months over a succession of years in the 1950s were spent convalescing—from pneumonia, shortness of breath, and simple tiredness. Farson vowed to give up cigarettes too many times to count, only to light up once more. His doctor pleaded with him to stop drinking. To no avail. He always found his way back to what Eve called the "inevitable bottle."[14]

Some relief arrived in the form of guests. Over their decades of traveling and living in London, the Farsons had made hundreds of friends and accumulated just as many colleagues. Now those friends periodically descended on Devon to spend a few hours at Grey House. Eve delighted in their company, and they in turn leaned in to let Farson regale them with his tales. One such visitor, writer and broadaster Ludovic Kennedy, stayed with the Farsons in the spring of 1958 and chronicled what must have been a commonplace conversation with Farson:

> He sat in the sun like some huge old lion, the wind gently ruffling his mane.
>
> He was wearing a sort of brown windcheater and scarf, and he talked with the gaiety and abandon of an undergrad.
>
> He spoke of Alan Moorehead's descriptions of the Russian Revolution ("Not as good as they ought to be"), of the huge trout he had caught in a river in Norway, of Germany just before the war, of Lenin at the ballet, of Lake Cowichan in Canada where for two years his rod had kept him alive . . . , of Colin Wilson (a frequent name in the visitors' book), of Liberalism, of almost everything under the sun.
>
> There was something of Winston Churchill about him, something of Ernest Hemingway, something of Lionel Barrymore.
>
> He is 68 and age has not wearied him nor alcohol condemned. My God, I thought, what a tough old bird you are.[15]

Farson relished the opportunity to revel in past adventures—he often found his neighborhood too isolated and dull for words—but only for short periods of time. The frequency of guest arrivals, and the necessity to make sure their stays were short, prompted Farson to post a list of wry house commandments:

Negley Farson's rules for houseguests.

1. Put the Radio Times [Britain's version of *TV Guide*] on the table before placing the tea tray on it.
2. Keep the saucer holding the saccharin on top of the milk jug, do not put it on the table. The fact that no one can get at the milk has nothing to do with it.
3. Give me a cigarette.
4. Do not throw wood on the fire, it might break the fire-brick. It's no concern if you burn your fingers doing it.
5. Keep your great horse's ass off *The Daily Mail*. Apart from wanting to read it, I write for it.
6. If I'm reading *The Times*, you can read yesterday's. And don't grumble.
7. Give me a cigarette.
8. I like having guests around for half an hour after breakfast, one minute after lunch, and for a few minutes after dinner. What d'you think we built that room for?
9. Deck chairs must be folded a certain way, and put against the wall at a certain angle. Please listen to my orders when doing this, which may last longer than you expect. There's only one Master here.
10. If I suggest you walk down the steps to the beach, that means you have stayed long enough. There's a hole in the steps half way down, and we have got rid of quite a lot of guests that way.
11. Give me a cigarette.

Though Farson could see that his smoking and drinking were killing him, he no longer had the willpower to take another tack. He was sailing into a strong wind, unable to reach safe harbor. "I am sorry to say his leg has got very much worse lately and is really painful now," Eve wrote to Gollancz in February 1953. "Doc wants Negley in hospital but 'he won't go!' Says there are too few survivors from British hospitals."[16] Several years later, after Farson had once again vowed to stop drinking, she fretted to Gollancz that Farson would use a planned trip to London as an excuse to fall off the wagon. "Negley is genuinely most anxious and determined not to drink, but you and I know what London, plus that long train journey, always does to him, and I must say I feel worried about it," she wrote to Gollancz on August 1, 1957.[17]

In another letter to Gollancz, dated July 26, 1958, Eve said the family doctor had told Farson it was now imperative for him to live at least four months out of the year in a warmer, drier client. Farson's lungs were failing. Farson, meanwhile, wrestled with occasional bouts of complete immobility. The effort to walk was too much. This for the man who had pulled a boat over a mountain range in Europe, for the man who had climbed the high Caucasus Mountains, for the man who had limped seventeen miles to kill a buffalo. With the doctor's urgent advice in hand, the Farsons considered moving to Greece, or to the south of France, or to Portugal.

But in the end they decided to stay put. Instead of moving, they took a small holiday in Spain and France in 1959. Sadly, Farson spent whole afternoons sitting in cafés, drinking whatever whisky was available, and growing increasingly argumentative. It was to be Farson's last trip. To call it an adventure would be bitter irony—he was merely a tourist, and a surly, ungrateful one at that.

Back home in Devon, Farson settled into the comfort of his small home on the coast, but though he would go no more a 'roving, he was optimistic. In one of his periodic letters to Leland Stowe, he confided that he knew he had emphysema but noted that so had Dostoyevsky, who in spite of his terminal condition wrote *The Brothers Karamazov.* "I am going to do exactly the same thing," Farson wrote.[18] Though he felt no rush: Doubleday was bringing out its version of *Caucasian Journey* on March 3, 1958, and that, Farson told his Pulitzer-winning friend Leland Stowe, would buy him at least two more years before he would feel compelled to deliver another book. Likewise he gave Gollancz one of his periodic status reports—with a promise of a new book, eventually—in a letter dated July 21, 1959. After admitting that he had been "desperately ill" the previous year, he offered a small insight into his life with Eve and alcohol, and the necessity of penning another book:

If it hadn't been for Eve—and the companionship we've had from being all over the world together: bad times and good—I would be out of this place by the next train. Life down here is a veritable mental desert: no one to talk to, except some mouldy colonels, etc., . . . and the awful emptiness of feeling so out of things. That, I suppose, is one of the penalties one pays for having so much enjoyed a roving correspondent's life: we feel somewhat dead when we pull off the road. I have tried to kill this mental loneliness with periodic bouts of drink—but (and God be praised) I saw long ago—though I have not always acted on it—that I get melancholia and become defeatist with every drop. . . . Hence, I may say to you, quite honestly, I—who have been very near a nervous breakdown—now see that my only way out lies inside myself—my own mind—in other words: writing. This will be my salvation.[19]

Farson added that he was already at work on another book—in the mental, planning stage, anyway—and this one would be his best ever. Moreover, Farson confided, Doubleday had been in touch and was interested in a novel he was working on titled *The Tides of Barnegut*.

The books never materialized, of course. And his condition worsened. "He is terribly exhausted," Eve confided to Gollancz on March 25, 1960, "and his voice has about gone but his spirit is quite indomitable. Each time I go in he says, 'I'm better.' 'I'm stronger than yesterday,' but actually he is slipping downhill fast." Farson had lost twenty-eight pounds since Christmas, she added.[20]

On December 13, 1960, the Reuters news agency filed a story that almost instantly traveled across the worldwide web of telephone wires and undersea cables. In radio, television, and newspaper newsrooms across the globe, curious editors picked up the paper spilling out of their Teletype machines and read the opening line: "Farson, Globe Trotting Newsman, Author, Dies." A few crisp paragraphs followed:

EXETER, England, Dec. 13 [Reuters]—Negley Farson, 70, an American born adventure loving writer who trotted the globe in pursuit of news stories and novels, died in his home near here yesterday.

Farson, a native of Plainfield, N.J., ranged from czarist Russia thru the middle east and Asia as a business man, flyer, foreign correspondent, and author. . . . [21]

The following day, December 14, in an obituary that ran the full length of the left-hand column of page 35, the *New York Times* announced the death of James Scott Negley Farson with a bit more flair. The headline read, "Ex-Reporter in Britain for *Chicago Daily News* Wrote of World-Wide

Adventures."[22] Though the obituary did not treat as a miracle the fact that Farson had managed to survive seven decades—despite the fact that he had suffered multiple injuries, smoked several packs of cigarettes a day, and drank more alcohol than water—it laid out the highlights of his life in such a way that his longevity must have seemed divine providence to the newspaper's readers. "Mr. Farson was a classic example of the glamorous movie foreign correspondent to whom everything seemed to happen, but who always emerged with his story and most of his skin intact," the writer noted.[23] The obituary then quoted from the review of *Way of a Transgressor* that R. L. Duffus had written twenty-four years earlier: "He attracted thrilling and high-colored experience as a light attracts moths. Some of his success, no doubt, was luck. Most of it was due to his passionate unwillingness to adapt himself to a conventional, steady-going existence."[24] The obituary highlighted Farson's adventures in the Caucasus, Turkey, and Egypt; in India, where he interviewed Gandhi; along the Khyber, "where the Afridis were hostile"; in Sholapur, where he faced an angry mob.[25] Also noted were his years in revolutionary Russia, his days in the Royal Flying Corps, his crash, his lifelong limp, as well as his journey by boat across Europe and his time in London spent under bombardment by the Nazis. Though the obituary quoted Farson as saying the deadline pressures prompted him to drink four double-whiskies after sending his cables to Chicago, it did not let on that he was a long-standing drunk.

The *Guardian*'s obituary covered the same ground as the *New York Times*', summing up Farson's life by noting that his entry in *Who's Who* "reads like an adventure story."[26]

Farson died in his home along the Devon coast on December 13, 1960, as he rested in an armchair. An official document from the U.S. embassy in London, titled "Report of the Death of an American Citizen," listed the primary cause of death as coronary thrombosis—in layman's terms, a blood clot in the coronary artery.[27] The document, based on the observations of Farson's family doctor, also listed a hodgepodge of other ailments that helped push Farson to the grave—coronary atheroma, or fat-congested arteries; arteriosclerosis, the old-age-induced hardening of the arteries; cor pulmonale, the abnormal enlargement of the right side of the heart due to lung disease; and, of course, chronic hypertrophic emphysema, the result of five decades of unrepentant chain-smoking. Despite the death sentence his heart and lungs had pronounced upon him, Farson had retained his wanderlust to the end. Shortly before his death, according to his son, he had been tying labels onto his luggage, preparing for a trip to Portugal.

Two years earlier, in a trip across the Iberian Peninsula, Farson had driven more than 4,700 miles, much of it along rough roads; he was sixty-seven at the time and traveling as hard and as fast as he had in his youth. But it was a bit of a last hurrah, and Farson knew it. Travel no longer was the center of his life. Begrudgingly, almost, he had accepted that the coziness of his seaside home wasn't so terrible after all.

Sitting on the side-lines down here in North Devon, I often felt that I was letting the years slip away. I had made much too big a break, too quickly; and into the wrong setting. For me, if I could have a free choice, there would be only two alternatives: New York, with all its roars, dirt, discomfort, and the most exciting mental and emotional life that any of today's cities can give you—or a life in some part of the world where men are few and far between. But to live in the woods entirely on your own, as we had lived during those two wonderful years on Vancouver Island, requires an amount of physical strength that is now quite beyond me—and the places just aren't there anymore. A Canadian author wrote to me from our lake in British Columbia, asking permission to quote from what I had said about it in the *Transgressor,* and added: "Don't come back. It would break your heart." He enclosed a real-estate development map which showed that the shores of the lonely bay where we had lived in our unpainted shack—where occasionally we saw a deer come gently down to drink, and I could catch all the trout I wanted for our dinner by casting a fly along the reeds at sunset—were now a suburb of bungalow plots. Most of the good places are gone. It took me some years, and I can't say that I have succeeded yet, to realise that the one place where I shall have to live from now on is within myself. Not so easy as it sounds.

. . . Sometimes, sitting up on the downs and watching the ships headed in for the Bristol Channel; or worse, watching some ship going *out*—the smoke from her freshly-stoked fires trailing behind her like a black rope—I have felt a madness of frustration. The world could still be so beautiful, the world beyond. Yet, would it be? The East is awakening. Well, let it awaken. And in every country you will find men completely indifferent to the happiness or misery of their fellow men, as throughout Eastern Europe, and others who are making the glamorous East, even as I write, foul and ugly. Let younger, more credulous, more hopeful Westerners write about it. And in the Africa I had seen, and had no wish to go back to (though I did), which the white man is making ugly because of his failure to be decent, I had jettisoned the entire shipload of romantic ideas. I think the white man has served his time under the tropic sun. Therefore, when I thought things over carefully, I knew that I was lucky in my coastal paradise here in North Devon. I think it is one of the most noble stretches of sea and sand anywhere in the world.[28]

By 1960, he knew the end was near; and he had hinted as much to his son. Daniel had himself become celebrated in Britain as the host of a series of television shows, and he had interviewed his father three times, the last shortly before Farson's death. During the final interview, conducted at Farson's house on the beach, Farson pointed out to the rocks of Baggy Point and exclaimed, "This is the perfect place for journey's end."[29] So it proved to be.

Farson's death desolated Eve. Instantly forgotten by her were forty years of arguing, four decades of recriminations over her lack of sexual drive, decades of shouting matches about his alcoholic misbehavior and his affairs. Instead, there remained nothing but fond memories of the man she had married in 1920, a wounded pilot with an adventurous spirit who had promised her an interesting life. Watching Daniel interview his father on television nearly broke her heart, she confided in a letter to Stowe. Despite the heartache, she told Stowe, she took great comfort in the rush of condolence letters she received. Such letters, she said, were "the only sort of comfort one can draw in this bitter grief. One friend wrote, 'So that wonderful little boy is gone.' Others said they felt they had lost their father—brother—best friend—and many total strangers wrote of their sorrow. He was dearly loved."[30]

Stowe's letter of condolence was one of the first she received. Stowe said he had learned of his great friend's death in the pages of the *New York Times,* and he tried to console Eve by assuring her that Farson would not be forgotten:

He was one of the rare, great spirits—untamed and untameable. No wonder he so loved lions and tigers and all wild creatures, and wrote about them with such insight and beauty. If there is such a thing as reincarnation, he must have been or will be a lordly lion. He would have great fun being a lion—both with his leaps and his roars. And how he lived—a dozen or two lives compressed into one! Rashly and with his faults and his demons—but magnificently all the way. I think I never knew another man who lived so fully, nor so utterly in what he believed and in defiance of all conformities and senseless restraints. This one thing about him—among so many others—will always give us joy in remembering him. On the big things he remained unalterably true to himself. That, in our times, is an enormous achievement reached by very, very few. But he also left us so much of his kaleidoscopic richness all his own. In his books, too, Neg will always be with us.[31]

Though she had watched over Farson's declining health for years and knew his frailties better than anyone, she had in her innermost mind come to think of him as indestructible. He had always rallied before. Eve—who would die less than two years later—buried him by the banks of a creek in the small graveyard of St. George's Church in Georgeham, a few miles from their home. The simple tombstone described James Scott Negley Farson as a writer from Plainfield, New Jersey. Some days after the funeral, after she had composed herself, Eve wrote a letter to Stowe, describing Farson's final days:

He had been wretchedly ill all last year, often gasping for breath, hardly able to walk—worse still not able to write, though he was always struggling to, and was convinced he would. But never complaining—always courageous and kind and even gay. I have never admired him more.

Then quite suddenly he seemed to get wonderfully, miraculously better, and we were about to leave for a holiday in Portugal the next day. We were sitting together by the fire and he said, "I am looking forward to this trip. We will have a grand time." And then he gave a great gasp and died.

Lucky, lucky Negley—he deserved it. He was truly good.[32]

Daniel worked hard to keep his father's memory alive. He compiled an anthology of Farson's journalism and published it under the title

Wanderlust: The World of Negley Farson. He wrote introductions to later editions of his father's works and used the space allotted to him by publishers to praise his father unreservedly and to admit to yearning to be like him, to walk in his footsteps. And then he literally did walk in his father's footsteps, attempting and succeeding in crossing the Caucasus on foot. The book he wrote about his adventure, *A Dry Ship to the Mountains,* was a loving and tender hymn to his father's memory. "Negley Farson was an exceptional man who did the things that most men dream about," Daniel wrote in the opening pages.[33]

Farson did not possess a timid soul. Most clerks, most men, perhaps, lead half lives, leaving their dreams stillborn. Farson's obsessive need to experience life set him on a path of hard living that at times seemed beyond reason, forcing him to push through sundry obstacles and frictions—his injuries, his troubled marriage, his alcoholism, the sort of things that often destroy even strong men. Farson, the swashbuckler, was willing to endure them all because he feared only the numbness of a normal life. Whenever he found himself settled, that feeling of dread would descend upon him, and he ran. He had to obey his wanderlust. He took to the sea, to the mountains, and to the fields and streams. He was a foreign correspondent because it allowed him to run—to the Black Sea, to the Pyrenees, to India, to the Shetlands. There was no impulse to derive meaning or lessons from his adventures; the adventure was both the path and the destination, and it was enough. As Arthur Krock of the *New York Times* put it when he reviewed *Way of a Transgressor:*

> Farson does not look inward at himself or at his experiences. His philosophy is light, personal and scantily indicated. The things he saw he sings, and does not dig for reasons. Almost everything happened to him that befalls a living man. Experiences bright and painful lay in wait for him. He knew everybody, saw everything, and evaluated nothing. He would not live a conventional life, and he did not. His youth was incident, upset and change, and his life so continued. People he found wholly explainable, as he finds himself, their variances depending upon the degree in which they possess or lack the human components. He was a bad salesman of small things, a remarkable salesman of large ones. He was a college athlete who never lost

the consciousness of his tall, strong body and its well-being, of the love for the sports of wave, stream and field.[34]

Farson also proved himself a true writer, a man who needed to chronicle things. He needed to write as much as he needed to breathe. He wrote millions of words, some of them crafted for mercenary reasons. Not all his prose amounted to literature: His writing could be wildly uneven, but he produced several works of genius. And yet, despite his torrent of prose, he managed to hide the very deepest parts of himself. Why did he stay married to Eve if he was so dissatisfied with their marriage? How did he relate to Daniel? What drove him, over and over, to such alcoholic depths? Would he care that he has been forgotten?

To the last question, the answer is probably not. Fame, he had declared, was a chimera, and he regarded those who sought it as a unique species of jackasses. His death proved his views on fame accurate: he has been forgotten by the literary world. For those familiar with his name, he is simply a Big Man Yesterday, emphasis on yesterday.

But why, exactly? Why should a man once so widely known now be so universally forgotten? There are several answers. First, there was his alcoholism. Plenty of alcoholic writers remain famous decades and even centuries after their death, of course, but Farson's alcoholism almost certainly reduced the quality and quantity of his work. As exceptional as it was, who could seriously doubt that it would have been better if he had stayed sober for an extended period of time? *Transgressor in the Tropics* is a perfect illustration. The book started out so wry and insightful, so full of action and entertaining characters, really Farson at his best, but after weeks of drinking on balconies and on barstools, Farson virtually fled the South American continent. Whatever notes he carried back to England with him had to have been incomplete, if not illegible. And not only could Farson have written better if he had avoided liquor, he could have written more. He could have finished *Created Equal*—a book he was convinced would have been the best of his career. Who knows what other books he lost to alcohol? In short, Farson cheated himself out of his fair measure of lasting fame. That he took himself out of the game, moving to Devon on the isolated shores of the Irish Sea, far from London and its temptations, also contributed to his eventual obscurity. He was no longer in the mix. But that was the price he chose to pay: he wanted to free himself from the pubs and social whirl of London, and remote Devon was ideal.

The second reason Farson has sunk into oblivion has to do with the nature of travel and foreign correspondency. Farson traveled the world at a time when fewer people traveled beyond the borders of their country. He traveled extensively before the advent of the airplane. But much of the traveling he did is commonplace today—flights to India, train trips across Europe, car rides across Africa, etc. His travels are much less exotic today than they were to the people of his generation. And as for foreign correspondency—the job title "foreign correspondent" has much less the aura of romance and adventure than it once had. Before television, foreign correspondents traveled the globe and used a thousand words or fewer to paint pictures of foreign landscapes, foreign customs, and foreign threats. Correspondents often went to dangerous places, and they usually lived to tell the tale. Such characters seized the public's imagination, hence all the movies that feature square-jawed, ink-stained truth-tellers. But today, they have lost their attraction. Television news broadcasters still employ foreign correspondents, as do newspapers, but the correspondents have become a mere part of the background, lost among the thousands of pictures and blogs and videos posted online by regular people who have witnessed the news and want to share it with the world. Correspondents account for a tiny contribution of the overall news picture, and readers and viewers no longer look to them as the most definitive, authoritative sources. So why would anyone want to buy the memoirs and books of a foreign correspondent who wrote so long, long ago?

Farson was not a good enough novelist to be remembered for his novels today. If he had stuck with fiction and tried to master it the way he labored to master journalism, perhaps critics and historians would have reserved him a seat at the table of Lost Generation writers. But that's not how it happened. Farson excelled at journalism, not fiction writing.

Journalism is ephemeral, and so often are the reputations of its practitioners. But Farson, who galloped through the years, who whipped life into a lather, would not mind one bit that he has been forgotten. He had his fun. He took his turn with both hands.

ACKNOWLEDGMENTS

T HE AUTHORS WOULD LIKE to thank the University of Wyoming American Heritage Center, which received Negley Farson's papers from Daniel Farson in March 1980. The librarians and staff were wonderful and helped us locate many of Farson's photos in the collection. We would also like to thank Britain's National Archives and the University of Warwick for the assistance they provided. Finally, we thank all the kind people who encouraged us to keep working on this book and shared our enthusiasm for that incredible man, Negley Farson.

NOTES

Introduction

1. Arthur Krock, "Reviewed Works," *North American Review* 241, no. 2 (June 1936): 354–58.

2. Daniel Farson, *Wanderlust: The World of Negley Farson* (London: White Lion, 1972), 12, 16.

3. Daniel Farson, *A Dry Ship to the Mountains* (London: Penguin, 1994), 7.

4. David Alexander, review of *The Way of a Transgressor,* by Negley Farson, http://www .davidalexanderbooks.com/the_way_of_a_transgressor_book_review_by_david _alexander.htm.

5. Alexander Wicksteed, *Ten Years in Soviet Moscow* (London: John Lane, 1933), 183.

6. Malcolm Muggeridge, *Chronicles of Wasted Time 2: The Infernal Grove* (New York: Morrow, 1974), 14.

7. Albert Hubbell, "The World Was My Oyster," *New Yorker,* March 23, 1957, 145.

8. Alexander Cockburn, quoted in *Journalism's Roving Eye,* by John Maxwell Hamilton (Baton Rouge: Louisiana State University Press, 2009), 243.

9. George Seldes, *Lords of the Press* (New York: Julian Messner, 1938), 285.

10. Cyril Watling, *Ink in My Blood* (London: Purnell, 1966), 48.

11. Krock, "Reviewed Works," 354–58.

12. Stephen Bodio, *A Sportsman's Library* (Guilford, Conn.: Lyons, 2013), 15.

13. Stanley Reynolds and John Moynihan, "Sacred and Monstrous," *Guardian,* November 29, 1997.

14. Daniel Farson, *Dry Ship,* 7.

15. Robert Ruark, "Papa Had No Use for Sham," *Field & Stream,* October 1961, 8.

16. Jeremiah Kitunda, "Knowing What Hemingway Knew: Hemingway's Reading in Natural History, Hunting, Fishing, and Africa," in *Hemingway and Africa,* ed. Miriam B. Mandel (Rochester. N.Y.: Camden House, 2011), 54.

17. Charles Lillard, "Negley Farson," British Columbia Book World, Spring 1987, https:// abcbookworld.com/writer/farson-negley/, accessed January 1, 2020.

1. Europe, 1925

1. Negley Farson, *Sailing across Europe* (New York: Century, 1926), vii.

2. Negley Farson, *The Way of a Transgressor* (New York: Literary Guild of America, 1936), 395.

3. Farson, *Way of a Transgressor,* 396.

4. Farson, *Way of a Transgressor,* 296.

5. Charles H. Dennis, *Victor Lawson* (New York: Greenwood, 1935), 347, 390.

6. Farson, *Way of a Transgressor,* 396.

7. Hamilton, *Journalism's Roving Eye,* 157.

8. Dennis, *Victor Lawson,* 273–74.

9. Dennis, *Victor Lawson,* 273–74.

10. Dennis, *Victor Lawson,* 276.

11. Dennis, *Victor Lawson,* 275.

12. Dennis, *Victor Lawson,* 7–8.

13. Dennis, *Victor Lawson,* 71.

14. Dennis, *Victor Lawson,* 296.

15. Farson, *Way of a Transgressor,* 396, 296.

16. Farson, *Way of a Transgressor,* 397.

17. John Hohenberg, *Foreign Correspondence: The Great Reporters and Their Times* (New York: Columbia University Press, 1964), 151–52.

18. Farson, *Way of a Transgressor,* 397.

19. Farson, *Way of a Transgressor,* 399.

20. Farson, *Way of a Transgressor,* 406.

21. Farson, *Way of a Transgressor,* 408.

22. Farson, *Way of a Transgressor,* 417.

23. Farson, *Way of a Transgressor,* 418.

24. Negley Farson, "Sailing across Europe," *Chicago Daily News,* August 26, 1925, 8.

25. Farson, *Sailing across Europe,* 52.

26. Farson, *Way of a Transgressor,* 419.

27. Eve Farson, diary entry, July 17, 1925, Negley Farson Collection, American Heritage Center, University of Wyoming.

28. Farson, *Way of a Transgressor,* 420.

29. Eve Farson, diary entry, July 21, 1925, Negley Farson Collection, American Heritage Center, University of Wyoming.

30. Eve Farson, diary entry, July 22, 1925, Negley Farson Collection, American Heritage Center, University of Wyoming.

31. Farson, "Sailing across Europe," *Chicago Daily News,* September 4, 1925, 10.

32. Benjamin Carter Hett, *The Death of Democracy* (New York: Henry Holt, 2018), 53.

33. Farson, *Way of a Transgressor,* 414.

34. Farson, "Sailing across Europe," *Chicago Daily News,* September 11, 1925, 10.

35. Farson, *Sailing across Europe*, 65.

36. Charles Dennis to Negley Farson, August 5, 1925, Charles Dennis Papers, University of Chicago.

37. Charles Dennis to Negley Farson, September 21, 1925, Charles Dennis Papers, University of Chicago.

38. Farson, *Way of a Transgressor*, 422.

39. Farson, *Way of a Transgressor*, 422.

40. Farson, *Sailing across Europe*, 233.

41. Farson, *Way of a Transgressor*, 425.

42. Farson, "Sailing across Europe," *Chicago Daily News*, December 23, 1925, 8.

43. Farson, *Way of a Transgressor*, 430.

44. Charles Dennis to Negley Farson, December 10, 1925, Charles Dennis Papers, University of Chicago.

45. Dennis to Negley Farson, December 10, 1925.

46. Farson, "Sailing across Europe," *Chicago Daily News*, February 17, 1926, 8.

2. The Old General

1. Negley Farson, *The Way of a Transgressor* (New York: Literary Guild of America, 1936), 28.

2. Farson, *Way of a Transgressor*, 1.

3. Josiah Seymour Currey, *Chicago: Its History and Its Builders* (Chicago: S. J. Clarke, 1918), 111.

4. Farson, *Way of a Transgressor*, 4.

5. Farson, *Way of a Transgressor*, 12.

6. Farson, *Way of a Transgressor*, 14.

3. Fish Mad

1. Farson, *Way of a Transgressor*, 15.

2. Farson, *Way of a Transgressor*, 17.

3. Farson, *Way of a Transgressor*, 17.

4. Farson, *Way of a Transgressor*, 19.

5. Farson, *Way of a Transgressor*, 19.

6. Farson, *Way of a Transgressor*, 20.

7. Farson, *Way of a Transgressor*, 20.

8. Farson, *Way of a Transgressor*, 17.

9. Farson, *Way of a Transgressor*, 23.

10. Farson, *Way of a Transgressor*, 40.

11. Farson, *Way of a Transgressor*, 31.

12. Farson, *Way of a Transgressor*, 35.

13. Farson, *Way of a Transgressor*, 36.

14. Theo Towe to Negley Farson, Negley Farson Collection, American Heritage Center, University of Wyoming.

15. Farson, *Way of a Transgressor*, 39–40.

16. Farson, *Way of a Transgressor*, 40.

17. Farson, *Way of a Transgressor*, 41.

18. Farson, *Way of a Transgressor*, 50.

19. Farson, *Way of a Transgressor*, 50.

20. Negley Farson, "Sport—The Great Civilizer of Individuals and Nations," *Chicago Daily News*, September 6, 1926, dateline Stockholm.

21. Farson, *Way of a Transgressor*, 63.

22. Farson, *Way of a Transgressor*, 50.

23. Farson, *Way of a Transgressor*, 54.

24. Farson, *Way of a Transgressor*, 69.

25. Negley Farson, *Mirror for Narcissus* (Garden City, N.Y.: Doubleday, 1957), 105.

26. Farson, *Way of a Transgressor*, 75.

27. Farson, *Way of a Transgressor*, 71.

4. England and War

1. Farson, *Way of a Transgressor*, 82.

2. Farson, *Way of a Transgressor*, 94.

3. Farson, *Way of a Transgressor*, 98.

4. Farson, *Way of a Transgressor*, 100.

5. Farson, *Way of a Transgressor*, 100.

6. Farson, *Way of a Transgressor*, 101.

7. Farson, *Way of a Transgressor*, 101, 102.

8. Farson, *Way of a Transgressor*, 104.

9. Farson, *Way of a Transgressor*, 107.

5. Russia

1. Farson, *Way of a Transgressor*, 115.

2. Farson, *Way of a Transgressor*, 117.

3. Timothy Wilson, "Broken Wings: The Curtiss Aeroplane Company, K-Boats, and the Russian Navy, 1914–1916," *Journal of Military History* 66, no. 4 (October 2002): 1061–83.

4. Joseph Vecchi, *The Tavern Is My Drum* (London: Odhams, 1948), 75, 85.

5. Farson, *Way of a Transgressor,* 191.

6. Farson, *Way of a Transgressor,* 139.

7. Farson, *Way of a Transgressor,* 140.

8. Farson, *Way of a Transgressor,* 143.

9. Farson, *Way of a Transgressor,* 156.

10. Farson, *Way of a Transgressor,* 174.

11. Farson, *Way of a Transgressor,* 181.

12. Farson, *Way of a Transgressor,* 181.

13. Farson, *Way of a Transgressor,* 203.

14. Farson, *Way of a Transgressor,* 204.

15. Farson, *Way of a Transgressor,* 210.

16. *Alumni Register of the University of Pennsylvania,* 1925, 427.

17. Farson, *Way of a Transgressor,* 213.

18. Farson, *Way of a Transgressor,* 225.

19. Farson, *Way of a Transgressor,* 225.

20. Farson, *Way of a Transgressor,* 233.

21. Farson, *Way of a Transgressor,* 234.

22. Farson, *Way of a Transgressor,* 245.

23. Farson, *Way of a Transgressor,* 263.

24. Farson, *Way of a Transgressor,* 264.

25. Farson, *Way of a Transgressor,* 264.

26. Negley Farson, "From the Diary of Lt. Negley Farson, RAF," *New English Review* 5 (May 1946): 395.

27. Farson, *Way of a Transgressor,* 265, 266.

28. Farson, *Way of a Transgressor,* 281.

29. Negley Farson, "It's Not So Bad If You Change Hospitals Often," *Chicago Daily News,* September 6, 1927, 2.

6. Crash Landing in Egypt

1. Farson, *Way of a Transgressor,* 283.

2. Terry Breverton, *Breverton's First World War* (Gloucestershire, U.K.: Amberley, 2014), 55.

3. Breverton, *Breverton's First World War,* 309.

4. Breverton, *Breverton's First World War,* 318.

5. Breverton, *Breverton's First World War,* 320, 321.

6. Breverton, *Breverton's First World War,* 328.

7. Daniel Farson, *Dry Ship,* 8.

8. Daniel Farson, *Never a Normal Man* (London: HarperCollins, 1998), 10.

9. Daniel Farson, *Never a Normal Man*, 10.

10. Negley Farson to Eve Stoker, March 12, 1920, Negley Farson Collection, American Heritage Center, University of Wyoming.

11. Negley Farson to Eve Stoker, March 24, 1920, Negley Farson Collection, American Heritage Center, University of Wyoming.

7. Life in the Wilds

1. Daniel Farson, *Never a Normal Man*, 17.

2. Daniel Farson, *Never a Normal Man*, 17.

3. Farson, *Way of a Transgressor*, 336.

4. Farson, *Way of a Transgressor*, 344.

5. John Aldridge, *After the Lost Generation* (New York: McGraw-Hill, 1951), 12.

6. Farson, *Way of a Transgressor*, 350.

7. Farson, *Way of a Transgressor*, 350.

8. Farson, *Way of a Transgressor*, 351.

9. Negley Farson, *Men of the World* (London: Pearson, 1946), 47.

10. Farson, *Way of a Transgressor*, 356.

11. Farson, *Way of a Transgressor*, 366.

12. Farson, *Way of a Transgressor*, 366.

13. Farson, *Mirror for Narcissus*, 56.

14. Negley Farson, *Going Fishing* (New York: Harcourt, Brace, 1943), 41.

15. William Willis to Negley Farson, undated, Negley Farson Collection, American Heritage Center, University of Wyoming.

16. Farson, *Going Fishing*, 42.

17. Negley Farson, "Camp-Fire," *Adventure*, November 22, 1922, 179.

18. Farson, *Men of the World*, 33.

19. Farson, *Way of a Transgressor*, 371.

20. Farson, *Way of a Transgressor*, 372.

21. Farson, *Way of a Transgressor*, 373.

22. Farson, *Way of a Transgressor*, 383.

23. Farson, *Way of a Transgressor*, 388.

24. Farson, *Way of a Transgressor*, 392.

8. The Exotic Life of a Foreign Correspondent

1. Negley Farson, "Turks Hang Seven More Reactionaries," *Chicago Daily News*, January 20, 1926, 2.

2. Farson, *Way of a Transgressor*, 442.

3. R. Sanger Wilkins, *Harvard College: Class of 1912, Twenty-Fifth Anniversary Report* (Cambridge, Mass.: Cosmos, 1937), 526.

4. Farson, *Way of a Transgressor,* 451.

5. Negley Farson, "Introducing, In Person: A Sage of the Far East," *Chicago Daily News,* July 23, 1926, 8.

6. Farson, *Way of a Transgressor,* 452.

7. Farson, *Way of a Transgressor,* 456.

8. F. V. Morley, "Writer vs. Surgeons," *Brooklyn Life and Activities of Long Island Society,* October 9, 1926, 27.

9. Review of *Sailing across Europe,* by Negley Farson, *New York Times,* September 26, 1926, 6.

10. "Charlemagne's Canal," review of *Sailing across Europe,* by Negley Farson, *Time,* October 25, 1926, 44.

11. Review of *Sailing across Europe,* by Negley Farson, *Wilmington (Del.) Morning News,* June 1, 1927, 4.

12. "Review: Sailing across Europe," *Westminster Gazette,* October 8, 1926, 5.

13. R. J. Hart, "The Log of a Trans-European Cruise," review of *Sailing across Europe,* by Negley Farson, *Travel,* April 1927, 41.

14. Hart, "The Log of a Trans-European Cruise," 41.

15. Dennis to Negley Farson, October 28, 1926, Charles Dennis Papers, University of Chicago.

16. Dennis to Negley Farson, January 5, 1927, Charles Dennis Papers, University of Chicago.

17. Dennis to Negley Farson, January 5, 1927.

18. Farson, *Way of a Transgressor,* 461.

19. Negley Farson, *Daphne's in Love* (New York: Grosset and Dunlap, 1927), 161.

20. Dennis to Negley Farson, March 25, 1927, Charles Dennis Papers, University of Chicago.

9. Whaling Adventure

1. Negley Farson, "Herrings and Whales," *Chicago Daily News,* November 29, 1927, 10.

2. Farson, "Herrings and Whales," *Chicago Daily News,* December 16, 1927, 10.

3. Farson, "Herrings and Whales," *Chicago Daily News,* December 23, 1927, 10.

4. Farson, "Herrings and Whales," *Chicago Daily News,* December 23, 1927, 10.

5. Farson, "Herrings and Whales," *Chicago Daily News,* December 27, 1927, 10.

6. Farson, "Herrings and Whales," *Chicago Daily News,* January 6, 1928, 8.

7. Farson, "Herrings and Whales," *Chicago Daily News,* January 27, 1928, 10.

8. Farson, "Herrings and Whales," *Chicago Daily News,* January 27, 1928, 10.

9. Farson, "Herrings and Whales," *Chicago Daily News,* January 27, 1928, 10.

10. Farson, "Herrings and Whales," *Chicago Daily News,* January 31, 1928, 10.

11. Farson, "Herrings and Whales," *Chicago Daily News*, February 3, 1928, 10.
12. Farson, "Herrings and Whales," *Chicago Daily News*, February 3, 1928, 10.

10. Among the Spaniards

1. Dennis to Negley Farson, June 16, 1927, Charles Dennis Papers, University of Chicago.
2. Dennis to Negley Farson, June 16, 1927.
3. *Chicago Daily News*, May 1, 1928, 10.
4. Negley Farson, "Across the Pyrenees," *Chicago Daily News*, June 15, 1928, 10.
5. Farson, "Across the Pyrenees," *Chicago Daily News*, June 15, 1928, 10.
6. Farson, "Across the Pyrenees," *Chicago Daily News*, July 17, 1928, 10.
7. Farson, "Across the Pyrenees," *Chicago Daily News*, July 20, 1928, 10.
8. Farson, "Across the Pyrenees," *Chicago Daily News*, July 20, 1928, 10.
9. Farson, "Across the Pyrenees," *Chicago Daily News*, July 31, 1928, 12.

11. Russia Again

1. "Enoch S. Farson Sr.," obituary, *New York Times*, September 1, 1928, 7.
2. Louis Fischer, *Men and Politics* (New York: Duell, Sloan and Pearce, 1941), 162.
3. Eugene Lyons, *Assignment in Utopia* (New York: Harcourt, Brace, 1937), 252.
4. Lyons, *Assignment in Utopia*, 172.
5. Ayn Rand, *Letters of Ayn Rand*, ed. Michael S. Berliner (New York: New American Library, 1995), 50.
6. Negley Farson, "Moscow's 'Third Floor Back' Packed Full," *Chicago Daily News*, January 16, 1929, 53.
7. Negley Farson, "Roving through Russia," *Chicago Daily News*, April 26, 1929, 14.
8. Farson, "Roving through Russia," *Chicago Daily News*, January 18, 1929, 10.
9. Farson, "Roving through Russia," *Chicago Daily News*, February 1, 1929, 12.
10. W. J. Tallman, letter to the editor, *Chicago Daily News*, February 19, 1929, 11.
11. Stephen Pogledic, letter to the editor, *Chicago Daily News*, February 13, 1929, 11.
12. Negley Farson, *Caucasian Journey* (London: Penguin, 1988), 22.
13. Farson, *Caucasian Journey*, 22.
14. Farson, *Mirror for Narcissus*, 237.
15. Farson, *Caucasian Journey*, 1.
16. "The Black Ace," review of *The Black Ace*, by Negley Farson, *Daily Mirror*, May 10, 1929, Special Collections, University of Birmingham, U.K.
17. "The Black Ace," review of *The Black Ace*, by Negley Farson, *Sunday Graphic*, May 12, 1929, Special Collections, University of Birmingham, U.K.
18. "The Black Ace," review of *The Black Ace*, by Negley Farson, *The Era*, May 15, 1929, Special Collections, University of Birmingham, U.K.

19. Farson, *Caucasian Journey*, 22, 23.
20. Farson, *Caucasian Journey*, 23.
21. Farson, *Caucasian Journey*, 30.
22. Farson, *Caucasian Journey*, 74.
23. Farson, *Caucasian Journey*, 83.
24. Wicksteed, *Ten Years in Soviet Moscow*, 183.
25. Farson, *Way of a Transgressor*, 542, 543.
26. Farson, *Caucasian Journey*, 148.
27. Farson, *Caucasian Journey*, 157.
28. Farson, *Caucasian Journey*, 158.
29. Farson, *Caucasian Journey*, 159.

12. Meeting Gandhi

1. Farson, *Way of a Transgressor*, 547.
2. Farson, *Way of a Transgressor*, 547.
3. Farson, *Way of a Transgressor*, 562.
4. Farson, *Way of a Transgressor*, 564.
5. Farson, *Way of a Transgressor*, 563.
6. Farson, "Unresisting Nationalists Beaten to Ground by British Police," *Chicago Daily News*, June 23, 1930.
7. Farson, "Unresisting Nationalists Beaten to Ground by British Police."
8. Farson, "Indian Hate Lyric," *We Cover the World*, ed. Eugene Lyons (London: George G. Harrap, 1937), 149.
9. Farson, "Bombay Fights Gandhi Arrest; Shops Closed," *Chicago Daily News*, May 5, 1930, 2.
10. Farson, "Indian Hate Lyric," 150.
11. Farson, "Bombay Fights Gandhi Arrest," 1–2.
12. Farson, "Indian Hate Lyric," 151.
13. Farson, "Indian Hate Lyric," 151.

13. Covering Hitler and the World

1. Walter Strong to Eve Farson, June 5, 1930, American Heritage Center, University of Wyoming.
2. Farson, "Hitler Roars His Denial of Rumor He Plans Putsch," *Chicago Daily News*, September 25, 1930, 2.
3. Farson, "Farson Seized by Poland for Ukraine Expose," *Chicago Daily News*, November 15, 1930, 2.
4. Claud Cockburn, *A Discord of Trumpets* (New York: Simon and Schuster, 1956), 253–54.

5. Hamilton, *Journalism's Roving Eye*, 171.

6. Hett, *Death of Democracy*, 200.

7. John Gunther, *A Fragment of Autobiography* (New York: Harper and Row, 1962), 6.

8. Hamilton, *Journalism's Roving Eye*, 178.

9. Hamilton, *Journalism's Roving Eye*, 178.

10. Farson, *Mirror for Narcissus*, 22.

11. Daniel Farson, *Never a Normal Man*, 183.

12. Farson, *Mirror for Narcissus*, 45.

13. Farson, *Mirror for Narcissus*, 167.

14. Negley Farson to Frank Knox, January 16, 1935, Negley Farson Collection, American Heritage Center, University of Wyoming.

15. Farson to Frank Knox, January 16, 1935.

16. Frank Knox to Negley Farson, February 8, 1935, Negley Farson Collection, American Heritage Center, University of Wyoming.

17. Drew Pearson, "Drew Pearson and Robert S. Allen," column, *Texas Daily Herald*, April 14, 1936.

14. Writing a Best Seller

1. Hamilton, *Journalism's Roving Eye*, 182.

2. Farson, *Mirror for Narcissus*, 15.

3. Daniel Farson, *Never a Normal Man*, 20.

4. Daniel Farson, *Out of Step* (London: Michael Joseph, 1974), 23.

5. Farson, *Mirror for Narcissus*, 17.

6. Farson, *Mirror for Narcissus*, 17

7. Farson, *Mirror for Narcissus*, 34.

8. Bob Davis, "Bob Davis Reveals," *New York Sun*, undated, Negley Farson Collection, American Heritage Center, University of Wyoming.

9. Muriel delaHaye, diary entry, September 10, 1916, in *Miss Daisy's Secret Russian Diary: 1916–1918* (Leicester, U.K.: Matador, 2017), 55.

10. Robert Bruce Lockhart, *My Europe* (London: Putnam, 1952), 201.

11. Review of *The Way of a Transgressor*, by Negley Farson, *Daily Herald*, undated, 1935, Negley Farson Collection, American Heritage Center, University of Wyoming.

12. Review of *The Way of a Transgressor*, by Negley Farson, *The Times*, undated, 1935, Negley Farson Collection, American Heritage Center, University of Wyoming.

13. Review of *The Way of a Transgressor*, by Negley Farson, *Sunday Times*, undated, 1935, Negley Farson Collection, American Heritage Center, University of Wyoming.

14. Review of *The Way of a Transgressor*, by Negley Farson, *John O'London's Weekly*, undated, Negley Farson Collection, American Heritage Center, University of Wyoming.

15. "A Reckless Rover," review of *The Way of a Transgressor*, by Negley Farson, *Sydney Morning Herald*, January 18, 1936.

16. "A Reckless Rover," review of *The Way of a Transgressor,* by Negley Farson.

17. Robert Van Gelder, "Books of the Times," review of *The Way of a Transgressor,* by Negley Farson, *New York Times,* February 14, 1936, 17.

18. Van Gelder, "Books of the Times," review of *The Way of a Transgressor,* by Negley Farson, 17.

19. Frank H. Simonds, "He Wrote What He Lived," review of *The Way of a Transgressor,* by Negley Farson, *Saturday Review of Literature,* February 15, 1936, 5.

20. Simonds, "He Wrote What He Lived," review of *The Way of a Transgressor,* by Negley Farson, 5.

21. Review of *The Way of a Transgressor,* by Negley Farson, *Indiana Evening Gazette,* February 24, 1936.

22. R. L. Duffus, "A Stirring Life of Adventure," review of *The Way of a Transgressor,* by Negley Farson, *New York Times,* February 16, 1936, BR1.

23. Theodore Hall, "White-Haired Boy of the World," review of *The Way of a Transgressor,* by Negley Farson, *Washington Post,* February 16, 1936, B8.

24. Hall, "White-Haired Boy of the World," review of *The Way of a Transgressor,* by Negley Farson, B8.

25. Frances Valensi, "The Way of an Adventurer," review of *The Way of a Transgressor,* by Negley Farson, *New Republic,* March 4, 1936, 116.

26. Valensi, "The Way of an Adventurer," review of *The Way of a Transgressor,* by Negley Farson, 116.

27. Farson, *Mirror for Narcissus,* 33.

28. Farson, *Mirror for Narcissus,* 35.

29. Farson, *Mirror for Narcissus,* 54.

30. Farson, *Mirror for Narcissus,* 60.

31. Farson, *Mirror for Narcissus,* 67.

32. Farson, *Mirror for Narcissus,* 69.

33. F. Scott Fitzgerald to Maxwell Perkins, October 16, 1936, in *Sons of Maxwell Perkins,* ed. Matthew J. Bruccoli and Judith S. Baughman (Columbia: University of South Carolina Press, 2004), 218.

34. Farson, *Mirror for Narcissus,* 72.

35. Farson, *Mirror for Narcissus,* 73.

36. Farson, *Mirror for Narcissus,* 90.

37. Farson, *Mirror for Narcissus,* 91.

38. Farson, *Mirror for Narcissus,* 98.

39. Daniel Farson, *Wanderlust,* 93.

15. South American Bender

1. Negley Farson, *Transgressor in the Tropics* (New York: Harcourt, Brace, 1938), 41.

2. Farson, *Mirror for Narcissus,* 108, 120.

3. Farson, *Transgressor in the Tropics*, 7.

4. Farson, *Transgressor in the Tropics*, 8.

5. Farson, *Transgressor in the Tropics*, 9.

6. Farson, *Transgressor in the Tropics*, 11.

7. Farson, *Transgressor in the Tropics*, 60.

8. Farson, *Transgressor in the Tropics*, 60–64.

9. Farson, *Transgressor in the Tropics*, 85.

10. Farson, *Transgressor in the Tropics*, 69.

11. Farson, *Transgressor in the Tropics*, 70.

12. Farson, *Transgressor in the Tropics*, 90.

13. Farson, *Transgressor in the Tropics*, 90.

14. Farson, *Transgressor in the Tropics*, 125.

15. Negley Farson to Leland Stowe, November 28, 1956, Negley Farson Collection, American Heritage Center, University of Wyoming.

16. Farson, *Mirror for Narcissus*, 128.

17. Farson, *Mirror for Narcissus*, 128.

18. Farson, *Mirror for Narcissus*, 128.

19. Farson, *Mirror for Narcissus*, 129.

20. Farson, *Mirror for Narcissus*, 129, 130.

21. Farson, *Mirror for Narcissus*, 133.

22. Farson, *Transgressor in the Tropics*, 155.

23. Farson, *Transgressor in the Tropics*, 254.

24. Farson, *Mirror for Narcissus*, 121.

25. Farson, *Transgressor in the Tropics*, 231.

26. Farson, *Mirror for Narcissus*, 135.

27. Farson, *Mirror for Narcissus*, 135.

28. *Amherst Graduates Quarterly* 26, no. 102 (1937): 166.

29. Farson, *Transgressor in the Tropics*, 4.

30. Farson, *Transgressor in the Tropics*, 296.

31. Farson, *Transgressor in the Tropics*, 299.

32. Farson, *Transgressor in the Tropics*, 299.

16. Taking the Cure

1. Farson, *Mirror for Narcissus*, 141.

2. Farson, *Mirror for Narcissus*, 141.

3. "Bestsellers," *New York Times*, February 21, 1938, 17.

4. Review of *Transgressor in the Tropics*, by Negley Farson, *Daily Mail*, October 7, 1937.

5. Review of *Transgressor in the Tropics*, by Negley Farson, *Bystander*, October 20, 1937.

6. Review of *Transgressor in the Tropics*, by Negley Farson, *Times Literary Supplement*, October 9, 1937.

7. Ernie Pyle, review of *Transgressor in the Tropics*, by Negley Farson, *El Paso Herald-Post*, February 7, 1939.

8. Farson, *Transgressor in the Tropics*, 40.

9. Farson, *Transgressor in the Tropics*, 295.

10. Farson, *Mirror for Narcissus*, 166.

11. Farson, *Mirror for Narcissus*, 149.

12. Farson, *Mirror for Narcissus*, 152.

13. Farson, *Mirror for Narcissus*, 153.

14. Farson, *Mirror for Narcissus*, 154.

15. Farson, *Mirror for Narcissus*, 164.

16. Farson, *Mirror for Narcissus*, 164.

17. Farson, *Mirror for Narcissus*, 162.

17. His Life in a Novel

1. British Columbia Bookworld, accessed January 1, 2020, https://abcbookworld.com/scripter/scripter-5301/.

2. Daniel Farson, *Never a Normal Man*, 183.

3. Daniel Farson, *Never a Normal Man*, 183.

4. Daniel Farson, *Never a Normal Man*, 185.

5. Daniel Farson, *Never a Normal Man*, 185.

6. Daniel Farson, *Never a Normal Man*, 186.

7. *Kirkus Reviews*, review of *Story of a Lake*, by Negley Farson, February 23, 1939.

8. Robert Van Gelder, "The End of the Lost Generation," review of *Story of a Lake*, by Negley Farson, *New York Times Book Review*, February 26, 1939, 88.

9. Van Gelder, "The End of the Lost Generation," review of *Story of a Lake*, by Negley Farson, 88.

10. "Books: Transgressor's Collapse," review of *Story of a Lake*, by Negley Farson, *Time*, March 6, 1939.

11. Joseph Henry Jackson, "A Bookman's Notebook," review of *Story of a Lake*, by Negley Farson, *San Francisco Chronicle*, March 2, 1939, 15.

12. Eleanor Roosevelt, "My Day," *El Paso Herald-Post*, August 18, 1939.

13. Farson, *Mirror for Narcissus*, 143.

18. Mired in African Mud and Acrimony

1. Farson, *Mirror for Narcissus*, 171.

2. Negley Farson, *Behind God's Back* (New York: Harcourt, Brace, 1941), 59.

3. Farson, *Behind God's Back,* 59.

4. Farson, *Behind God's Back,* 7.

5. Farson, *Behind God's Back,* 18.

6. Farson, *Behind God's Back,* 14.

7. Farson, *Behind God's Back,* 19.

8. Farson, *Behind God's Back,* 61.

9. Farson, *Behind God's Back,* 67.

10. Farson, *Behind God's Back,* 81.

11. Farson, *Behind God's Back,* 85.

12. Farson, *Behind God's Back,* 115.

13. Farson, *Behind God's Back,* 167.

14. Farson, *Behind God's Back,* 182.

15. Farson, *Behind God's Back,* 185.

16. Farson, *Behind God's Back,* 187.

17. Farson, *Behind God's Back,* 209.

18. Farson, *Behind God's Back,* 186.

19. Farson, *Behind God's Back,* 213.

20. Farson, *Behind God's Back,* 238.

21. Farson, *Behind God's Back,* 238.

22. Farson, *Behind God's Back,* 256.

23. Farson, *Behind God's Back,* 257.

24. Farson, *Behind God's Back,* 261.

25. U.S. Department of State, Bureau of African Affairs, *AF Press Clips,* August 1981, 23.

26. Farson, Farson, *Behind God's Back,* 313.

27. Farson, *Behind God's Back,* 309.

28. Farson, *Behind God's Back,* 309.

29. Farson, *Behind God's Back,* 310.

30. Farson, *Mirror for Narcissus,* 175.

31. Farson, *Behind God's Back,* 369.

32. Farson, *Behind God's Back,* 396.

33. Farson, *Behind God's Back,* 435.

34. Farson, *Behind God's Back,* 437.

35. Farson, *Behind God's Back,* 438.

36. Farson, *Behind God's Back,* 443.

37. Farson, *Behind God's Back,* 491.

38. Negley Farson, "French Equatorial Africa: The Vast Area in the Heart of the Black Continent Which Has Now Come under the Control of General de Gaulle," *Sphere,* September 14, 1940.

39. Farson, *Behind God's Back,* 512.

40. Daniel Farson, *Never a Normal Man,* 190.

41. Farson, *Behind God's Back*, v.

42. Farson, *Behind God's Back*, 181.

43. Farson, *Behind God's Back*, 524.

44. Daniel Farson, *Never a Normal Man*, 190.

45. Farson, *Behind God's Back*, 542.

46. Farson, *Behind God's Back*, 554.

47. Farson, *Behind God's Back*, 553.

48. Farson, *Behind God's Back*, 31.

49. Farson, *Behind God's Back*, 31.

19. A Bomber's Moon

1. Negley Farson, *Bomber's Moon* (New York: Harcourt, Brace, 1941), 35.

2. Farson, *Bomber's Moon*, 7.

3. Daniel Farson, *Never a Normal Man*, 28.

4. Farson, *Bomber's Moon*, 9.

5. Farson, *Bomber's Moon*, 27.

6. Farson, *Bomber's Moon*, 28.

7. Farson, *Bomber's Moon*, 52.

8. Review of *Behind God's Back*, by Negley Farson, *Observer* (London), September 1, 1940.

9. Review of *Behind God's Back*, by Negley Farson, *New Statesman & Nation*, September 7, 1940.

10. Review of *Behind God's Back*, by Negley Farson, *Scotsman*, October 3, 1940.

11. Review of *Behind God's Back*, by Negley Farson, *Daily Telegraph*, September 21, 1940.

12. Review of *Behind God's Back*, by Negley Farson, *Herald* (Glasgow), September 5, 1940.

13. "Something New out of Africa," review of *Behind God's Back*, by Negley Farson, *Washington Post*, March 16, 1941, L10.

14. R. L. Duffus, "A Broad View of Africa Today: Negley Farson's Account of His Journey," review of *Behind God's Back*, by Negley Farson *New York Times*, February 16, 1941, BR1.

15. Review of *Behind God's Back*, by Negley Farson, *New York Times*, March 24, 1941, 15.

16. Review of *Behind God's Back*, by Negley Farson, *Times Literary Supplement*, January 25, 1941.

17. Review of *Behind God's Back*, by Negley Farson, *Illustrated London News*, February 8, 1941.

18. Graham Greene, "A Pride in Bombs," *Spectator*, February 14, 1941.

19. "Negley Farson's Bomber's Moon," review of *Bomber's Moon*, by Negley Farson, *New York Times*, July 13, 1941, BR3.

20. Writing a Masterpiece

1. Christopher Wordsworth, review of *Behind God's Back*, by Negley Farson, *Observer* (London), July 1996, quoted on website of Merlin Unwin Books, http://www.merlinunwin.co.uk/bookDetails.asp?bookId=35&categoryId=.

2. Farson, *Going Fishing*, ix.

3. Farson, *Going Fishing*, 9.

4. Farson, *Going Fishing*, 36.

5. Farson, *Going Fishing*, 25

6. Farson, *Going Fishing*, 21.

7. Farson, *Going Fishing*, 9.

8. Farson, *Going Fishing*, 18.

9. Farson, *Going Fishing*, 30.

10. Farson, *Going Fishing*, 36, 37.

11. Farson, *Going Fishing*, 65.

12. Farson, *Going Fishing*, 65.

13. Farson, *Going Fishing*, 66.

14. Farson, *Going Fishing*, 82.

15. Farson, *Going Fishing*, 114.

16. Farson, *Going Fishing*, 116.

17. Farson, *Going Fishing*, ix.

18. Farson, *Going Fishing*, 72.

19. Maurice Richardson, review of *Going Fishing*, by Negley Farson, *Observer* (London), December 13, 1941.

20. Fowler Hill, "The Angler's Notebook," *New York Times,* October 3, 1943.

21. H. E. Bates, review of *Going Fishing*, by Negley Farson, *Cosmopolitans,* undated, Negley Farson Collection, American Heritage Center, University of Wyoming.

22. Review of *Going Fishing*, by Negley Farson, *Kirkus Reviews*, https://www.kirkusreviews.com/book-reviews/negley-farson/going-fishing/, accessed January 1, 2020.

23. Negley Farson, *Going Fishing* (London: White Lion, 1973), v.

24. Lillard, "Negley Farson," British Columbia Book World, Spring 1987, https://abcbookworld.com/writer/farson-negley/.

21. Back to Russia

1. Farson, *Mirror for Narcissus*, 259.

2. Farson, *Mirror for Narcissus*, 266.

3. Walter Graebner, "The Battle for Scoops," *Reporting World War II: Part One,* ed. Anne Matthews (New York: Library of America, 1995), 424.

4. Graebner, "Battle for Scoops," 421.

5. James McCargar, interview by Charles Stuart Kennedy, *Association for Diplomatic Studies and Training,* April 18, 1995, 20.

6. Eddy Gilmore, *Me and My Russian Wife* (New York: Doubleday, 1954), 72–74.

7. Farson, *Mirror for Narcissus*, 276.

8. Farson, *Mirror for Narcissus*, 275.

9. Daniel Farson, *Never a Normal Man*, 58.

10. Farson, *Mirror for Narcissus*, 35.

22. Back to Africa

1. Negley Farson, *Last Chance in Africa* (London: Victor Gollancz, 1953), 10.

2. Farson, *Last Chance in Africa*, 10.

3. Farson, *Last Chance in Africa*, 283.

4. C. S. Nichols, *Elspeth Huxley* (New York: St. Martin's, 2002), 200.

5. Farson, *Last Chance in Africa*, 6.

6. Farson, *Last Chance in Africa*, 6.

7. Farson, *Last Chance in Africa*, 94.

8. Farson, *Last Chance in Africa*, 92.

9. Farson, *Last Chance in Africa*, 139.

10. Farson, *Last Chance in Africa*, 284.

11. Farson, *Last Chance in Africa*, 284.

12. Farson, *Last Chance in Africa*, 344.

13. Orville Prescott, "Books of the Times," review of *Last Chance in Africa*, by Negley Farson, *New York Times*, May 5, 1950, 19.

14. John Barkham, "Report from Kenya," review of *Last Chance in Africa*, by Negley Farson, *New York Times*, May 7, 1950.

15. Review of *Last Chance in Africa*, by Negley Farson, *Kirkus Reviews*, May 4, 1950, https://www.kirkusreviews.com/book-reviews/negley-farson/last-chance-in-africa/, accessed February 10, 2020.

16. Elspeth Huxley, "Review: Last Chance in Africa," review of *Last Chance in Africa*, by Negley Farson, *African Affairs*, January 1950, 79.

17. BBC, "Review: Sons of Noah," review of *Sons of Noah*, by Negley Farson, March 10, 1949.

18. Review of *Sons of Noah*, by Negley Farson, *Punch*, February 23, 1949.

19. Leon Dorais, "Water Obsession: The Sons of Noah," review of *Sons of Noah*, by Negley Farson, *New York Times*, April 24, 1949, BR31.

23. Road's End

1. Daniel Farson, *Never a Normal Man*, 192.

2. Daniel Farson, *Never a Normal Man*, 192.

3. Daniel Farson, *Never a Normal Man*, 195.

4. "Journeys through Faraway Lands," review of *Caucasian Journey*, by Negley Farson, *Guardian*, January 28, 1993.

5. Robert Payne, "Journey into Yesterday," review of *Caucasian Journey*, by Negley Farson, *New York Times*, April 13, 1958, BR7.

6. Farson, *Mirror for Narcissus*, 312.

7. Negley Farson to Victor Gollancz, January 1951, Negley Farson Collection, American Heritage Center, University of Wyoming.

8. Eve Farson, diary entry, March 28, 1959, Negley Farson Collection, American Heritage Center, University of Wyoming.

9. Review of *Mirror for Narcissus*, by Negley Farson, *Sunday Times*, undated, Negley Farson Collection, American Heritage Center, University of Wyoming.

10. Review of *Mirror for Narcissus*, by Negley Farson, *Times Literary Supplement*, June 22, 1956.

11. Review of *Mirror for Narcissus*, by Negley Farson, *Kirkus Reviews*, https://www .kirkusreviews.com/book-reviews/negley-farson-3/a-mirror-for-narcissus/, accessed December 15, 2019.

12. John Mackenzie, "New Look at Life by Farson Shows 'Mirror' Clouded," review of *Mirror for Narcissus*, by Negley Farson, *Washington Post*, February 24, 1957, E7.

13. "Author Deplores Ways of Self, All Human Race," Review of *Mirror for Narcissus*, by Negley Farson, *Buffalo Courier-Express*, May 5, 1957.

14. Eve Farson, diary entry, May 19, 1959, Negley Farson Collection, American Heritage Center, University of Wyoming.

15. Ludovic Kennedy, "Meeting Him It Felt Good to Be Alive," *Star*, May 7, 1958.

16. Eve Farson to Victor Gollancz, February 17, 1953, Papers of Sir Victor Gollancz, University of Warwick, U.K.

17. Eve Farson to Victor Gollancz, August 1, 1957, Papers of Sir Victor Gollancz, University of Warwick, U.K.

18. Negley Farson to Leland Stowe, July 18, 1957, Negley Farson Collection, American Heritage Center, University of Wyoming.

19. Negley Farson to Victor Gollancz, July 21, 1959, Negley Farson Collection, American Heritage Center, University of Wyoming.

20. Eve Farson to Victor Gollancz, March 25, 1960, Papers of Sir Victor Gollancz, University of Warwick, U.K.

21. "Farson, Globe Trotting Newsman, Author, Dies," Reuters, December 13, 1960.

22. "Ex-Reporter in Britain for *Chicago Daily News* Wrote of World-Wide Adventures," *New York Times*, December 14, 1960, 34.

23. "Ex-Reporter in Britain for *Chicago Daily News* Wrote of World-Wide Adventures," 34.

24. "Ex-Reporter in Britain for *Chicago Daily News* Wrote of World-Wide Adventures," 34.

25. "Ex-Reporter in Britain for *Chicago Daily News* Wrote of World-Wide Adventures," 34.

26. "Negley Farson," obituary, *Guardian*, December 14, 1960, 10.

27. "Report of the Death of an American Citizen, February 5, 1961," available at Ancestry .com, https://www.ancestry.com/mediaui-viewer/tree/11875325/person/12251855197

/media/31070_B017607–00506?_phsrc=Onb1&_phstart=successSource, accessed July 1, 2019.

28. Farson, *Mirror for Narcissus,* 300–301.

29. Daniel Farson, *Never a Normal Man,* 278.

30. Eve Farson to Leland Stowe, January 1, 1961, Negley Farson Collection, American Heritage Center, University of Wyoming.

31. Leland Stowe to Eve Farson, December 15, 1960, Negley Farson Collection, American Heritage Center, University of Wyoming.

32. Eve Farson to Leland Stowe, January 1, 1961, Negley Farson Collection, American Heritage Center, University of Wyoming.

33. Daniel Farson, *Dry Ship,* 7.

34. Krock, "Reviewed Works," 354–58.

INDEX